COMPARATIVE EUROPEAN POLITICS

Parties and their Members

COMPARATIVE EUROPEAN POLITICS

Comparative European Politics is a series for students and teachers of political science and related disciplines, published in association with the European Consortium for Political Research. Each volume will provide an up-to-date survey of the current state of knowledge and research on an issue of major significance in European government and politics.

Parties
and their Members
*Organizing for Victory in Britain
and Germany*

SUSAN E. SCARROW

OXFORD UNIVERSITY PRESS
1996

Oxford University Press, Walton Street, Oxford OX2 6DP

Oxford New York
Athens Auckland Bangkok Bombay
Calcutta Cape Town Dar es Salaam Delhi
Florence Hong Kong Istanbul Karachi
Kuala Lumpur Madras Madrid Melbourne
Mexico City Nairobi Paris Singapore
Taipei Tokyo Toronto
and associated companies in
Berlin Ibadan

Oxford is a trade mark of Oxford University Press

Published in the United States
by Oxford University Press Inc., New York

British Library Cataloguing in Publicaton Data
Data available

Library of Congress Cataloging in Publication Data
Scarrow, Susan E.
Parties and their members: organizing for victory in
Britain and Germany/Susan E. Scarrow
(Comparative European politics)
Includes bibliographical references and index.
1. Political parties—Great Britain. 2. Party affiliation—Great
Britain. 3. Political parties—Germany. 4. Party affiliation—
Germany. I. Title. II. Series.
JN1121.S33 1995   324.241–dc20   95–40574

ISBN 0–19–827918–3

1 3 5 7 9 10 8 6 4 2

Typeset by J&L Composition Ltd, Filey, North Yorkshire
Printed in Great Britain
on acid-free paper by
Bookcraft (Bath) Ltd
Midsomer Norton, Avon

Preface and Acknowledgements

LARGE memberships were once regarded as valuable assets for parties in many electoral democracies. In recent years, however, many political scientists have come to view membership organizations as quaint—and potentially costly—anachronisms which can do little to help parties win elections in a mass media age. Yet, despite widespread scholarly acceptance of this view, there is surprisingly little supporting evidence to show that party leaders have come to share this assessment that party membership is an organizational burden. Few studies have asked why parties enrolled members in the first place, or have attempted to uncover the ways in which members fit into parties' organizational strategies, either before or after the advent of television campaigning. The purpose of this book is to begin to remedy this deficit. This study of four membership parties in Germany and Britain examines changing justifications for the practice of membership enrolment, and the effects that have flowed from these changes.

The initial idea for this book developed while I was working and studying in Germany and Britain during the campaigns which preceded each country's national election in 1987. Here I saw the leadership-centred battles and television-oriented campaign strategies which 'decline-of-party' literature had led me to expect. But as I toured both countries in search of local electioneering efforts, I was startled by the apparent vitality of many local campaigns. Some, though by no means all, of the parties I visited had once known stronger days, but all still maintained the support of loyal activists who believed that elections mattered, and who donated time and energy in order to give a local face to their party's campaign efforts. What was the explanation for what I saw? Was I encountering merely the unwanted remnants of former membership parties, or were there new reasons why parties continued to enrol members even in an era when television and direct mail gave party leaders unmediated contact with the entire electorate?

In exploring these questions, I incurred a debt of gratitude first and foremost to the many members of British and German parties who tried to help me understand politics in their countries, and who generously consented to be interviewed about organizational practices and problems in their localities. Hundreds of party members responded to my enquiries, and many also invited me to accompany them so that I could experience at first hand the routine of local business-meetings, the apolitical sociability of other party events, the drudgery of folding election leaflets, and the hoopla of campaign rallies. Without the help of these party activists, interpreting the terms and controversies in party documents would have been much more difficult; without their hospitality, conducting the research would have been much less interesting.

In the course of this project I have also acquired debts in the scholarly community which are too numerous to list in full. Nevertheless, several individuals and institutions are particularly deserving of public thanks for their support. First and foremost I want to thank those who commented on one or more versions of the manuscript, or who gave special help with my research arrangements: David Butler, David Cameron, Mark Franklin, Richard Katz, Thomas Koelble, Ruud Koole, Pippa Norris, Bruce Oppenheimer, Howard Scarrow, Hermann Schmitt, Byron Shafer, and Rudolf Wildenmann. Discussions with these and with many other, unnamed, colleagues have made the research process both challenging and rewarding. Four institutions also deserve special thanks for providing congenial settings for my research: Nuffield College, Oxford, and, at Mannheim University, the Forschungsstelle für Gesellschaftliche Entwicklung, the Zentrum für Europäische Umfragenanalyse, and the Mannheimer Zentrum für Europäische Sozialforschung. Many of the sources used in this study come from the following special collections and archives: the Conservative Party Archives (Oxford), the Labour Party Library and Archives (London); the SPD Libary and Archives at the Friedrich-Ebert-Stiftung (Bonn); the SPD Newspaper Clippings collection at Ollenhauer House (Bonn); the Archiv für Christlich-Demokratische Politik at the Konrad-Adenauer-Stiftung (St. Augustin). I am grateful to the directors of these institutions for giving me access to their collections, and to the archivists and librarians who helped me to discover relevant materials. The initial research for this book was completed with grants from the National Science Foundation, the Fulbright Commission, the Friedrich-Ebert-Stiftung, and Yale University. The University of Houston generously provided me with the time needed to carry out additional research, and a Conant Fellowship from the Center for European Studies at Harvard University provided me with the pleasant venue in which to complete the project.

Finally, I want to dedicate this book to my parents. They encouraged me to enjoy the opportunities and meet the challenges presented by study and research on two continents. I thank them for their unfailing support.

Contents

List of Figures

List of Tables

Abbreviations

APSA	American Political Science Association
BBC	British Broadcasting Corporation
CCO	Conservative Central Office
CDU	Christlich-Demokratische Union
CDU-BGSt	CDU-Bundesgeschäftsstelle
CLPD	Campaign for Labour Party Democracy
ConPar	Conservative Party
CSU	Christlich Soziale Union
ECPR	European Consortium for Political Research
FAZ	*Frankfurter Allgemeine Zeitung*
FDP	Freie Demokratische Partei
FES	Friedrich-Ebert-Stiftung
KAS	Konrad-Adenauer-Stiftung
LabPar	Labour Party
MP	Member of Parliament
NEC	National Executive Committee (of the Labour Party)
PDS	Partei des Demokratischen Sozialismus
PV	Parteivorstand
PCF	Parti Communiste Français
SED	Sozialistische Einheitspartei Deutschlands
SDP	Social Democratic Party (in Britain)
SPD	Sozialdemokratische Partei Deutschlands
SPD-PV	SPD-Parteivorstand

1

Party Members and Party Organization

PARTIES with large, formally enrolled memberships have been one of the most distinctive, and most successful, forms of political organization in the twentieth century. Indeed, this era has been dubbed the 'century of the mass party' because of the central roles such parties have played in structuring electoral choice in democratic systems.[1] The innovation of large-scale membership organization proved to be a rewarding response to the challenge of mobilizing support in newly enfranchised mass electorates. Because this organizational approach helped parties to win votes, it was widely imitated. As membership parties spread, they provided useful, and perhaps even essential, representative channels. In many countries, parties which enrolled their supporters, and which channelled their energies towards electoral contests, enhanced the democratic legitimacy and stability of political systems by integrating groups that might otherwise have been marginalized.

Today, however, membership parties no longer play a unique role in generating such support for governments or for political systems. Even where membership parties have remained large, they have lost much of their former power to mobilize voters or to inspire long-term allegiances. Furthermore, many such parties now find it difficult, if not impossible, to match their former levels of enrolment. Indeed, because membership parties once acted to reinforce political identities, declining enrolment may not only reflect, but also contribute to, the increasing disaffection with political élites and party-based political systems that has surfaced in many countries in recent years. In short, membership parties now seem to be an increasingly imperilled species, yet another victim of the twentieth century's rapid technological and social changes.

In retrospect, it seems easy to explain the apparent demise of the once-flourishing institution of the membership party. When the enrolments of membership parties began to stagnate or fall, it was soon recognized that the costs of attracting and retaining members were high enough to make it anything but inevitable that party leaders should continue to think of large memberships as a vital organizational tool. This was all the more true because new technologies made it increasingly easy for party employees to accomplish traditional tasks without the aid of member volunteers. Furthermore, in those countries where parties gained access to public subsidies, they had less of a financial incentive to enlist members. On the other side, as class differences levelled out and social mobility increased, citizens became less attached to class-based parties. Even those who maintained established voting patterns seemed less inclined to donate time and money to support their favoured party. Indeed, the logic of these explanations is so convincing that by the end of the twentieth century the observed weakening of membership parties has begun to seem as inevitable as their ascendancy previously did.

While these explanations for declining memberships are all plausible, they may or may not apply to every party. It is, in fact, not currently possible to judge the extent of their applicability, because few studies have investigated the reasons why party memberships have waxed and waned. Above all, little effort has been made to discover how the resource of membership has fitted into parties' changing electoral strategies. As a result, not much is known either about party organizers' original hopes concerning the ways in which members were to support their parties, or about how—if at all—party organizers have revised their assessments of members' potential utility. In short, although many parties may indeed have falling enrolments, not enough is known about the causes of this decline. It has not been clearly established whether such a drop shows that party organizers no longer find it worthwhile to invest in membership maintenance, that citizens have lost interest in enrolling in parties, or that there is a convergence of both these trends. Determining which of these possible causes is at work is important, because it will shape expectations about future developments. To the extent that party organizers no longer calculate that there are net advantages to be gained from enrolling members, they will probably make few efforts to counteract the pressures which are pushing them in the direction of developing small, vestigial membership organizations. On the other hand, if decline in membership solely reflects the diminishing appeal of traditional recruiting techniques, and of traditional perquisites for members, party organizers may well take steps to combat the decline by repackaging membership 'products'. However, even in the latter case, where party organizers continue to view membership as a useful organizational resource, the form and circumstances of such repackaging efforts will probably vary among parties.

In order to facilitate the choice between these scenarios, current debates about the possible demise of parties as membership organizations must be enriched by a more nuanced view of the many ways in which parties have sought to profit from their members. Establishing the changing reasons for which party organizers have valued membership will make it easier to understand the strategic dilemmas faced by organizers who have weighed the costs and benefits of enrolling members. This book seeks to develop such a perspective by examining changing views about membership in four parties that traditionally relied on, or acquired, large membership organizations: the British Labour and Conservative Parties, and the (formerly West) German Christian Democratic Union and Social Democratic Party. These parties evolved in different decades and under very different circumstances. Today, however, their membership organizations are all responding to similar societal and technological changes. As a result, a comparison of these four parties provides a way to begin to untangle the strands of circumstance, tradition, and calculation which together form the web of parties' organizational strategies.

THE RISE, AND POSSIBLE DECLINE, OF MEMBERSHIP PARTIES

More than a century ago Mosei Ostrogorski journeyed first to Britain, then to the United States, in order to complete one of the first cross-national studies of how political parties are organized. Whereas others before him had tried to distinguish between parties according to their fundamental principles,[2] Ostrogorski was interested in parties as organizational entities. In particular, he sought to understand the origins and operations of the relatively new phenomenon of political parties with permanent local structures. This future member of the Russian *Duma* was appalled by the parties which he encountered on his travels. For him, these year-round party associations seemed to be instruments for suffocating independent participation in the political process, and he denounced such structures as 'a virus strong enough to poison the blood of a community'.[3]

Yet, regardless of Ostrogorski's misgivings, in the early twentieth century such organizations flourished throughout Europe, where they were particularly characteristic of parties of the left. In countries such as Austria, Germany, and Denmark, socialist and social-democratic parties enjoyed early success in building up networks of enrolled members.[4] Here and elsewhere organizers of socialist parties sought to create cohesive class-based communities whose overlapping activities would reinforce a collective political identity. These communities enhanced life for party members and potential supporters by providing them with recreational clubs, insurance societies, newspapers, and even shops and banks. Membership parties also provided their ambitious and talented members with unmatched opportunities for advancement in party and in public offices. Access to political careers was particularly valuable to those from modest economic backgrounds (and often with modest educational histories). Individuals in this category who rose within the new membership parties to some of the highest ranks of public service included men such as Friedrich Ebert of the German Social Democratic Party (first president of the Weimar Republic), Karl Renner of the Austrian Social Democratic Workers' Party (first chancellor in the post-1918 Austrian Republic), and Ramsay MacDonald (Britain's first Labour prime minister).

But parties' efforts to enrol members, and to integrate supporters within organizational networks, were important not merely because they enabled a new class of citizens to rise to positions of political responsibility. These organizational strategies mattered above all because they produced the electoral dividends which enabled parties of the left to establish themselves in central positions within parliaments throughout Europe. In the 1920s, when countries such as Austria, Britain, Denmark, Germany, Norway, and Sweden all experienced (and survived) their first socialist-led governments, these parties won increasing credibility as plausible alternatives to bourgeois governments.

Socialist parties were not the only parties, and in some countries not even the first ones, to discover the advantages of recruiting and organizing supporters between election seasons. Most notably, years before the British Labour Party was founded, the British Liberal and Conservative Parties had already organized their supporters in response to new laws on electoral registration, and to the challenges of competition in multi-member districts. In many other countries, however, the apparent ability of Socialist parties to translate organizational strength into electoral gain prompted parties of the right to try to imitate their competitors' characteristic structures of mass enrolment.

In the 1920s and 1930s socialist and fascist parties demonstrated many of the organizational advantages of mass enrolment, and their successes convinced many scholars that parties with large formal memberships represented a new and higher step on the ladder of party evolution. One of these scholars was a German academic named Sigmund Neumann, who was fascinated by the clash of democratic and non-democratic membership parties in Weimar Germany. In 1932, only months before the collapse of the Weimar Republic, Neumann argued that democratic parties with large memberships offered the sole hope for the survival of modern democracy. He contended that, in an age when other ties between individuals and their communities had been shattered, it was only parties like these that were capable of integrating citizens into the polity.[5] Another prominent champion of mass-enrolment parties was Maurice Duverger, a French academic who wrote only a few years after the liberation of German-occupied France. Like Neumann, Duverger prophesied that the mass-membership model of democratic party organization would be the dominant force in future politics. According to Duverger, the electoral successes of parties with large, formally enrolled memberships would persuade their political rivals to imitate their organizational strategies.[6]

Yet such views about the inherent organizational superiority of parties with large memberships did not hold sway for long. Soon other scholars began to discover compelling reasons why such organizations would lose their comparative advantages. Their arguments about the probable, or even inevitable, decline of parties as membership organizations usually rested on complementary assertions about changes in the calculations made by party leaders ('demand-side' factors), and about changes in the calculations made by potential party members ('supply-side' factors).

Demand-side arguments about declines in membership highlight reasons why party élites are not, or are no longer, willing to invest either party resources or their own reputations in building and maintaining an inclusive party membership. According to such arguments, party leaders may come to view party membership as an inefficient, or even ineffective, tool for winning votes. They may even come to view enrolled members as electoral liabilities. Otto Kirchheimer used the latter argument in the mid-1960s, when he predicted that party leaders would abandon traditional mass-membership strategies once it became clear that voters had come to view large party-memberships (and the parties which organized them) as undesirably old-fashioned.[7] In Kirchheimer's words, leaders of parties that adopted catch-all organizational and electoral strategies would lose interest in cultivating party membership organizations. Other demand-side accounts have argued that leaders have good reason to try to reduce their support for organized memberships. Far from representing an electoral asset, members who are active in a party's voluntary organizations may actually diminish its electoral prospects (and thereby threaten leaders' office-holding ambitions) because volunteer activists have a tendency to impose vote-losing policy commitments.[8]

Probably the most common demand-side argument is that which asserts that party leaders lose interest in organizing supporters because they begin to view organized memberships as a comparatively worthless electoral resource. According to this argument, new tools for capturing electoral support make the strategy of membership organization obsolete. New communications technologies, including television, computer-aided direct mail, and opinion polls, all enable and encourage parties to employ small and efficient professional organizations to perform jobs once entrusted to large teams of member volunteers. Furthermore, the high costs of the new campaign tools dictate that parties no longer rely solely on the financial support of party members. Because they must inevitably look for other sources of funds, and because money can buy replacements for everything that members once did, party leaders are said to have little reason to invest in building or maintaining membership organizations.[9]

This variety of demand-side argument has been current for quite a while. As early as 1955 Robert McKenzie argued that in Britain, mass media communication had eroded the need for parties to enrol large memberships. He commented that, '[p]erhaps in retrospect it will be evident that the mass party saw its heyday during the period when the extension of the franchise had created a mass electorate, but there was as yet no effective means of reaching the voters in their own homes'.[10] A few years later Leon Epstein found that circumstances in the United States pointed to a similar conclusion. Epstein noted that parties and candidates in that country were increasingly reliant on new, professionally co-ordinated communications techniques, and that the new techniques cost far more than could be raised from membership dues. He thus concluded that 'membership organizations seem largely irrelevant to what has become the major campaign method for candidates and parties'.[11] Epstein speculated that these might not be isolated developments, and he asserted, '[i]f there are technological trends now working against the development of mass-membership party organizations in the United States, they ought by now also to be operative in Europe so as to reduce the importance of such organizations as have existed'.[12] As the political use of new communications techniques spread beyond the United States, developments in countries as far apart as Australia, Canada, and Norway seemed to confirm Epstein's conclusions about how newly available organizational resources would reduce party leaders' interest in, and dependence on, party membership.[13] More recently, other authors have restated versions of the now familiar demand-side argument about how new technologies (particularly televised communications) erode party leaders' commitment to membership-based organizational strategies, because they enable leaders to make direct contacts with voters. To this, they have added the similar demand-side argument about how the increased availability of public funding for political parties has eroded the incentives for parties to enrol members.[14] These were the reasons Richard Katz gave for labelling membership a 'vestigial' organ (a form without a function), and these were the circumstances which prompted Angelo Panebianco to pronounce the advent of the 'electoral-professional' party.[15]

In contrast, 'supply-side' arguments about why membership parties are waning emphasize the growing importance of factors which make citizens less interested in joining political parties. Such arguments contend that even if party leaders continue to find reasons to invest in membership enrolment, their efforts will meet with decreasing success. According to some supply-side explanations, a principal reason why membership recruitment becomes more difficult is that political dealignment is weakening the bonds which link citizens with particular parties. Dealignment may, in fact, be the result of parties' earlier successes in integrating new groups into the political community, and in diminishing the relevance of class cleavages by increasing access to social and economic opportunities. Whatever the cause, the result is that in many countries social-group loyalties are becoming much less important as sources of political identity. Issue-voting is replacing identity-voting, and even many committed partisans are loosening their party ties. These changes alter the nature of parties' electoral tasks; they also reduce the supply of loyalists from which parties can recruit their members.[16]

Other supply-side arguments emphasize how a different set of changes in society undercuts recruitment efforts by reducing the attractiveness of the non-political enticements parties can offer. In the mid-twentieth century most advanced industrial societies expanded their welfare-state provisions. This expansion drastically reduced the comparative value of party-linked welfare benefits. Similarly, and sometimes simultaneously, many countries reformed their administrative recruitment procedures in ways that made it difficult for parties to recruit members with credible promises of privileged access to state employment. Finally, the parallel expansion of both the leisure industry and public education reduced the comparative value of parties' offerings of entertainment and educational opportunities.[17] The implication of all these changes is said to be that parties will find it more difficult to recruit because they have less to offer to potential members.

In combination, these demand-side and supply-side arguments suggest that the decline, and perhaps even the eventual disappearance, of party membership organizations is inevitable. Today's party leaders apparently have few reasons for wishing to enrol members, and they would probably find it difficult to attract members even if they wanted to do so. However, though these arguments seem compelling, they have been challenged on both theoretical and empirical grounds. Epstein himself always argued that there were limits to the likely 'Americanization' of European party organizations, and he later reaffirmed this reservation, noting, for instance, that parties with alternative sources of funding might nevertheless try to retain members for even their 'marginal' contributions.[18] Klaus von Beyme argued in the 1980s that 'people's parties' might be more interested in having members than Kirchheimer had suggested.[19] More recently, Alan Ware has argued that there are legal and technological constraints which might lead party strategists to value membership organization even in an age of mass media.[20]

Such counter-arguments were prompted in part by evidence that seemed to counter expectations of a uniform decline in the strength and relevance of party membership organizations. For instance, French parties in the 1970s and early 1980s offered a striking counter-example to predictions of a decline of the membership party. In France, non-Communist parties only began strengthening their membership organizations after the advent of televised politics. The growth of these organizations was particularly notable because it occurred in a country that lacked a tradition of parties with large membership organizations, and in one in which the constitution had been intentionally designed to weaken political parties. Though French observers later questioned the true extent of the growth in party membership in this period, even the parties' eagerness to inflate their enrolment figures suggests that French party strategists have viewed large memberships, including paper memberships, as a useful source of political legitimacy.[21] In the 1980s, some parties outside France also appeared to be making new or renewed efforts to enrol members, long after television campaigning had become an established norm.[22]

These counter-arguments and counter-examples warn against too ready an acceptance of predictions about the inevitable obsolescence of broad membership enrolment as an organizational strategy. Moreover, they also suggest the need for discussions of organizational change that go beyond a debate about 'decline' or 'not decline'. What is needed instead are systematic ways to assess ongoing changes in relations between parties and their members. Chapter 2 turns to the problem of figuring out how to assess current organizational changes without needing to wait many years to test the plausibility of long-term predictions. Before this, however, it will be useful to review some of the reasons why scholars throughout the past century have bothered to pay so much attention to the development of parties' extra-parliamentary structures.

WHY DOES PARTY ORGANIZATION MATTER?

Political parties are such prominent actors in contemporary democratic politics that it would be easy to overlook the fundamental questions of whether, and in what ways, they matter. Indeed, a quarter of a century ago Anthony King complained that 'most writers on parties note what they take the functions of party to be, but they do not go on to ask whether parties actually perform these functions, and, if so, to what extent and under what conditions'.[23] Since King made this charge, however, many authors have attempted to remedy the deficit he described. Their efforts propose answers to versions of the question posed most succinctly by Richard Rose: 'Do parties make a difference?'[24]

One basic and important version of this question asks whether it matters which party wins an election. An affirmative answer to this question is obviously crucial if elections are to continue to act as devices which foster the legitimacy of political systems. The periodic civic rituals which allow voters to choose from among aspiring governors would be hollow charades if government policies were likely to be identical whichever of several competing parties actually attained office. In fact, it can be surprisingly difficult to demonstrate that parties in office do not merely act like Tweedledum and Tweedledee, because such a demonstration must rest on counterfactual arguments about what a defeated party would have done had it won, not lost, an election. Cross-national and cross-regional comparisons of party policies under similar circumstances have attempted to overcome these difficulties. Such studies have provided support for the assumption that different governing parties have distinct effects on policy outcomes.[25]

However, demonstrating that it matters which parties hold office does not directly answer the subquestion which is of greatest interest here: Do *party organizations* make a difference? Of course, many party scholars have assumed a positive answer to this question, and have implicitly or explicitly used this assumption to justify their investigations into the nature and origins of party structures. However, other researchers throughout the past century have taken the impact of party organizations as the object of their research. Their hypotheses and premises about the importance of parties' extra-parliamentary structures can be divided into two very general categories of arguments, the first of which link organization with outcomes, the second of which link organization with political processes.

Outcomes

Arguments which focus on outcomes may try to show that extra-parliamentary party organizations shape parties' choices of leaders and programmes. They may also seek links between party structures and election results. If variations in organizational structures have an impact on party policies, party leaders, or election outcomes, then these structures are important at least to the extent that it matters which parties win elections.

The question of whether parties' organizational forms influence their policy choices is a longstanding theme of party research. Some of the earliest students of party organization concluded that parties' extra-parliamentary arrangements were important because they could lead parties to endorse poor policies. Ostrogorski, for instance, argued that parties with well-staffed extra-parliamentary organizations, and with permanently enrolled memberships, were undesirable because they would not govern on behalf of the entire nation. According to him, countries had once been governed by independent representatives, but now they were controlled by party bosses who acted on behalf of special interests. Ostrogorski advocated solving the misrule of permanently organized parties by replacing them with temporary single-issue coalitions.

A few years later both Robert Michels and Max Weber reaffirmed Ostrogorski's assertions that strong extra-parliamentary organizations influenced policy choices by enhancing the power of party leaders. However, these friends disagreed about the significance of this finding.[26] Michels was convinced by his study of the German Social Democratic Party that membership parties would always be dominated by organizational élites, not by ordinary members. He claimed that this process was inevitable because party officials and party employees enjoyed privileged access to time, information, and influence within the party. Michels summed up his findings in his now famous 'iron law of oligarchy' ('Who says organization, says oligarchy'). He asserted that oligarchy could be mitigated, but not avoided, because 'oligarchy depends upon what we may term the PSYCHOLOGY OF ORGANIZATION ITSELF, that is to say, upon the tactical and technical necessities which result from the consolidation of every disciplined aggregate'.[27] Michels, at least initially, lamented this state of affairs because he thought that organizational leaders and ordinary party members had different, and often conflicting, priorities. According to him, members wanted to see the implementation of political ideals, whereas party employees wanted to strengthen the party bureaucracy, and party representatives wanted to guarantee their own re-election. His only consolation was that there were varying degrees of oligarchy in organizations, and that vigilant party members could employ party structures in ways that prevented leaders from gaining absolute control over their organizations. Thus, for Michels the relevant question to ask about extra-parliamentary organization was the extent to which it diminished members' control over party priorities.

Weber, unlike Michels, found the prospect of party oligarchy to be quite reassuring. He agreed with Michels's conclusion that party leaders were likely to manipulate the resources of extra-parliamentary party organizations in order to protect themselves from internal and external challengers. However, Weber considered such oligarchy to be good for society, because he thought that polities require strong leaders who are in a position to pursue effective, even if temporarily unpopular, policies. For Weber, well-organized but obedient extra-parliamentary support provided party leaders with useful insulation from the whims and extremes of public opinion and party factions.[28] In short, Weber and Michels reached very different conclusions about the impact and desirability of strong permanent party organizations because they started off with contrasting assumptions about the value of direct popular political control.

Decades later, John May formalized a slightly different argument about how party structures affect party policies. Like Michels, May reasoned that because active party members are motivated primarily by their support for party ideals, they will demand policies which are relatively extreme compared to those favoured by party voters, by inactive party members, or by those holding office within the party. (He named his proposition the 'special law of curvilinear disparity'.) But whereas Michels was concerned about the ways in which party structures might *enable* party élites to compromise party ideals, May was concerned about the circumstances in which party structures might *prevent* party élites from making precisely such compromises. May concluded that parties should not necessarily be expected to act like Downsian, vote-maximizing actors if their statutes gave programmatic control to party activists. Instead of moving toward the centre, such parties were much more likely to stick to ideologically pure policies even if these positions proved to be vote-losing ones.[29]

Thus, variations in the organizational structure of parties may affect political outcomes by imposing various constraints on the policy choices made by party leaders. In addition, they may also shape electoral outcomes. Indeed, some discussions of party organization take it as a given that there is a link between organizational forms and electoral success. Most notably, authors such as Duverger, Epstein, and Kirchheimer predicted that the characteristics of parties' extra-parliamentary organizations would converge as party organizers recognized the vote-winning effectiveness of their competitors' organizational innovations. Yet because many factors are known to influence how, and whether, individuals vote, it is much easier to assert that party organization affects outcomes than it is actually to prove that this is the case. Even so, some aggregate- and individual-level studies have managed to find evidence of links between the strength of party membership organizations and election results (measured either as electoral participation or as parties' share of the vote).[30] Such studies are of obvious importance, because it is the presumed electoral impact of organizational characteristics such as membership strength that provides one of the strongest justifications for continued scholarly attention to variations in extra-parliamentary party structures.

Process

Even if it were not possible to show that organizational variations had a direct impact on political outcomes, process arguments could nevertheless make a case for the importance of these variations.

The most common arguments about the connection between party organizations and political processes are those which explore how extra-parliamentary party organizations may facilitate—or stifle—individual political participation. As a result, much of the enquiry into links between parties' organizational styles and political processes has been motivated either by concern about how to maximize citizen participation, or by concern about the consequences of too much participation.

Ostrogorski, who has already been cited for his interest in the way that party organizations shaped outcomes, was also worried about parties' impact on the political process. He feared that certain party structures tended to distort participation in democratic decision-making. He believed that in the ideal world, parties would usefully contribute to citizens' political education. But instead of this, during his research he found that 'caucus' parties were trying to use permanent party membership as a mechanism for making free citizens into unthinking servants of the party, thereby '[b]lotting out independent thought and enervating the will and the personal responsibility of the voter'.[31] Ostrogorski's charges have been echoed by more recent advocates of participatory democracy, who likewise lament the ways that organized parties reduce individual citizens' opportunities for participation.[32]

Half a century after Ostrogorski described modern parties as a threat to democratic processes, Sigmund Neumann made a very different kind of assertion about the impact of party organizations on the fabric of political life. Neumann argued that in an age of mass politics, successful democracies must rely on parties to organize the 'chaotic public will', and to integrate private citizens into the political community. He pointed to the post-1918 rise of highly structured fascist and communist parties as evidence that loosely organized parties of notables ('parties of representation', in his terms) could not accomplish the tasks of civic integration once the electorate became very large. Neumann concluded that democratic parties also needed to enrol supporters and provide them with a sense of group identity if they were to be viable alternatives to more populist anti-democratic parties. Only if they organized as 'parties of democratic integration' could they successfully channel the demands of newly enfranchised mass publics into support for democratic institutions.[33]

Neumann and Ostrogorski started from very different assumptions about the desirability of citizens' unmediated impact on political decisions. However, both agreed that variations in party organization shape political processes, and can thereby affect the quality, and perhaps even the survival, of democracy itself. Much more recently, Peter Mair has drawn attention to yet another possible link between parties' organizational characteristics and political processes. Mair argued that the disappearance of membership parties may not merely be a reflection of electoral dealignment, but may itself contribute to the growing volatility of electoral preferences. According to this argument, parties which adopt a catch-all electoral strategy no longer try to forge strong ties with supporters, because they seek their main campaign support from professional organizations rather than from a community of enrolled volunteers. Once parties diminish their efforts to enmesh their core supporters inside a volunteer network, voters become more available to new political alternatives.[34] In this way a change in parties' organizational strategies can help to alter the entire environment of political competition.

The impact of party organizations on political processes has more often served as a premise than as a hypothesis for research about parties' structures. However, some recent studies of the correlates of political participation do buttress Neumann's assertion that parties which enrol supporters help to integrate citizens into the broader fabric of civic life. For instance, one five-country study found that party members were more likely to vote than were others with similar educational and economic backgrounds.[35] Similarly, a British study of various types of political participation found that it was those who had worked in party campaigns who were most likely to report that participation increased their political knowledge, and enhanced their favourable impressions of politics.[36] Such evidence buttresses the most striking contention of some 'process' arguments, namely, that certain types of party organization are particularly well-suited to increasing the legitimacy of democratic political systems.

As the preceding discussion shows, the century-old tradition of studying party organization has been sustained by a variety of perspectives about why, and how, variations in these organizations can affect the nature and quality of politics and policies. Because these contrasting perspectives have produced very different assessments about the links between parties and democracy, they can lead to very different conclusions about whether or not the apparent demise of membership parties is a matter for concern. However, all of them suggest that the diagnosis and explanation of variations in parties' membership organizations are worth pursuing because of their potentially broad impact.

PARTY MEMBERS AND MEMBERSHIP PARTIES

Before turning to the challenge of assessing changes in parties as membership organizations, it will be helpful immediately to confront two tricky definitional questions: what are party members, and what are membership parties? One reason why these definitions are not straightforward is that parties often maintain intentionally fluid membership boundaries.

At its most basic level, an acceptable definition of party membership must be able to distinguish party members as a subset within the broader universe of all party supporters. A useful way to make this distinction is by defining members as those whose relation to their party involves both obligations and privileges.[37] Two of the most common obligations imposed by parties on their members are the injunction to refrain from joining rival parties, and the requirement to contribute to party funds. Common privileges include the right to participate in candidate selection, and the right to influence programmatic decisions. In some countries, parties also (or alternatively) offer their members special access to goods and services. To qualify as membership indicators, these obligations and privileges should be provided by the party alone. This means, for instance, that party privileges are distinct from rights granted by the state to all elected officials. It also means that privileges granted to citizens by the state are not the same as privileges associated with party membership (though the state may require parties to offer their membership conditions in a non-arbitrary manner).

Actual parties vary widely both in the demands they impose on their members and in the benefits they offer to those who enrol. The extent of the differences is magnified by the fact that levels of privilege and of obligation do not necessarily vary in the same

OBLIGATIONS

		Very high	Very low
PRIVILEGES	Very high	Italy: Lombard League, 1991	West Germany: Greens, 1982
	Very low	France: Communist Party, 1970	United States: Republicans, Democrats, 1995

Fig 1.1. The privileges and obligations of membership
(Selected examples)

direction. That parties within democratic systems have a wide range of definitions of membership can best be illustrated by citing some of the most extreme combinations of formal obligations and privileges. These examples, depicted in Fig. 1.1 and described below, refer to specific times as well as to specific parties, because parties have the ability frequently to adjust both the rewards of membership and the requirements for enrolment.

The Italian Lombard League of the early 1990s was on the high end of the two scales of membership obligations and membership privileges. The 1990 statutes of this newly founded party made it difficult for any but the most committed supporters to become full members. Individuals qualified for membership only after they had proved their dedication to the party by performing at least two years of active work as registered 'militant supporters'. Even those who fulfilled this requirement were not automatically admitted to full membership. Full members were expected to pay dues and to continue their active work within the party. In return, however, these full members (in contrast to other supporters) were given direct or indirect (delegated) voting rights in all formal procedures to select candidates and party leaders, and to approve the party programme.[38]

The French Communist Party (*Parti Communiste Français*: PCF) of the early 1970s illustrated a second sort of arrangement. Its statutes imposed relatively high obligations on members but offered relatively low formal privileges. All PCF members were supposed to participate in party activities on a regular basis, in addition to paying party dues. On the other hand, party statutes gave ordinary party members only a small formal role in the selection of the PCF's leaders or in the formulation of its policies. Though members were represented at the party conferences where such decisions were initially formulated, party statutes gave leaders the final word about most decisions.[39]

The German Greens (*Die Grünen*) at the beginning of the 1980s fell into a third category, offering members comparatively high privileges but exacting few obligations. The party's federal statutes required only that members should support party goals, and should refrain from joining another party. At the time, the comparatively high privileges of party membership included the right to attend party meetings at all levels (including those of the parliamentary party and the party executive), and the right to participate in some state and federal policy-making conferences.[40]

Finally, some political parties fall into a fourth category, one in which both the obligations and privileges of membership are low. Parties in the contemporary United States fit this description. Here, parties offer extremely low privileges to members, in part because rights to participate in primary elections are created and regulated by state laws, not by party rules. Furthermore, parties in the United States can rarely offer their members credible promises of access to more material benefits. However, at the local and state level members of US parties in some cases are distinguished from other supporters by having opportunities to influence endorsements of party candidates or to select the individuals who will attend party conventions. Clearly, though, parties in the United States are hard to accommodate in this typology, because they are close to the boundary at which the differences between members and supporters become irrelevant.

Thus, party members can be distinguished from other party supporters by identifying privileges granted to them (or obligations imposed on them) by the party. The unmediated quality of these privileges helps to clarify another distinction, the difference between 'direct' and 'indirect' members. The discussion of privileges and obligations has so far considered only direct members. In contrast, the relationship of indirect members to their parties is mediated through associations which have organizational affiliation with the parties. Intermediary organizations define and impose the primary obligations on indirect members, and receive privileges from the parties. For instance, many British trade unions have traditionally affiliated most of their members to the British Labour Party, paying the party a set fee for every union member who becomes an indirect member of the party. (Swedish trade unions had a similar relation with the Swedish Social Democratic Workers' Party.) In return, the unions as organizations (not their individual members) have received voting privileges in the party. 'Direct' and 'indirect' members have thus had very different formal positions within party structures.

The preceding discussion helps to define what is meant by 'direct' party members. But what is meant by the term 'membership party'? As used here, the term is essentially equivalent to Maurice Duverger's more familiar category, the 'mass party'. Ever since Duverger published his wide-ranging study of the organizational development of parties, his terms of discussion have provided the foundation for many comparative analyses of party structures. Nevertheless, there are two compelling reasons for eschewing his 'mass party' label.

First, even though Duverger's term is now widely used, it can still easily be misunderstood. For Duverger, a true mass party is identified by its *aspirations* to enrol a wide segment of supporters, and to offer them year-round opportunities for participation. For reasons of both ideology and electoral strategy, Duverger's mass parties seek to convert supporters into members. In the French original, Duverger's *parti de masses* conveys the added sense of being a 'party of the masses', in other words, a party whose structures and recruitment policies are non-élitist. Duverger's mass parties are thus distinguished from cadre parties by their strategic goals and formal enrolment-procedures, but not by their success in implementing these strategies. As Duverger wrote, 'The distinction between cadre and mass parties is not based upon their dimensions, upon the numbers of their members: the difference involved is not one of size but of structure.'[41] To the ears of English speakers, however, a 'mass' party sounds confusingly like a party which has a 'massive' membership—something that a *parti de masses* may or may not possess.[42] The same confusion arises when the term 'mass-membership party' is used as a substitute for Duverger's 'mass party' label. The term 'membership party' avoids this potential confusion by stressing self-image (parties which seek to enrol members), not size.

The second reason for using the 'membership party' label is that this term makes it easier to treat some of Duverger's assumptions about 'mass party' characteristics as hypotheses, rather than axioms. Most importantly for present purposes, the more neutral term leaves open the question of whether the decision to seek large memberships eliminates all other choices about the nature of party structures. Although Duverger begins by distinguishing between membership strategies and organizational structures, he ultimately asserts that, '[c]adre parties correspond to the caucus parties, decentralized and weakly knit; mass parties to parties based on branches, more centralized and more firmly knit'.[43] For Duverger, and for many who have used his writing as a starting-point, expansive enrolment and branch-party structure are synonymous. As a result, the 'mass party' label is often used as shorthand for what Duverger sometimes refers to as the 'mass/branch' party. Because it is not encumbered with these prior associations, the term 'membership party' does not carry any implications about structure, such as whether cadre parties might develop strong centralized structures, or whether parties with aspirations to enrol members might nevertheless abandon hierarchic, branch-based structures.

Membership parties are thus distinguished by certain aspects of their organizing strategies. In true membership parties, efforts to enrol members and to involve them in year-round activities are not merely inspired by tradition; in these parties, leaders view members as potentially valuable electoral assets. This definition suggests that indicators of strategy, not of size, will be needed in order to answer the question of whether membership parties are disappearing.

Membership parties can also be defined negatively, by specifying what they are not. Their extra-parliamentary organizations are not *ad hoc*, unlike those of Duverger's cadre parties. Nor are they composed exclusively of professional employees. Membership parties may well have large paid bureaucracies, but they also rely on formally enrolled member-volunteers (not just on informal supporters) to help realize party goals. As these few stipulations suggest, the term 'membership party' is a very inclusive one. This deliberate inclusiveness makes it possible to go beyond Duverger's mass-to-cadre organizational spectrum by considering variations in the ways that membership parties structure relations with their members. The task of systematically describing such variations is taken up in Chapter 2.

EVALUATING ORGANIZATIONAL CHANGE IN GERMANY AND BRITAIN

The aim of this book is to provide a party-centred perspective on the possible decline of membership parties. In pursuing this goal, the book adopts a long-term view of recent changes in the formal links between parties and their supporters. In the past, far-ranging predictions about organizational decline or organizational convergence have tended to be undermined by both the complexity and the non-finality of party change. The current study seeks to avoid both these problems by resisting the temptation to focus on the broadest question of whether 'party decline' is a general, inevitable phenomenon. Instead, the following chapters develop a framework for assessing the origins, and the likely impact, of ongoing alterations in parties' extra-parliamentary organizations. As will be shown, it is rewarding to pay attention to both large and small organizational changes as they occur, because it is the cumulative impact of these incremental movements which most significantly alter the parties, and which may also affect their political environments.

When change is understood as an ongoing process, institutional evolution is seen to be a complex phenomenon which can best be studied by looking for patterns of development in specific parties. In keeping with this view, the current study seeks to uncover the sources and dimensions of change in membership parties by concentrating on organizational reform and innovation in four parties, two British and two German. Comparing these four parties makes it possible to observe processes of change under a variety of circumstances which are said to shape the evolution of relations between parties and their members.

The four parties—the British Labour and Conservative Parties, and the German Social Democratic Party (*Sozialdemokratische Partei Deutschlands*: SPD) and Christian Democratic Union (*Christlich-Demokratische Union*: CDU)—are obvious choices for such a study of the organizational development of parties. In the first place, all four have figured prominently in past studies of party organization. From Ostrogorski, Michels, and Weber, through Kirchheimer, Ware, and Panebianco, students of comparative party organization have regularly examined British and German cases when they have wanted to make general statements about the course of party development. For this reason alone, new assessments of trends in this area must be able to take account of changes in established parties in both countries. However, the second and more important reason to examine these four cases is that their similarities and differences can aid in assessing the impact of factors which may influence the direction of organizational change within parties.

To begin with, all four parties have been affected by factors which are said to produce organizational convergence. All four define electoral success in terms of vote maximization. All have led national governments, and define this as their primary electoral goal, but all have also spent time as opposition parties. As election winners they have enjoyed access to political resources which could supplement, or even replace, membership resources (government patronage, for example, or large private donations). As election losers, they have experienced conditions which are commonly described as catalysts for organizational reform.

Other, more fundamental factors also point to organizational convergence. Britain and Germany are large democracies of the type for which Kirchheimer predicted a trend towards catch-all parties. In the years since Kirchheimer wrote, ongoing technological and social changes seem only to have confirmed his description of the pressures on parties to adopt less differentiated appeals, and to employ similar organizational approaches. In Britain and Germany the technological change during the past half-century that has most affected the practice of politics has been the rise of television as the dominant medium for top-down political communication. Television has assumed this status in both countries even though parties' opportunities to purchase broadcasting-time have been limited (Germany) or non-existent (Britain). In both countries, social changes since the 1950s have had almost as strong an impact on the development of party organizations. Most importantly, changes in labour markets and in access to education have helped to erode the formerly strong links between social class and political behaviour. For these and other reasons,

British and German citizens' attachments to parties have apparently weakened in past years.[44] Such weakened links can lead parties to alter their electioneering strategies, encouraging them to spend less time mobilizing supporters, and more time trying to convince 'floating voters'. They can also make it more difficult for parties to enrol supporters as members. Furthermore, social changes in both countries have not only weakened ties to established parties; they have also produced constituencies for new parties, and for new approaches to politics. As a result the parties studied here have been forced to react to the advent of new electoral competitors. In sum, all four parties have been exposed to many factors which might be expected to leave similar imprints on their organizational strategies.

But not all circumstances point to organizational convergence among these parties. Indeed, it could be argued that organizational idiosyncrasy is the pattern of development most likely to emerge in a study of these parties, because they differ widely in terms of two factors which have been named as strong and ongoing influences on parties' organizational decisions: initial organizational circumstances, and institutional environments.

Scholars differ in their assessments about the extent to which organizational legacies have a continuing impact. Duverger started his analysis of party organizations by proclaiming that 'just as men bear all their lives the mark of their childhood, so parties are profoundly influenced by their origins'.[45] Panebianco's analysis echoes and amplifies this declaration. He stresses the enduring importance of organizational choices made during the initial phase of party institutionalization.[46] To emphasize organizational legacies is to emphasize the power of inertia. These legacies not only make it easier for parties to maintain traditional practices than to change their organizational habits and structures; they also limit parties' options when they do change. Few scholars would deny that past organizational choices have enduring effects; what is still at issue is the extent to which past practices constrain future developments, and thereby limit the degree of possible convergence towards new or existing organizational models.

If organizational origins impose tight constraints, the four British and German parties should continue to develop in very different ways, because all four experienced very different organizational 'childhoods'. In both countries, the parties of the left initially formed outside parliament, and both tried to mobilize support by highlighting similar economic conflicts. However, their original organizational choices and developmental circumstances were very different. The British Labour Party was established as an extension of the trade-union movement, and during its first decade and a half it did not even permit individuals to be direct members. In contrast, the German Social Democrats emerged as a membership party even before German trade unions were legalized, and the SPD never relied on trade unions as formal organizational affiliates. From the first, SPD organizational strategies focused on individual membership, and on enmeshing individual supporters in a multi-faceted organizational community. In each country the parties of the centre-right also arose out of different philosophical traditions and social milieux. The British Conservative Party already had a long involvement in parliamentary politics when it began organizing a broad membership-base in the 1880s, a strategy it adopted as part of its response to Liberal Party successes. In contrast, the German Christian Democratic Union did not emerge until 1945, when it was the heir to the Catholic Centre Party (*Zentrum*) of earlier German regimes. Like the Centre Party, the CDU started as a party of local notables which initially relied on church-based associations to mobilize individual supporters. As a bi-confessional party the CDU played down its reliance on Catholic organizations, but it was nevertheless slow to build up its own membership structures.

How much continuing impact we ascribe to these parties' organizational legacies and ideological origins partially depends on the importance we attribute to institutional environments, another set of factors which is said to shape organizational strategies. The structures of electoral competition are key elements of these institutional environments; they include rules which determine eligibility for participation, and others which govern the translation of votes into legislative seats. Where elections are conducted on the basis of proportional representation (as in Germany), parties have relatively greater incentives to develop strong, nationwide organizations which can maximize overall votes. In contrast, where elections are decided in single-member-district contests (as in Britain), parties have strong incentives to target their organizational efforts on marginal districts.[47] Levels of public funding for political parties have also been linked to variations in parties' organizational decisions, and this is another area of difference between the German and British competitive environments. High public subsidies (such as exist in Germany) may enable, or even encourage, parties to shed their membership organizations, because subsidies provide parties with alternatives to using members as volunteers and as fundraisers. In short, because institutional environments are usually national in scope, and because they affect the competition of all parties within the system, focusing on institutional factors produces expectations of intra-national organizational convergence, and of cross-national organizational divergence.

As the preceding discussion suggests, competing theories about the organizational development of parties lead to very different expectations about which trends might emerge from an examination of half a century of change in these four parties. If technological imperatives and social changes are dominant, a pattern of cross-national convergence of organizational characteristics should emerge. If the rules governing electoral competition, or the configurations of the national electorates, are more important than either party traditions or technological possibilities, the most likely pattern is one of similarity between party organizations within the same country. Finally, if historical legacies are particularly important, a pattern of organizational idiosyncrasy may be revealed, because each of the four parties institutionalized in very different ways.

If the third pattern (idiosyncrasy) emerges, it will not be possible to disentangle the relative impact of different influences on party strategies. On the other hand, if the first pattern (convergence) prevails, it would suggest that factors such as electoral rules or organizational traditions have only a circumscribed effect on parties' strategies for adapting to external change. Thus, comparison of these four cases may provide an opportunity for drawing tentative conclusions about the relative importance of each of these different sets of influences during a long span of the parties' organizational development.

The following analysis of post-1945 developments in four parties takes the non-finality and complexity of organizational change as starting-points rather than as impediments to perfect prediction. Chapter 2 begins by discussing approaches for diagnosing and interpreting ongoing changes in the ways that membership parties structure their relations with enrolled supporters. This initial discussion provides a basis for examining a half-century of organizational change in the two German and two British membership parties. Instead of looking solely for evidence of the decline or persistence of the parties' membership structures, the accounts in the chapters that follow seek clues about how and why the parties have modified their organizational strategies. Chapter 3 introduces each of the parties, and describes long-term changes in their organizations and competitive environments. Chapters 4 and 5 look at changes in the specific ways in which party strategists have sought to convert enrolled members into electoral assets. These discussions of the changing roles for members during and between election campaigns show that party organizers have discarded some roles for members, but have simultaneously thought up new ways in which members can be of use to their parties. Chapter 6 analyses recent organizational debates and decisions in three of the parties, and asks whether the resulting structural changes reflect party strategists' calculations about the costs and benefits of party membership. Chapter 7 approaches the question of party decline from a different angle by examining evidence of growth or decline in each of the parties' reliance on members' contributions. The concluding chapter returns to the models introduced in Chapter 2 and re-evaluates their utility for facilitating judgements about cross-party patterns of organizational change.

As will become evident in these accounts, the story of 'party decline' from a party perspective is more complex, but ultimately more revealing, than are attempts to infer the aims of party strategies by looking only at organizational results. Above all, recognizing changes in the specific reasons for which party organizers value members helps to explain otherwise unexpected party-led efforts to restructure relations with their enlisted supporters.

2

The Costs and Benefits of Enrolling Members

[W]e have recognised the need, not so much for a Constitution which seems tidy to the student of political history or logical in all respects, as for an organisation which is an educative political force and a machine for winning elections. A political organisation must be judged by its efficiency in securing victory for the fundamental principles for which the Party stands.

Conservative Party report[1]

MANY parties' organizational experts would undoubtedly endorse this report's assertion that the success of a party organization should be judged not on grounds of logic or political theory but on whether it contributes to the attainment of party goals. Yet because such a yardstick may be quite elastic, it may produce a changing array of assessments about the adequacy of party structures and practices. Even if a party's long-term goals are stable, views about how best to reach these goals may be altered if election results indicate that current methods are not working. In the wake of lost elections, party planners may reassess the value of specific organizational features as they develop new tactics for securing victory. Party organizers may also alter their tactics in response to social or technological changes which make old approaches obsolete, or if party leaders begin to seek support among new segments of the electorate. Whatever the underlying causes, when party leaders and professional party organizers adopt new strategies for attaining party goals, they may find it useful to attempt to restructure the party's extra-parliamentary organization.

Parts of this chapter are taken from the author's article 'The "Paradox of Enrolment": Assessing the Costs and Benefits of Party Memberships', *European Journal of Political Research*, 25 (1994); 41–60, © Kluwer Academic Publishers. The material is reprinted by permission of Kluwer Academic Publishers.

The process of organizational change in membership parties is still only partially understood, despite recently renewed scholarly interest in the dynamics of that change. Many who have turned their attention to this area have sought to provide comprehensive models for describing the circumstances and constraints on organizational change, and for depicting complex relations between facets of parties inside and outside legislatures. In contrast, the aim of the present study is narrower, though no less ambitious in its own way. The intention is to illuminate a set of calculations found in most models of party development, namely, the costs and benefits party leaders identify when they assess the value of party members as organizational resources.

Although studies of party change have long been concerned with the rise and apparent demise of membership parties, most relevant theories nevertheless start with very rudimentary views about the ways that members may aid their parties. Because of this, they run a high risk of presenting vastly oversimplified explanations of parties' efforts to reshape their relations with the most committed partisans. The current chapter tries to remedy this deficit by making explicit the most common assumptions about the ways in which members can aid their parties, and then exploring some of the predictions that can be generated from a broader understanding of why parties might want to enrol members. Such a perspective will make it easier to understand the forces which produce the net balance of change. However, before considering possible explanations of organizational change in membership parties, the necessary first step is to introduce a set of tools for recognizing and interpreting such change as it occurs.

THE ORGANIZATIONAL DIMENSIONS OF MEMBERSHIP PARTIES

In biology, taxonomy is the science of identifying and classifying species in a way that highlights relevant differences or similarities. In the study of political parties, classification has also played an essential role in efforts to describe and understand differences between parties. Some of the most influential proposals for the comparative classification of party organizations have been mentioned already: Maurice Duverger's famous mass and cadre labels;

Sigmund Neumann's parties of representation and parties of integration; Kirchheimer's catch-all parties. Other well-known party taxonomies include Fred Riggs's classification of party structures according to their reliance on various inputs,[2] Herbert Kitschelt's distinction between left-libertarian and mass-bureaucratic parties,[3] and Angelo Panebianco's contrast between mass-bureaucratic and electoral-professional parties.[4] Though each of these authors proposes slightly different categories, all their classifications take account of the formal structures and actual practices which link party leaders with extra-parliamentary organizations.

These structures and practices are often described with the aid of answers to three fundamental questions: does the party attempt to assemble a large, formally enrolled, individual membership; how much control do the party's supporters have over the selection of the party's leader, its candidates for public office, and its policies; and how hierarchical and centralized are the structures in which the party organizes its supporters? Answers to these questions may be used to determine how closely a political party approximates to some taxonomical ideal. In addition, if these questions are asked at several points in time, they can also be used to chart the course of a single party's development.

In order to make such cross-temporal comparisons, parties can be located on three intersecting organizational dimensions which correspond to the preceding questions. These dimensions describe the ease of access to membership, the degree to which decision-making is centralized, and the directness of contacts between supporters and party élites. The three dimensions, which closely resemble those proposed by Austin Ranney to describe variations in the procedures by which parties select candidates, can also be useful for making cross-party comparisons.[5] Attempts to explain why parties move along these dimensions will probably need to concentrate at least as much on internal choices as on external circumstances, because all three dimensions direct attention towards changes which parties can implement on their own. Like Duverger's definition of the mass party, which highlighted parties' enrolment aspirations instead of their achieved membership size, these dimensions describe parties in terms of elements which are largely under their own control.

Dimension 1: Inclusiveness

The dimension of inclusiveness indicates the height of barriers separating party members from other supporters. The level of these barriers is partly determined by the extent of duties and privileges attached to party membership; in addition, however, it also reflects the ease or difficulty of enrolment. The latter is a function of factors such as the degree of formality of membership procedures (is there an application form? is there a probationary period?), and the party's actual accessibility to would-be members (does it recruit? can would-be members easily locate and contact the party?). The level of inclusiveness is also determined by the reasons for which a party chooses to exclude supporters from membership privileges. These may be of a kind which all individuals can sooner or later overcome (for example, the parties may exclude those under a particular age), or they may more permanently bar certain individuals (for example, some parties may refuse to admit those not of a certain race or religion). The most inclusive parties are those which blur all distinctions between members and supporters. Highly inclusive parties lack set schedules of dues and procedures for national membership, and they may even grant non-enrolled supporters full rights to participate in decision-making processes and party-sponsored events.

Dimension 2: Centralization

The second dimension for describing extra-parliamentary party organizations shows the location of control over party decision-making. This dimension indicates, for instance, whether national party leaders make all relevant decisions, or whether they share responsibility, either with regional party leaders, or with the entire party membership. In practice, the location of control over decision-making probably varies most in three areas: the selection of party leaders; the selection of party candidates for public office; the designation of party programmes. In highly centralized parties, a small core of self-appointed and self-replacing national leaders takes most decisions, and retains power of veto even in those areas in which the centre does relinquish partial control. In less centralized parties, institutions such as party conferences may be used as devices to include a wider segment of the membership in decision-making. However, determining the degree of centralization is more than just a matter of assessing formal structures, because party conferences and other institutions that apparently provide member democracy may actually be used to strengthen the control of central leaders.

Dimension 3: Mediation

The third dimension shows the extent to which party structures mediate contacts between individual members and those who lead the national party.[6] As with the other two dimensions, the degree of mediation in a party is a function both of its formal structures and of its practices. Organizational links within a party provide important channels of communication from party leaders to supporters, and from members to all levels of the organization. The degree of mediation is signalled by the nature of contacts in both directions: attempts by national party leaders to communicate with members may be more direct (for instance, through targeted mailings), or less direct (through officers of regional or local parties, or through pamphlets distributed by local parties); similarly, members' opportunities to communicate with national party élites may be more direct (internal advisory primaries, membership-only surveys) or less direct (summaries of views conveyed by intermediary sources such as regional employees or delegates to party conferences).

Tracing movement along these three dimensions is a useful way to summarize a party's organizational changes. Fig. 2.1 gives an example of such a summary. It plots the organizational characteristics of two hypothetical parties at two separate times. Over the period shown, Party A has become more inclusive and slightly less mediated, but its level of centralization has remained unchanged. In contrast, Party B has become less inclusive, more centralized, and more mediated.

Using all three dimensions to describe the direction of ongoing changes in actual parties may reveal significant patterns in what otherwise might appear to be only isolated and insignificant alterations in the relations between parties and their supporters. Conceiving of change in terms of movement along three dimensions is preferable to looking for shifts along a single spectrum (cadre to mass, mass to catch-all, etc.), because it does not impose

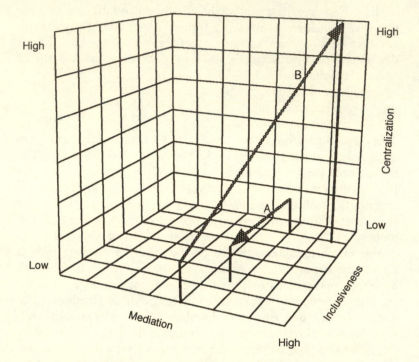

Fɪɢ 2.1. Membership party characteristics: Organizational change in a three-dimensional space

the assumption that change in these separate areas will necessarily be either unidirectional or simultaneous. Describing movement along multiple organizational dimensions, instead of working with more rigid taxonomies, may therefore make it easier to discover cross-party trends in organizational development.

The dimensions presented here can serve as useful tools for uncovering and comparing patterns of development in membership parties. However, description alone does not provide an explanation of change. Any perspective which proposes to account for trends in the evolution of party forms, or to predict the likely nature of future organizational transformations, must specify the causal motor(s) of change. The next section draws on existing theories of organizational development to introduce one such set of motors.

THE SOURCES OF CHANGE

The causes of organizational evolution can be sought both inside and outside the parties themselves. Many studies of party development have focused on the latter aspect, and have considered ways that exogenous pressures and opportunities can shape and reshape parties' modes of organization. As the previous chapter noted, some external factors which have figured prominently in explanations of party change include, in the words of one observer of parties in the United States, 'changes in the resources [a party] recruits, in the competitive pressures it feels from other political organizations, in the environmental limits on its organization and activities, and in the goals, demands, and perceptions of the electorate'.[7]

Yet, while alterations in parties' legal, social, and technical environments may all act as important catalysts for organizational change, it would be a mistake to assume that external factors alone propel development. Such a view would overlook the fact that party leaders often have more than one choice about how, or whether, to respond to outside pressures. It would also ignore the possibility that parties may act in anticipation of change, and that they may even be the cause of external changes (for instance when they alter their competitive environments by revising electoral laws). Focusing exclusively on external sources of change is thus likely to provide an inaccurate picture of the processes involved in the organizational development of parties. Because of this, many accounts of party development have looked not only at external changes, but also at parties' internal reactions to new circumstances. Some such studies have found internal pressures to adapt in the motivations of members and other supporters, others have emphasized the ways that party élites shape organizational choices, and still others have accounted for change by attributing aspirations to parties as organizational actors.

The first of these approaches explores how the presumed interests of members, and of would-be members, shape parties' organizational strategies. When the interests of party members are viewed through a rational-choice lens, levels of party membership and party activism appear to be the joint products of individuals' priorities and parties' menus of membership incentives. Authors who write from this perspective treat individual participation in voluntary organizations as something which needs to be explained in terms of individual calculations about the benefits membership brings. They note that party membership may be financially costly, and that party activism demands the valuable resource of time; for these authors the puzzle consists in explaining why some individuals are willing to assume such costs. In one of the earliest efforts to solve this puzzle, James Q. Wilson argued that participation in parties is explicable in terms of a party's incidental or deliberate provision of some combination of the following: material incentives (for example, patronage positions); specific solidary incentives (non-material benefits enjoyed selectively, that is, by only some members, such as party honours or offices); collective solidary incentives (non-material 'identity' benefits which can be enjoyed by all members of the group, such as social opportunities); and purposive incentives (non-material benefits which can be enjoyed by all members, such as satisfaction derived from helping to achieve goals which are perceived to be worthwhile).[8]

Wilson's terms have been widely adopted. To take a notable example, Kitschelt did not stray far from Wilson's earlier categories in his analysis of the development of the Belgian and German Green parties in the 1980s. He distinguished three types of party supporters according to their primary motivations: those who are most attracted by solidary incentives and collective goods (the ideologues); those who are most attracted by short-term selective policy benefits (the lobbyists); and those who seek long-term selective policy benefits (the pragmatists). Part of what was so valuable about Kitschelt's analysis was that he used these categories to emphasize how parties can adjust the combination of membership incentives they offer, and to explore how the motivations of activists can in turn shape parties' structures and policies.[9] This is a particularly useful perspective, for while it acknowledges that state laws and party traditions may impose restrictions on what parties may offer their members, it calls attention to parties' efforts to flourish within these constraints.

Those who view decisions about enrolment as something that should be explicable in terms of membership rewards must expect party membership to shrink whenever there is a decline in the absolute or relative value of the incentives which parties provide. This is the logic that underlies the assertion that the rising benefits of the welfare state, and the growing availability of leisure alternatives, have both threatened the persistence of membership parties by diminishing the relative value of the material incentives that parties can offer to their members.

One way to explain change in party organizations is thus to examine changes in the calculations made by party supporters. A second way is to examine changes in the calculations made by party leaders. Panebianco emphasized the latter when he asserted that it is the 'dynamics of the struggle for power within an organization' which 'offer the key for understanding its functioning as well as the changes it undergoes'.[10] He suggested that the nature of basic organizational changes should be interpreted by studying the ambitions and cohesiveness of those who belong to a party's 'dominant coalition'. For example, in parties with divided leaderships, factions may block the expansion of membership because they fear that new members might upset existing internal power-balances. Furthermore, Panebianco saw leaders' interests as crucial for explaining variations in the size of party membership:

Size can sometimes vary independently of the elites' decisions to change it, but their deliberate choices still play a greater role on most occasions. Our thesis is that party size mainly depends on each party's internal power structure, i.e. on the conformation of its dominant coalition.[11]

Panebianco thus argued that environmental crises could act as catalysts for change, and that a party's initial institutionalization could constrain its subsequent organizational choices, but he also stressed that the strengths and interests of competing party élites would nevertheless help shape the direction of party development.

A third perspective on organizational change in membership parties looks at parties as if they were unified actors which pursue electoral goals. From this perspective, organizational change can result from party leaders' changing interpretations of whether, or how, members can improve the party's electoral chances.

By examining the calculations of members, the first of these approaches offers a supply-side account of why membership parties may find it easy or difficult to enrol members. The latter two approaches offer demand-side explanations for change in membership parties. Such demand-side approaches are surprisingly underdeveloped, despite the many predictions that parties will alter their organizational strategies in response to technological change.

Whereas supply-side considerations of party development have often sought to explain why individuals affirm their partisan support through the act of enrolling as party members, far fewer studies have looked at the membership equation from the perspective of parties. Indeed, for many years there were very few attempts to uncover the calculations party leaders make when they decide to pay the costs necessary to attract and retain the support of enrolled members. As Robert Harmel and Kenneth Janda noted recently, 'most statements about party change have given little attention to the parties' own decision-making processes in effecting organizational change'.[12] This deficiency is now rapidly being remedied, and recent studies in this area have begun to gather new data and shed new light on these processes.[13] However, much remains to be done.

In the present study, the focus is on understanding how parties' internal decision-making processes shape the direction of development when changes do occur. The argument is that demand-side calculations about what makes membership useful provide clues about the specific nature of changes in particular structures and practices. While this perspective will surely not be adequate to account for all organizational change, a less simplistic view of parties' organizational calculations will certainly improve the more comprehensive models of organizational change. Unlike money, the value of members as an organizational resource is a subjective one, and it is precisely this subjective view that can shed light on parties' organizational manifestations.

In exploring the implications of changing assessments of member utility, the present chapter follows the Downsian tradition of examining predictions generated when parties are viewed as electorally-motivated unitary actors. The Downsian approach admittedly overlooks complex and important relations among actors within organizations. However, it is used here precisely because it is the one most commonly employed by those who make the bleakest predictions about the future of parties as membership organizations. Furthermore, it constitutes the toughest challenge, because, as will be explained shortly, predictions of the decline of membership organizations are hardest to refute from this perspective.

The scenario that most commonly produces predictions about the inevitable decline of membership parties is that party leaders lose interest in enrolling large memberships once new technologies and new social conditions diminish the comparative electoral utility of members. One way to refute this prediction is to change the assumptions that underlie it (that parties are unitary actors whose decisions are driven by electoral considerations). For instance, a convincing argument can be made in favour of viewing parties as collections of competing élites and their supporters. Panebianco adopted this approach when he showed how the utility of members can lie in their ability to help individual party leaders attain personal goals. If parties' organizational decisions are seen in terms of the priorities of competing party leaders, it should not be surprising to find parties investing in schemes to attract members even if there is no evidence that members help the party as a whole to win votes. An alternative approach for refuting predictions concerning the disappearance of membership parties is to argue that party decisions are not solely, or even primarily, motivated by electoral considerations. Kitschelt employed this perspective in his study of left-libertarian parties when he focused on how members contribute to the realization of parties' non-electoral goals. Of course, Kitschelt himself argued that parties motivated only secondarily by electoral considerations were only a small subset of parties in liberal democracies, and he implicitly accepted that an electoral perspective is valid for what he calls 'mass-bureaucratic' parties. Still, as both these examples make clear, one way to explain why membership parties might persist is by shifting the assumptions of the debate.

However, neither of these perspectives says anything about the validity of the original prediction. They leave unanswered the more difficult question of whether unitary vote-maximizing parties would have any reason to invest in memberships once they have gained access to financial and technological resources which equal or exceed the potential contributions of party members. This is the question which will be explored in the following pages, where parties are initially viewed as vote-maximizing unified actors in order to investigate whether contemporary party strategists might see reasons for parties to pay the costs of recruiting and retaining members.

Studying the organizational strategies of parties as if they were developed by unified actors is thus a way of directly confronting one of the more explicit predictions about parties' organizational calculations. Use of this perspective can be further defended on the grounds that it does not require a very big leap of abstraction. In fact, the studies in this book make clear that party organizational strategies are usually developed by a small, easily identified, group of 'role incumbents' who carry out their assigned tasks.[14]

The terms 'party leaders', 'party organizers', and 'party strategists' are used throughout this book to refer to individuals who gain formal or *de facto* control over the financial and personnel resources of a party's extra-parliamentary organization. The leadership group often includes the party chair, the party manager (if independently elected), the head of the party's parliamentary delegation, and some or all members of the party's national executive. Party organizers are party employees who have the job of directing the year-round work of the extra-parliamentary party. Party leaders and party organizers have strong incentives to pay attention to organizational strategies and tactics because their professional reputations are usually enhanced if they introduce apparently successful (vote-winning) organizational innovations. The intra-party support that initially helped leaders and organizers to win their offices gives them a good chance, but no guarantee, of being able to implement their organizational ideas. Party leaders and party organizers may not share identical organizational strategies, but they are likely to hold many common perspectives, particularly if leaders control or influence the appointment of top party employees. Finally, the term 'party strategist' refers to all those who articulate organizational plans for the party, and who possess some influence with the current party leadership. Those who act as party strategists may do so from within the ranks of party leaders or party organizers, but more junior parliamentarians, journalists, or academics may also provide their parties with new ideas and new strategies. Thus, viewing a party as if it had a single set of preferences about party organization only aggregates the views of, at most, a dozen readily identifiable individuals, all of whom are members of a party's 'dominant coalition'; these are the individuals who usually must give at least tacit assent to official organizational strategies.

For the reasons just described, the chapters that follow employ an electoral perspective in examining changes in the ways that British and German party leaders and party organizers have assessed the net value of membership organization. The focus adopted here is similar to the one advocated by Stefano Bartolini, who argued that in order to understand the organizational decisions of parties

party membership has to be viewed as an organizational resource, and as the result of organizational incentives offered by the party leadership and officers. In this case, the problem is knowing how party leaders perceive and value the basic resource of membership . . . To maintain, increase, or even decrease the levels of membership and activism is, from the leadership perspective, an organizational effort, which might or might not be rewarded in terms of money, work, and time.[15]

Although the following discussions emphasize demand-side calculations about the utility of members, they do not ignore the effects of the supply-side forces which affect enrolment. Instead, external changes are viewed here as factors which shape party leaders' calculations about the costs and benefits of party membership.[16] As will be explained in the following sections, if organizational change in membership parties is driven by changed perceptions of member utility, such changes are likely to coincide with reassessments about the kind of supporters parties should attempt to enrol. This means that understanding why parties want members may yield predictions about what parties will be prepared to do to enrol such supporters.

Of course, as Bartolini makes clear in the excerpt cited above, party leaders may be just as likely to consider membership a liability as to view it as an asset. Indeed, arguments about the costs imposed by members, like arguments about the costs of enrolment, are quite familiar in the wake of years of articles which take for granted that party organizers are interested in shedding party memberships. Nevertheless, this is only part of the story—even in a mass-media age, members can be assets as well as liabilities. The interesting questions are whether party leaders consider the benefits of membership to outweigh the costs, and what they will do to maximize the former and minimize the latter. However, because the demand-side calculus of membership utility is so understudied, these questions cannot be answered until after an explicit consideration of the reasons why party strategists might categorize enrolled supporters either as electoral assets or as liabilities. Only then will it be possible to complete the argument about how changing strategic assessments can propel organizational change in membership parties.

ASSESSING THE UTILITY OF MEMBERSHIP ORGANIZATION

To portray party members as generic organizational assets, uniformly valuable or worthless, would be to make the mistaken assertion that membership is a resource which is as fungible as money. Whereas money is an asset which can be stored and used as needed, members may be a meaningless resource unless party leaders can mobilize them at appropriate times and in useful ways. Of course, party strategists may hold very different ideas about which times are 'appropriate', and what tasks are 'useful'. Yet despite the long history of studies of party organization, there are surprisingly few efforts to describe the broad range of uses which party strategists might envisage for enrolled members.[17] To remedy this deficit, the following discussion brings together a wide variety of claims about the ways in which members may constitute organizational liabilities or organizational assets. Of these, it is the arguments about members as liabilities which are most familiar, because these are arguments that explain why party leaders may consider enrolled supporters to be more trouble than they are worth.

Members as Liabilities

There are two general types of argument about why party members may be harmful to party interests. The first focuses on ways in which members may directly undermine electoral support for their own party. The second points to the opportunity costs incurred by the recruitment and retention of members, and concludes that enrolment is an inefficient use of organizational resources.

1. Programmatic Costs

According to arguments about the programmatic costs imposed by party members, the latter are an electoral liability because they tend to support vote-losing policies. Individuals who become party members, and especially those who become active members, are said to come from the most ideologically extreme segment of party supporters. Unlike the holders and seekers of party office, many committed members would rather see their party lose an election than see it compromise on the purity of its principles.[18] At its most extreme, this argument leads to the conclusion that wherever party members have a formal, or even an informal, role in the selection of party leaders and party policies, parties are likely to become inflexible and unresponsive to shifts of preference among the broader electorate. As a result, such parties will find it difficult to win elections. The conclusion of this argument is that party leaders who want to win or retain office may see members as a burden, because they can hamper the party's ability to act as an efficient vote-seeking organization.

The premise of this argument is by no means universally accepted in the scholarly community, and there are both theoretical and empirical reasons for rejecting the notion that active members always impose programmatic costs.[19] However, even if it is not inevitable that members will make vote-losing programmatic demands, if party leaders believe it to be likely, the argument may nevertheless shape party organizational development.

2. Opportunity Costs

Another argument that can be used to oppose membership enrolment is that the resources used to recruit and retain members are poorly invested. Incurring such opportunity costs is almost unavoidable for membership parties. Even parties which do not provide selective incentives for members usually pay expenses associated with formally enrolling individuals in the party. At the minimum, in most membership parties professionals or volunteers must spend time keeping membership records. Furthermore, party activists and employees at both local and national levels usually spend time and party money organizing membership meetings and sending information to members and possible recruits. These are resources which might instead be used to reach out to the broader community. Thus, it can be argued that the opportunity costs of organizing and maintaining the party membership exceed any potential benefits which could be provided by these members.

Members as Assets

On the other side of the ledger, members can be portrayed as organizational assets, and it may be thought that parties improve their electoral fortunes by formally enrolling some, or even many, of their supporters. There are eight common arguments about how members may help their parties to win votes. The benefits they describe can be roughly ranked according to the increasing difficulty of the tasks that individual members must undertake in order to aid their parties.

1. Legitimacy Benefits.

One reason that party strategists may value members is because they believe that undecided voters will be swayed by their perceptions concerning the extent and the nature of parties' support. In this case, party organizers may value new members simply because they improve membership statistics. Such statistics may be considered to be particularly important wherever journalists use membership growth or decline to assess a party's standing, or to predict its future electoral prospects. Good membership statistics may also be especially useful for boosting the legitimacy of fledgling parties, a point noted by Michels when he argued that for a young socialist party 'every decline in membership and every loss in voting strength diminishes its political prestige'.[20]

'Political prestige' may be won from membership statistics in other ways than by enhancing overall totals. For instance, party organizers may also attach special value to members who possess the characteristics of electoral segments to which the party is trying to appeal. Because of this, party organizers may seek to alter the demographic composition of party membership either more closely to reflect the party's existing votes or better to match the types of voter the party would like to attract. Thus in certain contexts statistics on ethnic-minority or female enrolment may be seen as a useful tool for increasing the credibility of a party's claim to represent these groups.

At a slightly more abstract level, enrolled members may boost party legitimacy, and thereby help parties' electoral fortunes, by allowing parties to present themselves as popular organizations controlled by ordinary members, rather than by 'professional politicians'. Members may provide these kinds of legitimacy benefits even if membership control is more apparent that real, as long as party leaders can plausibly claim to be deferring to the wishes of a broad membership. In either case, whether members are wanted because they improve membership statistics or because they enhance the appearance of intra-party democracy, arguments concerning legitimacy benefits provide reasons why party leaders might find electoral value even in members who are completely inactive within their parties.

2. Direct Electoral Benefits

In some parties, members may be particularly valued for the electoral support they provide. This may be particularly likely where members are known or assumed to vote more regularly, and more consistently, than other voters. Research in some countries has provided support for such a view of party members.[21] Of course, in most countries party members represent only a small portion of the electorate, and electorally ambitious parties must usually seek votes beyond the boundaries of their own membership. Nevertheless, party strategists may believe that members are able to provide a crucial margin of victory, particularly in elections with low turn-out levels or in very competitive contests.

3. Outreach Benefits

Party leaders may value members for the support they can mobilize by means of their everyday contacts. For instance, those under the influence of theories such as Paul Lazarsfeld's two-step communication model may consider members who are local notables ('opinion leaders') to be particularly valuable, because such citizens are thought routinely to influence the political views of those in their communities.[22] Others may view even non-notable members as potentially valuable ambassadors to the community, as people who can multiply votes through their willingness openly to declare, and even to explain, their personal political allegiances. Party members' everyday contacts may be especially valued in parties which are struggling to gain, or regain, public recognition and acceptance.

4. Financial Benefits

Party organizers may view membership enrolment as a useful means of generating revenue. Duverger expressed this idea most picturesquely when he equated the invention of mass-membership organization with the invention of the national-defence bond, both of which were devices to assemble large sums through the collection of many small donations.[23] According to Duverger, parties without other resources were the pioneers in developing membership-based funding. However, party leaders may also value members' financial contributions where members are not the sole, or even the primary, source of party funds.

5. Labour Benefits

Party members may be valued for the free labour they can contribute both during and between election campaigns. This is probably the benefit political scientists most frequently mention when they describe the ways in which members help their parties, even though studies of specific parties usually emphasize the small proportion of active members.

Labour benefits are qualitatively different from the preceding benefits. Whereas the first four describe ways in which all members, even those who never show up at a party event, can boost a party's electoral fortunes, labour benefits are provided only by members who actively work within the party.

6. Linkage Benefits

Party leaders may see members as an essential source of information about public concerns, and they may consider the membership organization to be a channel of communication which keeps the party in touch with 'grass-roots' opinion. Leaders of parties which have intentionally narrow electoral appeals are particularly likely to consider messages from the party membership to be more revealing of supporters' attitudes than is information from general surveys of public opinion. Note, of course, that this argument about linkage benefits directly contradicts the argument that members impose progammatic costs because they tend to keep party leaders out of touch with relevant popular opinions.

7. Innovation Benefits

Members can also be viewed as a source of new ideas that can improve party policies, or that can make party practices more effective. In order to provide such benefits, members must be more than mere receptors which gather and transmit widespread public concerns; they must also independently generate ideas that have the potential to capture the popular imagination. If party leaders look to members to provide new perspectives, they may be particularly amenable to procedures which facilitate intra-party debates.

8. Personnel Benefits

Party leaders may view the party membership as a greenhouse for cultivating new generations of political talent. Though parties may well have additional channels of leadership recruitment, existing leaders may favour candidates who have already demonstrated commitment to current party goals (and to current party leaders) through their prior service within the party's membership organization. Furthermore, party strategists may argue in favour of recruiting members with particular demographic attributes (women, ethnic minorities) in order to build up a reservoir of potential candidates who can visibly embody the party's commitment to specific groups.

The eight benefits listed above are not mutually exclusive. Indeed, it is likely that party leaders will simultaneously advance several arguments about why it is useful for their parties to recruit. However, it is plausible to assume that leaders of specific parties have different primary reasons for valuing members, just as it is plausible to assume that individuals have different primary reasons for enrolling in parties. It is also likely that parties' reasons for enrolling members will change over time. As social and political circumstances change, party leaders are likely to alter their assessments about which are the most important mechanisms for converting the potential resource of membership into an actual electoral asset. Changing circumstances may even encourage leaders to conclude that the potential costs of membership outweigh any benefits that members might provide.

Recognizing this possibility for recalculation is important because, as the next section shows, party leaders' changing ideas about the utility of members can have an important organizational impact. The likely nature of the impact can be shown by employing the preceding lists of arguments about the costs and benefits of

membership enrolment as a foundation for more general statements about links between strategies and organizational changes
within parties.

THE CALCULUS OF MEMBERSHIP INCENTIVES

When party strategists determine how members can and should aid
their parties, they are also making implicit calculations about the
characteristics of the members the party should attempt to attract.
Some benefits can be provided by completely passive members,
but others will be provided only by members who are willing to be
continually active on behalf of their party. The demands associated
with providing various benefits can best be described by answering
two questions: what intensity of engagement is demanded of those
who provide this benefit, and to what extent does the envisaged
activity take place within formal party structures? Fig. 2.2 uses
answers to these two questions to display in graphic form the wide
range of differences in the nature of tasks which individual
members may be expected to perform. This figure shows, for
instance, that if parties are to reap labour benefits from membership enrolment, members must be actively and visibly engaged
within their local parties. It also shows that parties can reap other
rewards, such as legitimacy benefits, whether or not members ever
show up at party meetings.

Because of the wide variations in demands, and because individuals are assumed to enrol and remain in parties for a variety of
reasons, it is unlikely that all members will be equally interested in
performing every task. For instance, the members who are most
likely to enjoy active and public proselytizing are those who are
motivated by fervour for the party cause; in contrast, those who
join a party because they want the more tangible benefits of
membership may have little interest in volunteering for such
time-consuming and highly visible outreach activities. As a result
of variations in members' motivations, when party strategists
change their ideas about the best ways for members to aid their
parties, they are also likely to change their ideas about which type
of members the party most needs to attract. Organizational change
within a party may thus occur because party leaders deliberately

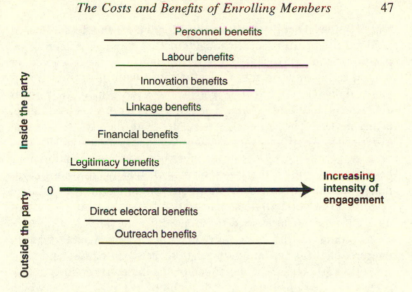

FIG 2.2. Reaping benefits from members: The costs to members

alter structures and practices in order to make membership more appealing to individuals with distinct interests or characteristics.

At this point it will be helpful to summarize the sequence of premisses introduced so far.

1. If party leaders value members, it is because members perform specific tasks which increase the party's electoral chances.
2. If party leaders value members, they are willing to spend party resources or to sacrifice leadership privileges in order to encourage supporters to enrol.
3. Members and potential members have a variety of reasons for enrolling, and therefore have different degrees of interest in performing particular tasks within their party.
4. If party leaders value members, they will try to ensure that their party offers incentives which will attract individuals most likely to perform the specific tasks which they, the party leaders, value most.

This sequence of arguments does not assume that party professionals or elected leaders are familiar with the discussions about participation incentives which are conducted in the realms of political science. In fact, in today's parties those who plan organizational strategies may well have training in political science, or may at least draw on the advice of those who do. More importantly, however, political scientists have developed their ideas about why individuals join parties by observing behaviour in actual parties. The arguments presented here merely assume that experienced party organizers and the political scientists who observe parties develop similar intuitions about why individuals become, and remain party members—whether or not these organizers would express their intuitions in the terms of political science. Like good anglers, party organizers must be aware that different types of lures tend to attract different types of fish.

According to the view developed here, one useful way to interpret changes in top-down relations between parties and their supporters (such as those described on the three dimensions in Fig. 2.1) is by viewing them as reflections of the reasons for which party leaders value members. Do party leaders primarily want to realize greater legitimacy-benefits from their membership organizations? Then they will probably be content to add mostly passive members. Hence, we should expect them drastically to lower the barriers to membership (increased inclusiveness). What if party leaders want greater outreach-benefits? Then they may consider it essential to enrol more individuals who are willing to speak out about politics in formal or informal settings. Such individuals are more likely than others to appreciate purposive rewards. Party leaders may therefore calculate that it is worth trying to attract politically-motivated members by offering increased opportunities for members to shape party policy or select party candidates (decreased centralization).

Decisions about specific ways to change the package of membership incentives may also reflect party leaders' assessments about the value of continuously active local parties. If campaigning for national elections is conducted exclusively in the national media, and if local government is non-partisan, parties may choose to offer only those benefits which the national political organization can provide directly to individual members. In these circumstances, party leaders may see no direct electoral benefits in having intermediaries from local parties acting either as benefit providers, membership mobilizers, or campaign organizers. However, even in these circumstances national party organizers may still recognize an indirect value in maintaining local associations—for instance, if they want to attract the type of members who appreciate solidary benefits. Local parties are probably the best providers of such collective solidary rewards as holiday festivities, or services for older members; no amount of direct mail from national head-quarters can replicate the experiences offered by involvement within a local party community.

Few, if any, parties will try to limit their recruitment to a single type of member, because in most parties there will be more than one answer to the question of how members can help the party. Accordingly, parties will offer a mixture of incentives designed to attract a variety of members. However, this mixture is likely to change as party leaders alter their assessments about the relative value of particular benefits. Looking for changes in parties' organizational strategies can thus help to integrate short-term interpretations of current events with longer-term predictions about organizational trends.

But what precisely is an 'organizational strategy'? Sjöblom's definition is a useful starting-point for defining this term:

'Strategy' . . . is meant to indicate an actor's extensive and comprehensive planning of the use of available means with the object of attaining certain goals attempted in competition with others. The actor is presumed to have the option of choice. The result of various alternatives cannot be precisely determined . . . .[24]

Parties' organizational strategies are distinct from their electoral strategies, though the latter may well influence the former. For a vote-seeking party the electoral strategy is a plan for winning votes from specific segments of the electorate. In contrast, its organizational strategy is a plan for optimizing the use of available and potential organizational resources in order to promote the realization of the electoral strategy.

A party's organizational strategy at least implicitly ranks the value of different resources (money, members, etc.), and it assesses how each type of resource can most usefully be deployed. An organizational strategy also incorporates judgements about the prices which should be paid for each type of resource. Because organizational strategies bring together assessments about the best means for achieving electoral ends, they can influence party decisions about how to shape formal structures of the extra-parliamentary organization, about the proper uses of professional and volunteer campaigners, and about the appropriate ways to conduct relations with non-party supporters (including wealthy patrons, trade unions, and businesses). In short, parties' organizational strategies may be at least as important as institutional constraints and opportunities in influencing the course of party development.

However, this importance does not make organizational strategies any easier to identify. It is relatively straightforward to ascribe policy preferences to parties, even to opposition parties, because party élites regularly endorse written programmes and election platforms, but they only rarely lend their support to documents which summarize organizational strategies. Indeed, quite the opposite may be the case, because many party discussions about organizational failures and planned improvements are conducted in secret, and in ways that may leave few traces even in party archives. Fortunately, on most organizational matters there is not only an 'official story' about what the party looks like;[25] there is also an 'official story' about how the ideal party should function. Pieces of this story can be found in a variety of sources, including documents issued by central-party bureaucracies, leadership-supported conference resolutions, and statements made by parties' national chairs and professional organizers. Though this official story is likely to contain a good measure of wishful thinking, it can nevertheless be quite revealing. Most importantly, as long as the official story is not static, it provides good evidence of underlying changes in a party's organizational aspirations.

APPLYING THE FRAMEWORK

Organizational changes have been characteristic of parties throughout the past century, and there is no reason to expect party organizations to stop evolving in the future. The twentieth century may indeed have been the century of the mass party, but even so, there has never been a single recipe for describing how such parties were actually organized. Instead, the structures of membership parties have varied across time and between countries. Because organizational change appears to be the norm for parties, it is the development of dynamic models, not the proliferation of static categories, which is likely to prove most helpful for interpreting organizational relations in today's political parties.

The present chapter has argued that existing models of change in membership parties can be improved by developing a more nuanced view of party leaders' calculations concerning the costs and benefits of enrolling members. It has also proposed that invoking such demand-side assessments may help to make sense of seemingly unconnected or minor organizational changes. The case for adopting such a perspective would be strengthened if evidence were available to show that party leaders and party organizers actually do alter their views about how and why members constitute a useful organizational resource, and about how best to attract members. Put differently, if such calculations about the costs and benefits of members are shown to be fixed, these calculations cannot possibly account for changes in a party's organization. As a result, one basic test of the plausibility of the proposed perspective is to ask whether parties' organizational experts do take the time and effort to revise their assessments of what it is that members are good for. Furthermore, using such a perspective would seem more appropriate if in at least some cases there is indeed sufficient evidence to link changes in leaders' strategic calculations with specific top-down efforts to change party structures or practices.

Looking for this kind of evidence of strategic thinking about membership utility is the task for the remainder of this book. The following chapters systematically consider the 'official organizing stories' of four German and British parties, and they search for evidence that organizers and leaders in these parties have deliberately cultivated party memberships as an organizational resource. These chapters examine published and unpublished party records for clues about how party leaders have thought about the utility of membership organization, and about how their assessments have led them to promote specific organizational initiatives. As will become clear, party records provide a rich and rewarding resource for uncovering changing ideas about the costs and benefits of enrolling and maintaining membership networks.

3

The Development of Membership Parties in Germany and Britain

> The organizational structures of the CDU as a people's party have grown and further developed in the past forty years under different conditions as [both] government- and opposition-party. Today it is a matter of adapting these organizational structures to changed external circumstances. . . . In a competitive society like that in the Federal Republic, success comes only on the basis of constant innovation.
>
> CDU party conference report[1]

'CONSTANT innovation' and willingness to reinvent organizational structures may be a virtue, or even a necessity, for any party which tries to survive over decades. But what form will this innovation take? Innovation is unlikely to be a random process, and a party's possibilities for adaptation are probably not unlimited. Instead, organizational change is likely to be constrained by a party's organizational origins, and shaped by the specific nature of the 'changed external circumstances' to which it responds. The impact of such factors can best be recognized by observing organizational change as a long-term process carried out on several levels. The chapters which follow look closely at organizational innovation and the development of organizing strategies in four parties in Britain and Germany. These chapters examine party leaders' changing ideas about the uses, and the costs, of enrolled membership, and they ask how changed ideas have contributed to changed structures and changed procedures.

However, the first step in this examination is formally to introduce the parties and their electoral environments. The remainder of the current chapter thus presents broad sketches of post-1945 organizational developments in the German SPD and CDU, and in the British Labour and Conservative Parties. These histories highlight changes in the parties' leaderships and in their electoral fortunes, and they provide an overview of some of the period's most important party decisions affecting membership structures and rules.

GERMANY

The development of parties in the Federal Republic of Germany was shaped by reaction against perceived failures of political parties in the Weimar Republic. Most notably, the politicians and jurists who drafted the country's new Basic Law responded to the strong anti-party rhetoric of the Weimar period by granting democratic parties a constitutionally protected role. The Basic Law stipulates that 'parties help form the political will of the people', and that parties' 'internal organization shall conform to democratic principles', with details to be regulated by federal laws.[2]

Despite the Basic Law's injunction, the German parliament (*Bundestag*) did not actually get around to passing legislation to regulate parties until 1967, when it adopted the first Parties Law. Since then, the Parties Law has affected two important aspects of German political organization. First, it stipulates that the highest governing body in every party and party sub-unit is the party conference, which must convene at least once every two years to elect the party chair and other party leaders. Parties may choose whether all members, or merely their representatives, will have voting rights at these conferences. The Law also states that only individuals, and not organizations, may belong to German parties.

The Parties Law accounts for, and perpetuates, certain similarities in the formal structures of the SPD and CDU. Most importantly, from the passage of the Parties Law until very recently, both SPD and CDU operated almost exclusively on the principle of delegate democracy, with representatives to regional and federal conferences having the final authority to select party candidates and leaders, and approve party programmes. (In both the CDU and SPD, the chair of the federal party is usually, but not always, the chancellor or designated chancellor-candidate.) However, this uniformity in decision-making structures eroded in the 1990s, when units in both parties began experimenting with direct democracy inside the party, the other option permitted by the Parties Law.

The Parties Law also encourages the convergence of party statutes by stipulating that all members of a single party must enjoy formally equal privileges and obligations. These obligations have seldom been very onerous. In the early 1990s, a person who wished to become a member of either the SPD or CDU had to pay monthly dues (according to a schedule established by the respective party conferences), agree to support party goals, and abstain from simultaneously enrolling in a second party. In 1994 employed individuals were supposed to pay a monthly minimum of DM5 as a CDU member (the equivalent of approximately £24 or $US44 per year), and of DM7 as an SPD member (approximately £34 or $US51 per year). In both parties, those who earned more were supposed to pay higher dues.

A third reason the Parties Law has been so important in German politics—and the real impetus for the Law's passage—is that it establishes the legal framework for state subsidies to political parties. The legislators who established the state payments, and the judges who approved a succession of funding plans for parties, argued that public subsidies to parties are legal and proper because they help parties fulfil their constitutionally mandated role of 'helping to form the political will of the people'. Though the levels and conditions of this funding have changed several times since the adoption of the Parties Law, in all their forms the subsidies have enabled German parties to develop comparatively large professional bureaucracies.

The Parties Law and the constitutional protection for democratic parties were two products of the reaction against the experiences of the Weimar Republic; West Germany's electoral system was another. Many German politicians and political scientists of the 1940s and 1950s blamed Weimar's system of pure proportional representation for fostering parliamentary instability and undermining links between citizens and their representatives, and they were determined that the new republic should not make the same mistakes. The new electoral system modified proportional representation in two ways. First, it added a 5-per-cent hurdle for parties seeking to enter the *Bundestag*; this was intended to encourage party consolidation. Second, it grafted single-member constituencies onto a list-system of proportional representation; this was intended to strengthen links between voters and their elected representatives. Since 1953, half the members of the *Bundestag* have been elected from these single-member constituencies, while the other half have been chosen from party lists. The formula governing the distribution of list seats ensures the approximate proportionality of the overall outcome.[3]

Germany's federal constitution gives state governments a potentially powerful role in national politics. In 1995 there were sixteen states (*Länder*), each with its own parliament and state minister-president or mayor. Because they need to contest state elections and to participate in state-level governments, both the SPD and CDU have gradually adjusted their own multi-tiered structures to reflect state boundaries, although the correspondence is still not exact. For instance, in some areas the SPD's state parties are less important than its lower-tier regional parties (*Bezirke*). Furthermore, the CDU does not organize in Bavaria, the home of its 'sister party', the Christian Social Union (*Christlich-Soziale Union*: CSU). The CDU and CSU have always co-operated in the federal parliament, but they have completely separate (and rather different) organizational structures, policy platforms, and party leaders.[4]

In both the SPD and CDU, state- or regional-level party sub-units play important roles, including compiling lists of candidates for federal elections. In addition, party organizations and government offices at state level provide regional party élites with important power-bases. Below the state and regional levels are the 'county parties' (usually known as *Kreisverbände* in the CDU, *Unterbezirke* in the SPD), units whose boundaries sometimes coincide with those of parliamentary districts. At the lowest organizational level, each of the parties enrols individual members in neighbourhood or village units. (These are known as *Ortsverbände* in the CDU, *Ortsvereine* in the SPD.) The local parties are responsible for organizing all members who reside within specified geographic boundaries.[5]

Both federal parties support their extra-parliamentary organizations with well-staffed national headquarters, and the state and regional parties have an even larger network of employees dispersed throughout the country. Both parties have federal business managers (*Bundesgeschäftsführer*), who oversee the work of their professional bureaucracies. The CDU also has a general secretary who supervises the work of the entire party. Although both the general secretary of the CDU and the party manager of the SPD are now formally elected by party conferences, they need the support of the party leader to obtain, and retain, their positions. The parties' headquarters figure prominently in the following discussions of the development of the individual parties, because central organizers have sponsored many of the initiatives for extra-parliamentary party reform.

Social Democratic Organization since 1945

In 1945 most SPD members believed that their party was well placed to prosper in any reconstituted German state. This optimism stemmed in part from the fact that the re-established SPD inherited from its Weimar predecessor a clearly defined electorate, a strong organizational tradition, an experienced leadership, and a pre-war record of steadfast opposition to the National Socialists. Kurt Schumacher, the party's first post-war chair, had served as a party official and *Reichstag* member in the Weimar SPD, and he had strengthened his political stature while serving as a political prisoner during most of the years of National Socialist rule. The refounded SPD grew rapidly under Schumacher's leadership. As early as 1946 SPD membership in the Western zones and Berlin exceeded the party's 1932 totals for these areas[6] (see Table 3.1 and Fig. 3.1). The SPD also did well in many of the first state-level elections. Thus, it came as a shock to many within the SPD when the party's strong organization did not triumph in the first federal elections in 1949 (see Table 3.2). The impact of this loss was magnified because the party was unable to surpass the psychologically important 30-per-cent barrier.

Leading party officials disagreed about how the SPD should react to these disappointing results. National party leaders appointed a committee to study the implications of the 1949 defeat. This committee concluded that the best response was to strengthen the party's traditional organization by increasing activity in workplaces, expanding the network of party functionaries, and enhancing efforts to enrol women and young voters.[7] As part of its resultant efforts to build up the party organization, the federal headquarters sponsored (in 1950) what was to be the first of many party-wide recruiting drives.[8] However, not everyone in the party agreed with this strategy of relying on traditional

TABLE 3.1. *CDU and SPD membership 1946–1994*

Year	CDU	SPD	Year	CDU	SPD
1946		711,000	1970	329,000	820,000
1947	400,000	875,000	1971	356,000	847,000
1948		845,000	1972	423,000	954,000
1949		736,000	1973	457,000	974,000
1950		684,000	1974	531,000	990,000
1951		650,000	1975	590,000	998,000
1952	200,000	628,000	1976	652,000	1,022,000
1953		607,000	1977	664,000	1,006,000
1954	215,000	585,000	1978	675,000	997,000
1955		589,000	1979	683,000	982,000
1956	245,000	612,000	1980	693,000	986,000
1957		626,000	1981	705,000	956,000
1958		624,000	1982	719,000	926,000
1959		634,000	1983	735,000	926,000
1960		650,000	1984	730,000	916,000
1961		645,000	1985	719,000	916,000
1962	248,000	647,000	1986	714,000	913,000
1963	252,000	648,000	1987	706,000	910,000
1964	280,000	678,000	1988	677,000	912,000
1965	288,000	710,000	1989	663,000	921,000
1966	281,000	728,000	1990	790,000	950,000
1967	286,000	733,000	1991	757,000	920,000
1968	287,000	732,000	1992	714,000	886,000
1969	304,000	779,000	1993	685,000	861,000
			1994	674,000	854,000

Note: The figures for 1990 and afterwards are for the unified parties.

Sources: CDU: for 1947–69, from Ute Schmidt, 'Christlich Demokratische Union Deutschlands', in Richard Stöss (ed.), *Parteien-Handbuch*, i (Opladen: Westdeutscher Verlag, 1983), 643; for 1970–94, CDU, *Bericht des Bundesgeschäftsstelle*, various years. SPD: information provided by the SPD party headquarters, Bonn.

practices. In particular, some junior party leaders saw the poor election results as a signal that 'more of the same' was precisely the wrong response. At the beginning of the 1950s, however, internal critics of SPD traditions faced an uphill struggle.

When Kurt Schumacher died in 1952, he was replaced by Erich Ollenhauer, another leader who had formed his ideas about party

(in thousands)

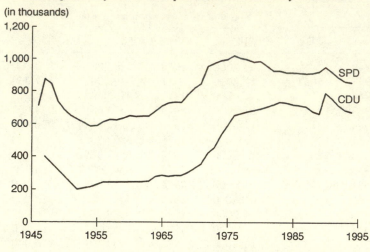

Fɪɢ 3.1. German party membership 1946–1994

organization during an apprenticeship in the Weimar SPD. Though the party's second defeat, in 1953, brought renewed calls for organizational and programmatic reform, Ollenhauer insisted on the importance of maintaining party traditions. In one revealing example of this loyalty to the party's past, Ollenhauer and his supporters in the party executive rejected the argument that the party could broaden its appeal to new members by abandoning such 'old-fashioned' SPD traditions as the red flag and the familiar 'thou' (*du*) and 'comrade' forms of address. Instead, the party executive described the retention of these symbols as 'a sign of solidary strength'.[9]

SPD reformers finally gained the upper hand in organizational battles after the CDU won an absolute majority in the 1957 *Bundestag* election. In the wake of the party's third consecutive defeat, reformers on the SPD executive pushed through new procedures for selecting top officials. These procedures opened the way to further organizational and programmatic reforms because they diminished the influence of the party's career bureaucrats. The most important and well-known legacy of the subsequent period of reform was the 1959 Bad Godesberg Programme, a document in which the SPD staked its claim to be a party for *all*

TABLE 3.2. *German federal-election results 1949–1994 (%)*

Year	CDU/CSU		SPD		FDP		Greens		PDS	
	Votes	Seats	Votes	Seats	Votes	Seats	Votes	Seats	Votes	Seats
1949	*31.0*	*34.6*	29.2	32.6	*11.9*	*12.9*[a]	n.a.		n.a.	
1953	*45.2*	*49.9*	28.8	31.0	*9.5*	*9.9*[a]	n.a.		n.a.	
1957	*50.2*	*54.3*	31.8	34.0	7.7	8.2	n.a.		n.a.	
1961	*45.3*	*48.6*	36.2	38.1	*12.8*	*13.4*	n.a.		n.a.	
1965	*47.6*	*49.4*	39.3	40.7	*9.5*	*9.9*	n.a.		n.a.	
1969	46.1	48.8	*42.7*	*45.2*	*5.8*	*6.0*	n.a.		n.a.	
1972	44.9	45.4	*45.8*	*46.4*	*8.4*	*8.3*	n.a.		n.a.	
1976	48.6	49.0	*42.6*	*43.2*	*7.9*	*7.9*	n.a.		n.a.	
1980	44.5	45.5	*42.9*	*43.9*	*10.6*	*10.7*	n.a.		n.a.	
1983	*48.8*	*49.0*	38.2	38.8	*7.0*	*6.8*	5.6	5.4	n.a.	
1987	*44.3*	*44.9*	37.0	37.4	*9.1*	*9.3*	8.3	8.5	n.a.	
1990	*43.8*	*48.2*	33.5	36.1	*11.0*	*11.9*	5.1	1.2[b]	2.4	2.6
1994	*41.5*	*43.8*	36.4	37.5	*6.9*	*7.0*	7.3	7.3	4.4	4.5

Notes: Figures in italic indicate parties which formed the first federal government after the election; n.a. = not applicable.

[a] Figures for 1949 and 1953 are combined vote of FDP and the German People's Party (*Deutsche Volkspartei*: DVP).

[b] 5.1% is the combined vote of the Greens in western Germany and of their east German partner, Federation '90. Because of rules which applied only to the first post-unification election, the Greens, which received only 3.9% of the western vote, won no *Bundestag* seats. Federation '90 received 1.2% of total votes, and thus 1.2% of the total seats, as a result of the over 5% of the votes it received in the the eastern states.

Sources: Alf Mintzel and Heinrich Oberreuter (eds.) *Parteien in der Bundesrepublik Deutschland* (Opladen: Leske & Budrich, 1992), 510–13. For 1994, 'CDU/CSU und FDP können mit knapper Mandatsmehrheit weiterregieren', *Deutschland Nachrichten*, 21 Oct. 1994, 1.

citizens, not just for industrial workers. These programmatic and organizational changes apparently began to pay electoral dividends in the 1960s, when the SPD gained votes in federal and state elections, and when party membership climbed back towards pre-1950 levels.[10]

Social and political changes helped reshape all the German parties in the 1960s and early 1970s. The popular protests which brought French and American students onto the streets in the 1960s had their counterparts in Germany, where increased interest in politics and in political participation transcended student circles. The 1960s also brought the end of the CDU's uninterrupted government of the Federal Republic. In 1966, the CDU/CSU and the SPD formed a grand coalition after the CDU's long-time coalition partner, the Free Democrats (*Freie Demokratische Partei*: FDP), refused to continue supporting the CDU's economic policies. The years of the grand coalition (from 1966 to 1969) were important ones for the SPD, because they gave party leaders ministerial experience, and because they polished the SPD's image as a reliable political alternative. This era is also notable in party histories because it was during the grand coalition that the SPD finally dropped its opposition to public financing for political parties. In 1967 the SPD co-operated with the CDU in passing the long-awaited Parties Law, the statute which authorized public subsidies for political parties.

After the 1969 election the SPD finally reached its goal of becoming the senior partner in a federal government (with the FDP). Their coalition increased its very small majority in the 1972 elections, when the SPD won its highest-ever proportion of the national vote. The SPD's extra-parliamentary organization also flourished in this period. As public funding for parties increased at the end of the 1960s, the SPD rapidly enlarged its federal staff, and it built a much larger national headquarters to accommodate expanded operations. In addition, the party's membership increased yearly during the late 1960s and early 1970s. However, it is notable that even during a decade of overall expansion of membership, some officially sanctioned SPD membership-drives were quite unsuccessful. The SPD's central organizing staff responded to these failures by trying to develop and promote more effective recruiting techniques.[11]

National party organizers wanted to ensure that the SPD would profit from its expanding membership. This concern led the party's 1970 conference to appoint a 'Commission on the Reform of Party Organization', which was charged with suggesting ways of improving intra-party communication and party electioneering. This commission concluded that the party needed a more informed membership and an improved (better-trained and better-equipped) local network of party employees.[12] Bolstered by this report, SPD headquarters established a central database of membership records. Those responsible for the computerized database described it as an

essential tool which would enable the party to distribute a magazine to all members. The expanding party was said to need such a
magazine because many of the party's new members were 'only
infrequently touched by the traditional intra-party information and
communications networks (membership meetings, SPD newspapers, workers' welfare society, etc.)'.[13]

Despite the party's electoral and organizational successes in the
early 1970s, those who oversaw the SPD organization were not
entirely complacent. The party executive's 1974 report on the
work of local parties identified deficiencies in staff and equipment, in communication with party members, and in communication with those outside the party.[14] A party study conducted after
the 1976 election once again found signs of poor communications
between the central party and its members.[15] Leaders of the party-
in-government did not respond to such warnings about problems of
intra-party communication, and they found it increasingly difficult
to retain the support of the party's more leftist members and
voters. In the late 1970s, SPD Chancellor Helmut Schmidt faced
growing hostility from these segments, who blamed him for
ignoring their views on economic and social policies.

At the electoral level, party differences were temporarily
papered-over in 1980, when the CDU/CSU fielded as its chancellor-candidate the conservative Bavarian minister president Franz
Josef Strauß. SPD supporters rallied when confronted with such a
controversial opponent. However, within months of winning the
1980 election, SPD leaders were facing renewed dissent within the
party, and renewed discord with their coalition partner, the FDP.
The SPD/FDP coalition broke apart in 1982, after thirteen years in
government.

Subsequent SPD struggles over how to re-create an electable
party focused much more on programme and leadership than on
organizational reform. Indeed, it was partly because they wanted to
counteract the negative publicity generated by intra-party struggles
over policy that federal organizers repeatedly tried to persuade
local branches to devote more attention to community-outreach
activities. However, in the early 1980s this increased emphasis on
outreach work was not inspired solely by intra-party disputes. It
was also a response to the electoral success of the new Greens
party, and to the new-found success of single-issue citizens'
initiatives in mobilizing politically interested community members.

In the 1980s SPD headquarters demonstrated continuing interest in membership by its ongoing investments in national recruiting drives. Despite these efforts, SPD membership began to decline.[16] Still, the SPD leadership could console itself that the party's recruitment difficulties were not unique, because in the 1980s the rapid growth of the CDU's membership was also halted. Furthermore, by the end of the 1980s opinion polls and the outcomes of state elections gave SPD leaders good reason to hope that in the 1990 federal election the SPD could reverse its 1983 and 1987 election losses. Such optimism was confounded by the sudden and unanticipated opportunity for German unification, an opportunity seized by Chancellor Kohl, and one which temporarily overshadowed all other political issues. Partly as a result of its reaction to unification issues, the SPD lost badly in the first modern all-German election. Oskar Lafontaine, the SPD's chancellor-candidate, seemed ambivalent about unification, and he campaigned by offering stark, though perhaps realistic, warnings about the costs of unification; these warnings proved to be much less popular than the rosy optimism offered by Helmut Kohl, the 'chancellor of unity'. In the 1990 federal election, the SPD's overall share of the vote fell below its 1987 level: even more ominous was the fact that the party gained only 23.6 per cent of the eastern German vote.[17]

The SPD's 1990 campaign was not made any easier by the extremely weak state of its organization in the former East Germany. In 1946 the SPD in the Soviet Occupation Zone had united with the Communist Party to form the Socialist Unity Party (*Sozialistische Einheitspartei Deutschlands*: SED), and an independent East German social-democratic party was not re-established until the autumn of 1989, only a few weeks before the collapse of that country's Communist government. As the old regime collapsed, the party's dissident founders initially had high hopes that they would profit from the region's pre-1933 strong social-democratic tradition. They also hoped to be able to construct a non-hierarchical citizens' party (more like the Western Greens than the Western SPD). Both these hopes were soon disappointed.[18] The new party lacked financial and personnel resources, and it soon discovered that it lacked strong electoral support as well. The results of various elections in 1990 showed that the eastern SPD would have to lower its short-term expecta-

TABLE 3.3. *CDU and SPD membership in united Germany 1990–1994*

Year	CDU		SPD	
	Western Germany	Eastern Germany	Western Germany	Eastern Germany
1990	655,200	134,000	911,600	24,400
1991	645,300	111,200	892,700	27,200
1992	619,600	94,300	860,200	25,700
1993	601,500	83,800	835,500	26,000
1994	594,800	79,400	826,800	27,500

Sources: CDU: for 1947–69, Ute Schmidt, 'Christlich Demokratische Union Deutschlands', in Richard Stöss (ed.), *Parteien-Handbuch*, i (Opladen: Westdeutscher Verlag, 1983), 643; for 1970–94, CDU, *Bericht des Bundesgeschäftsstelle*, various years. SPD: information provided by the SPD party headquarters, Bonn.

tions while it proceeded with the difficult work of finding voters, recruiting candidates, and enrolling members.

The two German social-democratic parties united in the autumn of 1990. Leaders of the united SPD tried to secure the support of western state and local parties in building up the eastern SPD. In addition to encouraging local parties in the west to enter into partnerships with associations in the east, party leaders also persuaded the SPD conference to approve a three-year 'solidarity contribution'. This dues surcharge was levied on all party members in order to provide equipment and campaign materials for the tiny eastern parties. But the eastern SPD continued to struggle despite this help, and it attracted few new members even in areas of rapid trade-union expansion (see Table 3.3). Because of its recruitment problems, in some eastern areas the SPD had trouble fielding candidates in the 1994 local elections.[19]

In spite of the grave problems of the eastern SPD, not all of the party's efforts at organizational reform were targeted eastward. In 1992 and 1993 the SPD party executive asked local parties to discuss a major new report on organizational reform. This report, which dealt almost exclusively with the problems of the western party, concluded that party work needed to be more interesting, that local parties should be more open to non-members, and that membership should be made more attractive by giving members new privileges.[20] (This report and its consequences are discussed in greater detail in Chapter 6.) The most immediate innovation to result from these discussions was the party's use of a membership ballot to help a 1993 party conference select the party's new leader. With a turn-out of 56 per cent this 'primary' proved quite successful, and it helped Rudolf Scharping to enjoy a few months of broad popularity after he was selected as party chair. However, as the party's 1994 chancellor-candidate, Scharping proved unable to unseat Helmut Kohl. At the end of 1994 Social Democrats led state governments throughout much of Germany. As a result, the SPD had a dominant position in the *Bundesrat*, the parliament's federal chamber, which gave it an important role in national policy-making. Yet, for the fourth time in a row the SPD had failed to win the chance to lead a national government.

Christian Democratic Organization since 1945

The Christian Democratic Union was a new party which was formed through the efforts of local and regional initiatives in occupied Germany in 1945. Members of the party's founding groups shared a determination to avoid Weimar's sectarian split of the democratic centre-right, and they were committed to building a bi-confessional (Protestant and Catholic) party. However, not all of them shared identical organizational and programmatic visions. Furthermore, because the party initially formed as a coalition of regional élites, national party leaders found it difficult even weakly to centralize party work. As a result, the CDU was able to conduct only a loosely co-ordinated campaign in the first federal elections in 1949. It did not even formally organize as a national party until a year after these elections. The party's first federal conference (in 1950) established a party headquarters (the *Bundesgeschäftsstelle*), but this only began functioning in 1952, when the second federal elections were already imminent.[21]

However, the CDU's organizational decentralization did not prevent it from winning the first five *Bundestag* elections. Indeed, in 1957 the CDU/CSU won an unparalleled absolute majority of seats in the *Bundestag* (see Table 3.2). These electoral successes gave CDU leaders little reason to find fault with the party's relatively small and passive membership, or with its weak central organization. Moreover, in the 1950s some regional leaders actively opposed both the expansion of membership and organizational centralization, because they saw these as threats to their own roles as brokers within the party. Nor was Chancellor Konrad Adenauer, the party's first and long-serving chair, interested in strengthening the role of party membership. Adenauer preferred to have an extra-parliamentary party which was too weak to challenge him.[22] With no strong pressures for change, the CDU's local voluntary organization remained underdeveloped, and its professional organization remained understaffed.

As early as the mid-1950s one of the CDU's federal party managers wrote wistfully about 'The Road to Becoming a Membership Party'.[23] Yet it was not until the 1960s, when the CDU simultaneously confronted the end of the Adenauer era and the rising appeal of the post-Godesberg SPD, that the national party began allocating significant resources to expanding and activating the party membership. The 1961 federal election served to remind many in the CDU of the party's political vulnerability. Though the CDU was still the largest vote-getter in this election, the loss of nearly 5 per cent of its 1957 vote seemed like an ominous trend. In the wake of the 1961 election, CDU regional leaders reluctantly approved moves to strengthen the central party by appointing a full-time federal business manager (*Geschäftsführender Vorsitzender*). Josef Herman Dufhues held this position from 1962 to 1966. Bruno Heck followed him, taking over the job in 1966, and in 1967 the post was transformed into the more powerful office of general secretary. Both Heck and Dufhues viewed stronger central organization, and a larger and more active membership, as prerequisites for the party's future electoral success.

Under the influence of these two managers the CDU organized its first nation-wide recruiting drive in 1963, and its second one in 1968. Membership expansion was only one part of their plans to move the extra-parliamentary party out from under the shadow of the national and regional leadership. Dufhues outlined his wish-list for party reform at the 1962 party conference. Among his prescriptions were that party branches should make their inter-election activities more interesting, and that every regional party should have full-time staff and premises. He argued that these reforms were necessary because, 'Above all, the party must be able to exist if the day should come when—may God shield the German people from it—the Party is not in Government.'[24]

Under Dufhues the national party began to standardize its procedures for enrolling and administering membership, and it began to compile a central file of members; this task was almost completed by the mid-1960s despite the resistance of some regional leaders. The membership file provided CDU organizers with their first good look at the geographical and demographic characteristics of the party's membership. In 1964 the federal party further centralized membership procedures by adopting its first national schedule of dues.

About the same time that the CDU began to strengthen its central organization, the new Parties Law had the effect of forcing the CDU formally to democratize its procedures for choosing candidates and party leaders. These new procedures in turn gave regional parties new incentives to register all their members with the federal CDU, because now intra-party votes were allocated according to membership size rather than regional electoral success. The scope of these organizational reforms prompted one observer to call 1967 the CDU's true natal year as 'an effective federal party'.[25]

Events in the next years further fuelled CDU organizational reforms. After the 1969 federal election the CDU/CSU was forced out of the federal government for the first time since 1949. This was a defeat which was easy to excuse, because the CDU/CSU still formed the largest single parliamentary block, and the SPD led the government only because it was the FDP's choice as coalition partner. The CDU's first experience of being out of federal government thus seemed to many in the party more like a fluke than a verdict against the party. As a result, this loss did not occasion rapid changes either in the party's organization or in its leadership. However, after the CDU's more clear-cut electoral loss in 1972, the party conference showed that it was ready to abandon vote-losing traditions by electing Helmut Kohl as the party's new chair.

In 1972 Kohl was a relatively young state minister-president who was already known for his skill in intra-party politics, and for his interest in party organizational reform. During the early years of Kohl's tenure, the opposition CDU changed its organizational self-image under the prodding of organizational specialists such as Kurt Biedenkopf and Heiner Geißler (Kohl's first and second general secretaries, from 1972 to 1977 and 1979 to 1989 respectively), and Peter Radunski (CDU publicity-director 1973-81, and business manager 1981-1991).[26] Kohl and Geißler, like many of those who rose within the CDU in the 1970s, gained their initial political experience in the party's youth organization, the 'Young Union' (*Junge Union*). Soon after the CDU's loss of office in 1969, several rising organizational experts from the Young Union (including Radunski) published thirty-four theses on party reform. They demanded expansion of the federal organization, improved publicity-work at all levels, expansion and activation of party membership, and a greater decision-making role for members.[27] The goals they articulated were to become central to the party's organizational self-understanding during the CDU's period in opposition. Also crucial to the party's image during the 1970s was the emergence of a strong parliamentary party, something that had been impossible as long as there was a CDU-led federal government. The development of a more active membership and of a more self-sufficient parliamentary party were important for aiding the work of the CDU as an opposition party, but both features began to erode after the CDU returned to power in Bonn in 1982.

In the early 1970s the CDU, like the SPD, used rapidly increasing public subsidies to expand its federal bureaucracy and build a new party headquarters. In this period, the party also easily achieved its goal of expanding party membership. CDU membership doubled between 1969 and 1976 and then continued to grow, reaching a reported peak of almost 735,000 in 1983 (see Table 3.1). The federal headquarters did what it could to encourage this growth, reportedly sponsoring twenty-three national recruiting initiatives between 1970 and 1980.[28] Although even CDU organizers attributed much of their party's recruiting success to changes in the broader political environment, they nevertheless sponsored local efforts at recruitment in order to ensure that the party would profit from increased public interest in political participation.[29] In this period the CDU's membership magazine described recruitment as 'the foremost party activity',[30] and party pamphlets recommended recruiting drives as a standard feature of local pre-election campaigning.

As membership expanded, CDU organizers were confronted with the challenge of defining what it meant to be a membership party. To begin with, they recognized that the central party needed to improve communications with all its new members. In response, party headquarters transformed the CDU's monthly newspaper (*Deutsches Monatsblatt*) into an attractive magazine featuring policy discussions and suggestions for members' political activities. The party executive also appointed a committee which sponsored local experiments in organization as a way of generating ideas about how the CDU could best profit from its new members. This committee concluded that the efforts of the central party should focus on making local parties more active agents of party outreach, something which could only be achieved by boosting the activity of individual party members.[31]

In the 1970s neither the CDU's growth in membership nor its changes of leadership produced immediate triumphs in federal elections. Though the CDU/CSU's share of the vote was consistently above SPD totals after 1972, and though the CDU won state-level victories throughout the 1970s, it was not until after the collapse of the SPD/FDP coalition in 1982 that the CDU once again took over leadership of the federal government. The CDU maintained this position in federal elections in 1983, 1987, 1990, and 1994, although between these elections the party's popularity fluctuated widely.

Like their SPD counterparts, CDU strategists in the 1970s and 1980s debated the appropriate organizational responses to the increasingly popular citizens' initiatives. The appeal of these new (generally leftist) social movements even prompted organizers in the centre-right CDU to reflect anew about how to cultivate ties with supporters. One response from CDU headquarters in the late 1980s was a series of discussions and documents addressing the theme of 'the CDU as a modern people's party'. A 1989 report on 'Modern Party Work in the 1990s' reaffirmed the importance of the party's membership organization. It urged local parties to recruit a broader range of members and candidates, to offer members more interesting opportunities to participate, and to make public events more topical and more inviting for non-members.[32] Although this report represented a harsh attack on the CDU's organizational *status quo*, it was overshadowed by other events at the CDU's 1989 party conference. Subsequently, organizational reform of the party was put on hold as the difficulties of unifying Germany absorbed the energies of party leaders.

(The recommendations and impact of the 'Modern Party Work' report are discussed in more detail in Chapter 6.)

The Western CDU united with its Eastern namesake in October 1990, immediately before German unification. The East German CDU was started in 1945 (like its Western counterpart), but it had survived the Communist era as an official partner of the SED, the Communist party which ran the German Democratic Republic. Because of this, whereas the unified SPD inherited only the weak financial and personnel resources of the newly refounded Eastern SPD, the unified CDU inherited from its Eastern predecessor a relatively large membership, solid financial reserves, and desirable property-assets. These resources undoubtedly contributed to the CDU's initial electoral successes in the east.[33]

In 1990 the CDU was the clear winner in federal elections in both east and west; in addition, it won the right to lead governments in four out of five of the new states. Such success suggested that the CDU could be the east's dominant political force for years to come. However, within a few years the CDU's support slipped, and it became clear that this region would remain a politically contested one. Furthermore, the party's eastern inheritance eventually proved to be a mixed blessing. By the time of the second round of local, state, and federal elections, in 1993 and 1994, CDU membership was so diminished in the east that the party had difficulty fielding candidates for local-government races (see Table 3.3). In many places, the party's local organization was burdened by internal struggles between CDU members who had joined the party before the collapse of the Communist regime and those who had joined thereafter.[34]

Chancellor Kohl led his party to the narrowest of triumphs in the 1994 *Bundestag* elections. Meanwhile, the health of the extra-parliamentary party looked as precarious as that of the CDU's federal legislative contingent. The party's long years in government had drained much of the vitality of the CDU's membership organization, and the unified CDU had yet to sink deep roots among eastern Germany's generally apolitical citizens.

Thus, at least until the mid-1980s, Germany's two largest parties seemed to confound predictions of the decline of parties as membership organizations. Most strikingly, in the 1960s and 1970s the CDU transformed itself from a party of local notables into a party with a large membership enrolled in branches throughout the country. The SPD's membership also expanded in this period. Furthermore, as the party broadened its class appeal, it also strengthened its organizational network outside industrial cities. The boom in party memberships in the 1970s suggests that television—which was well established by the end of the 1960s—was not the immediate cause of decline in the German membership parties.

However, the growth of the German parties in the 1970s may have represented only a temporary reprieve. At the beginning of the 1990s the biggest German parties were much less healthy than they had been only a decade earlier. By this time both the SPD and CDU were faced with declining membership, increasing electoral abstention, and rising support for parties that challenged traditional patterns of German politics. The SPD and CDU were also nursing very weak organizations in eastern Germany. Thus, as the end of the twentieth century approached, the future electoral and organizational prosperity of these two German membership parties seemed less than assured.

GREAT BRITAIN

Britain, unlike Germany, has little legal regulation of party organization, so that British parties have been relatively free to develop their own distinctive formal structures. Yet, despite such freedom, the Labour and Conservative membership organizations display several basic similarities. Both parties have traditionally built their local organizations around parliamentary districts, and both reorganize these constituency parties whenever electoral boundaries are changed (about every ten to twenty years). The two British parties have traditionally required individual members to be enrolled within the parliamentary district in which they reside. The residence requirement simplifies procedures for selecting parliamentary candidates, which is the most consequential task entrusted to Conservative and Labour constituency parties.[35] For other purposes, constituency Labour parties and Conservative constituency associations divide themselves into smaller branch or ward parties, whose boundaries may, but do not necessarily, reflect local-government divisions. Britain is a unitary state, without state-level governments, and it is undoubtedly because of this that the parties' regional organizations have always been less important than those of their German counterparts.

The Labour Party has much more precise, nationally stipulated, membership requirements and procedures than does the Conservative Party. Prospective Labour Party members must accept the party constitution and programmes, must join a trade union if eligible, and must pay an annual subscription to the national party (at a rate determined by the party conference). In 1994 members in employment were required to pay a £15 annual subscription (the equivalent of about $US23, or about DM37—in other words, less than half of what employed SPD members were expected to pay each year). The Conservative Party's non-binding 'model rules' for constituency associations merely recommend that prospective members should pay some (unstipulated) annual subscription, and should state their support for the party goals.

The Labour Party has always had a much smaller individual membership than the Conservative Party. Indeed, as noted earlier, the notion of individual membership was something of an afterthought in the Labour Party; it was almost two decades after its establishment before the party officially recognized individual (direct) membership (in 1918). In contrast, indirect membership has been an essential component of Labour organization from the beginning. Indirect, or affiliated, membership is the mechanism which allows trade unions to enrol their members *en masse*. The dues paid on behalf of indirect members have been the party's most important source of funding, and votes cast at the party conference on behalf of these indirect members have been the mechanism for formally maintaining trade-union influence over party policy. The Labour Party's indirect membership has always been many times larger than its individual membership.

As in the two German parties, the Labour Party's annual conference has formal responsibility for deciding party policy. However, Labour conferences differ from their German counterparts in one crucial respect: delegates representing the party's individual membership are joined, and outvoted, by delegates representing the party's affiliated membership (primarily trade unionists). Until 1981 Labour MPs had sole responsibility for choosing the party leader, but since then the process has included both the individual and the affiliated membership. Constituency parties, affiliated organizations (primarily, trade unions), and the party conference all elect a specified number of members of the party's leadership body, the National Executive Committee (NEC). The NEC officially oversees the work of Labour Party headquarters.

In contrast, the Conservative Party differs from the other parties studied here in the extent to which it formally separates the leadership of the parliamentary party from the membership organization. (The latter is officially known as the National Union of Conservative and Unionist Associations, or 'National Union' for short.) Since the mid-1960s, party procedures have called for the 'party leader' (the leader of the parliamentary party) to be formally elected by Conservative MPs. The leader in turn appoints the party chair,[36] who oversees party fundraising and the work of the party's professional bureaucracy, Conservative Central Office (CCO). The membership organization has no formal role in policy-making or leadership selection, although the reactions (or even anticipated reactions) of local activists at annual party conferences may guide party leaders.[37] In short, formal rules and party traditions combine to make the leader of the Conservative Party much less dependent on the party membership than is the leader of the Labour Party.

Labour Party Organization since 1945

In the summer of 1945, even before the war in the Pacific had ended, British voters expressed their hopes for a new era of peacetime prosperity by giving their overwhelming support to Labour Party candidates. The size of the Labour Party's success in 1945 can best be appreciated in the context of its record in the 1930s, when the party's electoral fortunes were at a low ebb. In the 1931 general election the Labour Party returned only fifty-two MPs (8 per cent of total seats); this constituted a loss of 236 seats in two years.[38] While it recovered some of these seats in 1935, the party's extra-parliamentary organization continued to suffer. Individual (direct) membership halved between 1937 and 1942, when it dropped below 219,000 members (see Table 3.4). However, unlike the Conservative Party, the Labour Party was able to use the wartime suspension of elections to help consolidate its organization. As a result it was able to mount a comparatively well-run campaign in 1945.

TABLE 3.4. *Direct membership of the Labour Party 1928–1945*

Year	Members	Year	Members
1928	215,000	1937	447,000
1929	228,000	1938	429,000
1930	277,000	1939	409,000
1931	297,000	1940	304,000
1932	372,000	1941	227,000
1933	366,000	1942	219,000
1934	381,000	1943	236,000
1935	419,000	1944	266,000
1936	431,000	1945	487,000

Source: Labour Party, *NEC Report to Conference 1991*, 5.

Good organization was one of many factors which contributed to the Labour Party's stunning victory in the 1945 general election (see Table 3.5). The party's organization continued to prosper, and the 1945 election victory was followed by a surge in individual (direct) and affiliated membership enrolment (see Table 3.6 and Fig. 3.2). National organizers played their role in trying to sustain the growth of the direct membership by sponsoring party-wide recruiting campaigns. Such campaigns resurfaced regularly over the next four decades. For the most part, however, Labour Party leaders in the late 1940s were busy trying to enact an ambitious legislative programme, and they devoted little attention to questions of party organization.

The Labour Party's electoral success eroded quickly, and in 1951 the party was forced into opposition after losing an election in which it received more votes, but fewer seats, than the Conservative Party. The circumstances of this loss slowed the search for organizational scapegoats, but the party's more resounding defeat in the 1955 general election unleashed a spate of internal critiques of Labour's organizational deficiencies.[39] In response, the party's National Executive Committee appointed a 'Subcommittee on Party Organization' (chaired by Harold Wilson), which was given the task of assessing party weaknesses. The subcommittee's interim report delivered a famous indictment of Labour's organi-

TABLE 3.5. *British general-election results 1945–1992*

Year	Conservative		Labour		Liberal[a]		Other[b]	
	Votes	Seats	Votes	Seats	Votes	Seats	Votes	Seats
1945	39.8	33.3	*48.3*	*61.4*	9.1	1.9	2.7	3.4
1950	43.5	47.8	*46.1*	*50.4*	9.1	1.4	1.3	0.3
1951	*48.0*	*51.4*	48.8	47.2	2.5	1.0	0.7	0.4
1955	*49.7*	*54.8*	46.4	44.0	2.7	1.0	1.1	0.3
1959	*49.4*	*57.9*	43.8	41.0	5.9	1.0	1.0	0.2
1964	43.4	48.3	*44.1*	*50.3*	11.2	1.4	1.3	0.0
1966	41.9	40.2	*47.9*	*57.6*	8.5	1.9	1.6	0.3
1970	*46.4*	*52.4*	43.0	45.7	7.5	1.0	3.1	0.9
1974[c]	37.8	46.8	*37.1*	*47.4*	19.3	2.2	5.8	3.1
1974[d]	35.8	43.6	*39.2*	*50.2*	18.3	2.0	6.7	4.1
1979	*43.9*	*53.4*	37.0	42.4	13.8	1.7	5.3	2.5
1983	*42.4*	*61.1*	27.6	32.2	25.4	3.5	4.6	3.3
1987	*42.3*	*57.8*	30.8	35.2	22.6	3.4	4.3	3.6
1992	*41.9*	*51.6*	34.4	41.6	17.8	3.0	5.8	3.8

Notes: Figures in italic indicate party which formed government after election.

[a] Includes SDP 1983 and 1987, and Liberal Democrat 1992.

[b] Includes Northern Ireland.

[c] February.

[d] October.

Source: David Butler and Dennis Kavanagh, *The British General Election of 1992*, (London: Macmillan, 1992), 284–5.

zation: '[C]ompared with our opponents, we are still at the penny-farthing stage in a jet-propelled era, and our machine, at that, is getting rusty and deteriorating with age.'[40] Yet the subcommittee's recommendations aimed more at improving the existing vehicle than at developing a new means of transport. The report's most lasting effect came as the result of its advice on how to increase the revenue of the central party. To achieve this, the party began to require constituency parties to purchase memberships for at least 800 members (instead of only 240 members) if they wanted to send delegates to the annual party conference. The side-effect of this change (and of subsequent similar ones) was a long-term reduction in the accuracy of the party's membership statistics.

After the Labour Party's third consecutive general-election

TABLE 3.6. *Conservative Party and Labour Party membership 1945–1994*

Year	Conservative	Labour	Year	Conservative	Labour
1945		487,000	1970	1,500,000	690,000
1946		645,000	1971		700,000
1947	1,2000,000	608,000	1972		703,000
1948	2,249,000	629,000	1973		665,000
1949		730,000	1974	1,500,000	692,000
1950		908,000	1975		675,000
1951		876,000	1976		659,000
1952		1,014,000	1977		660,000
1953	2,806,000	1,005,000	1978		676,000
1954		934,000	1979		666,000
1955		843,000	1980		348,000
1956		845,000	1981		277,000
1957		913,000	1982		274,000
1958		889,000	1983		295,000
1959		848,000	1984		323,000
1960	2,800,000	790,000	1985		313,000
1961		751,000	1986		297,000
1962		767,000	1987		289,000
1963		830,000	1988	1,000,000	265,000
1964		830,000	1989		294,000
1965		817,000	1990		311,000
1966		776,000	1991		261,000
1967		734,000	1992	750,000	280,000
1968		701,000	1993		266,000
1969		681,000	1994		280,000

Sources: Conservative Party: for 1947–74, Alan Ball, *British Political Parties* (London: Macmillan, 1980), 150, 215; for 1988, Nicholas Wood, 'Tories Hope for 10% Rise in Membership', *The Times*, 11 Oct. 1988, 6; for 1992, Paul Whitely, Patrick Seyd, and Jeremy Richardson, *True Blues* (Oxford: Clarendon Press, 1994), 25. Labour Party: *NEC Reports* 1985–8, 1992, and 1994; for 1989, 'Membership Drive Disappointment', *The Independent*, 1 Oct. 1990, 2; for 1990 and 1991, Ralph Atkins, Ivo Dawnay, and Emma Tucker, 'Snags Mar Party's Recruitment Drive', *Financial Times*, 1 Oct. 1991, 14; for 1994, 'Labour to Hold Economy Debate', *Financial Times*, 17/18 Sept. 1994, 6.

defeat in 1959, and again after its narrow victory in 1964, party leaders looked to improved presentation of policy as a way to increase votes.[41] This concern for image improvement did not

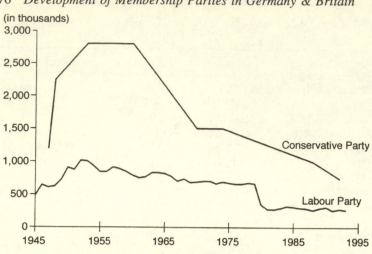

(in thousands)

FIG 3.2. British party membership 1945–1993

produce any lasting organizational reforms, though it did prompt Labour headquarters to sponsor such efforts as a competition to encourage the refurbishment of constituency-party premises, and, on a grander scale, a summertime 'Festival of Labour' in London's Battersea Park. In short, although the party remained out of government for more than a decade after its 1951 loss, during this period its organizers did not fundamentally change their views about the tasks and structures of membership organization.

Once the Labour Party returned to government in 1964, party leaders again became too preoccupied with governing to devote much attention to organizational questions. Yet such attention was urgently needed. Although the party won the two general elections of the 1960s, its organization was deteriorating rapidly. This decline showed up even in the party's artificially inflated figures for individual membership, which dropped by 150,000 between 1964 and 1969. The loss of membership weakened the finances of local parties, which in turn made it more difficult for them to hire professional election-agents or to rent permanent offices. By 1970 the party's corps of locally based (and locally financed) professional organizers was only half as large as it had been in 1950.

According to one assessment, 'a combination of social change, neglect and political disillusionment almost destroyed the Labour

Party as a mass party' during Labour's two terms in government in the 1960s.[42] This neglect persisted even after the party was defeated in the 1970 general election, with few Labour Party leaders viewing organizational reform as essential to electoral success. Such a verdict seemed to be vindicated by the party's rapid return to government in the 1974 elections.

In the 1970s and early 1980s, the biggest pressures for Labour Party organizational reform came not from the top, but from 'bottom-up' campaigns led by factions which were hoping to increase their relative influence in party decision-making. After 1974, some of the left-wing party and trade-union activists who were unhappy with the policies of the Labour government banded together in the Campaign for Labour Party Democracy (CLPD), a group which aimed to increase the power of constituency parties at the expense of the party's parliamentary wing. The CLPD scored its first big success shortly after the Labour Party's crushing defeats in the 1979 local-government, Westminster, and European elections. In the wake of five years of hard campaigning by the CLPD, the party's 1979 annual conference adopted the requirement that each constituency must formally select or reselect its candidate prior to every general election. This change was promoted as a way of making incumbent members of parliament more accountable to their constituency parties. The CLPD achieved a further big success in 1981, when a special party conference approved a new procedure for selecting the party's leader (an 'electoral college'). Under the new mechanism, the parliamentary party was forced to share decision-making control with trade unions and delegates from constituency parties.[43] The well-publicized procedural change had the immediate effect of prompting a handful of Labour MPs to break with the party; they immediately formed the new Social Democratic Party (SDP). However, their departure did not resolve intra-party controversies, and throughout the early 1980s the Labour Party suffered from unfavourable media reports about the local and national struggles which accompanied these and other changes in the party's organization, leadership, and policies.

The full extent of the decline in individual Labour Party membership became clearer after 1980, when affiliation rules were once again changed to permit constituency parties to present more accurate enrolment statistics.[44] Reports of the sharp decline in membership coincided with a further drop in the party's electoral fortunes. In 1983 the Labour Party suffered a humiliating defeat when it received 27.6 per cent of the British vote, only 2.2 per cent more than the combined votes for SDP and Liberal Party candidates. In the wake of this election, the Labour Party conference replaced its defeated party leader, the left-wing champion Michael Foot, with Neil Kinnock, another man who originated on the party's left. Yet Kinnock kept his eyes firmly fixed on electoral verdicts in the following years, and he proved much more willing than Foot to confront the party's left wing on both organizational and policy questions. One result was that after the party's disastrous 1983 defeat, (new) party organizers began promoting revised ideas about how individual members should fit into party organizational strategies.

For Kinnock, and for his team in party headquarters, organizational change was one of several steps which were needed in order to boost public acceptance of the party and its policies. Their first efforts in this direction aimed to limit the influence of, and the publicity given to, 'hard-left' activists. In pursuit of this goal, central-party leaders adapted the CLPD's democratization rhetoric to their own purposes. In the late 1980s and early 1990s it was thus top-down initiatives which did the most to transfer power from local activists to the entire membership (which leaders thought was more moderate), and to circumvent local élites by strengthening links between the central party and individual members.[45] As part of the latter plan, in 1986 Labour's national headquarters began to distribute messages from the central party using a new, free magazine for all members (*Labour Party News*). Initially, members who wished to receive the magazine could get it merely by adding their names to a central mailing-list. This list provided the national party with its first detailed records of membership.

After the Labour Party lost its third consecutive general election in 1987, the national leadership won the approval of the party conference for a new system of national membership. The system gave the national party responsibility for processing approvals and renewals of membership, a change which was supposed to improve membership retention and regularize national income from dues. The system was also designed to deprive constituency leaders of much of their power to exclude newcomers who might be seen as challengers to local oligarchies. The party's general secretary optimistically speculated that the new approach to membership could help the Labour Party grow to half a million, or even one million, individual members.[46] In fact, the decline in party membership was only temporarily reversed. Other dividends from the new system were also elusive, because mastering computerized registration proved to be much more difficult than expected.[47]

The Labour Party's standing in opinion polls revived more quickly than did its membership organization. Indeed, the defeat suffered in the 1992 general election was quite a blow to the newly confident party, which seemed to have victory snatched away from it at the last minute. John Smith, who replaced Kinnock as party leader shortly after this fourth consecutive Labour defeat, continued his predecessor's efforts to revise the organization in ways that would produce a more marketable image. He pursued reforms designed to draw clearer boundaries between the party and the trade unions, and he promoted changes which were intended to boost the party's individual membership by persuading affiliated trade-unionists that it was worth their while to become direct members. Tony Blair, who was elected party leader in mid-1994, after John Smith's untimely death, continued to pursue organizational and policy reforms which were designed to give Labour a winnable identity. (For more on these reforms, see the discussion in Chapter 6.)

Conservative Party Organization since 1945

When Prime Minister Winston Churchill and his Conservative Party left office in the summer of 1945, it was the party's first experience in opposition in fourteen years. This long span in government clearly showed that the Conservative Party had been much more successful than the Liberal Party, its nineteenth-century rival, in adapting to the post-1918 era of mass suffrage. In the 1930s, as the Liberal Party slipped into its seemingly permanent third place in parliament, the Conservatives reached new heights of electoral success. In the 1931 general election they even won an astounding 473 (77 per cent) of the 615 parliamentary seats.[48] Yet, despite, or perhaps even because of this electoral success, many Conservative constituency associations apparently withered during

the 1930s. This organizational decline continued during the subsequent wartime suspension of elections.

The 1945 general election—the first in a decade—dispelled
Tory dreams of a return to pre-war politics (see Table 3.5). At
the time, journalists and other analysts blamed weak Conservative
constituency organization for the defeat, and this diagnosis added
urgency to discussions of organizational reform which had begun
even before the end of the war.[49] The changes that followed
marked important and lasting adjustments in accepted Conservative ideas about how members and local associations should
support the work of the national party.

The activities of Conservative Central Office expanded after the
1945 election, and this increased the central party's need for
revenues just as one of its traditional sources of funds—very
wealthy individual donors—was becoming harder to tap. The
new head of the party's extra-parliamentary organization, Lord
Woolton, and the newly-appointed 'Committee on Party Organization' both responded to this financial squeeze by arguing that
constituency associations should, for the first time, provide funds
for Central Office. The 1948 party conference demurely assented
to the committee's proposed quota-scheme for voluntary payments
from constituencies. Those attending did not even raise a recipro-
cal demand for constituency association oversight of central budgets, a demand that had been fearfully anticipated by some
members of the committee.[50] As a result of another of the committee's proposals, constituency parties accepted strict limits on
the size of contributions they could accept from MPs and from
parliamentary candidates. These new limits were adopted with the
aim of combating the widespread perception that wealthy people
could buy nominations for safe Conservative seats. However, their
side-effect was to force many local associations to seek new
sources of income.[51]

Members were an obvious potential source of funds for local
parties, and during the immediate post-war period both financial
pressures and national membership-drives encouraged local Conservative associations to recruit. These expansion efforts apparently met with resounding success. It is, however, hard to
determine precisely how much the party grew, because Conservative Party statistics about membership have always been summaries of (probably optimistic) local estimates. In the 1950s, as in the

1990s, the Conservative Party did not have party-wide rules about membership, nor did it require local associations to report to Central Office the names of individual members. Thus, although party membership almost certainly did expand while the party was in opposition, lax local record-keeping, generous definitions of membership, and wishful thinking all played roles in boosting estimated Conservative Party membership from about one million in 1947 to its all-time high of almost three million in 1952 (see Table 3.6).

The Conservative Party's electoral popularity rose along with its membership, and the party rapidly recovered electoral support in constituencies which it had lost in 1945. By 1951 the Conservatives were once again leading the government, and they retained this position for more than a decade. However, parliamentary strength did not protect the party against an erosion of its extra-parliamentary organization. Retention and recruitment of members clearly became more difficult once the party was back in government, which probably explains why Conservative Central Office stopped publishing membership estimates in the mid-1950s. In this period, party-wide membership-drives met with diminishing success and enthusiasm. By 1962 one assessment of that year's recruiting campaign read like an obituary for traditional recruiting practices: 'The day of the short term highly publicized membership campaign seems for the present to have passed.'[52]

In the 1950s and 1960s the Conservative Party fell into a routine of appointing committees on party reform which investigated organizational deficiencies but made only modest proposals for change. In 1957, for instance, a committee chaired by Lord Colyton was asked to examine ways of reducing committee work in local parties in order to 'release supporters for canvassing, collection of subscriptions, and the many other essential tasks which made for efficient constituency organization and helped to win elections'.[53] The committee's mandate reflected Central Office suspicions that recent increases in membership had not produced corresponding increases in local political activity. Yet the Colyton Committee concluded that complaints about over-bureaucratization were largely unfounded, and it recommended no major changes. Two slightly later committees on organization also refrained from recommending major reforms.

The most important organizational change in the Conservative

Party during the 1960s was its adoption of new procedures for selecting the party leader. This change did not originate from any of the reform commissions, but was instead a product of the circumstances surrounding the party's 1963 transition in leadership (when an ailing Prime Minister Harold Macmillan was replaced by Sir Alec Douglas-Home). These new procedures, which were once again revised in the mid-1970s, replaced unstructured backroom bargaining among party élites with opportunities for Conservative MPs to elect their party leader. Without these new rules, Margaret Thatcher would not have been selected as party leader in 1975, but she also would probably not have been so suddenly forced to leave her post in 1990.

The new procedures for leadership selection did nothing to increase party members' roles in decision-making. Several symbolic changes of the 1960s did, however, suggest that there was at least a small shift in ideas about how to foster communication between party leaders and party members. Most notably, starting in 1965 the party leader began attending the entire Conservative Party conference, and in 1967 party conferences began to include votes after some debates.[54]

During the 1960s and 1970s, national organizers made only sporadic efforts to reverse the continuing slump in membership. One of these attempts, dubbed 'Project '67', was an ambitious new 'scientific' approach in which local parties were urged to target their recruiting efforts so that local memberships would more closely match constituency demography. Despite complicated preparations by the national party, the idea was apparently not a success, and it was not repeated. Indeed, in the 1970s and 1980s Central Office organized few party-wide recruitment campaigns. More typically, national organizers urged local parties to recruit but did not suggest specific times or provide special materials. Financial difficulties throughout the 1970s constricted other Conservative Party attempts to reform the work of either local associations or of the party's Central Office. One of the few innovations which did survive into the 1990s was a new, subscription-only magazine for members (*Conservative Newsline*).

During the long period of Conservative government in the 1980s and 1990s, Conservative Central Office concentrated on planning and financing expensive publicity-campaigns, not on revitalizing membership associations. Yet even though the health of the party's constituency associations was clearly a secondary concern for party strategists in this period, the central party nevertheless continued to subsidize local employees, and to encourage and facilitate local membership-recruitment. In 1988 Central Office sponsored a full-scale party-wide recruiting drive for the first time in years. As in the recruitment campaigns of the 1940s, the national party supported this campaign by issuing leaflets, stickers, press announcements, and advice brochures for local recruiters.[55] Central Office proclaimed a new interest in remedying organizational deficiencies when it announced a drive to open 1,000 new branches during 1990. As the Conservative Party's director of party campaigning explained at this time, party organizers believed that healthy local associations remained important to party success even in an age of computers, direct mail, and television, because

the only really effective way of getting in touch with the electorate, and continuing to stay in touch with them, is by having an active organization in each town, village and ward in EVERY constituency in the country.[56]

However, such declarations were not matched by equal efforts on behalf of organizational renewal, and affirmations alone were unable to stop the apparent unravelling of the party's local organization. This decay was aggravated by the ageing of the party's post-1945 recruits.[57] Yet, despite the party's organizational difficulties, in 1992 the Conservatives managed to win their fourth consecutive general election, this time under the leadership of John Major.

Thus, during the long period of Conservative Party government in the 1980s and early 1990s, observations about organizational decline did not translate into intra-party debates about membership privileges and structures (in contrast to the situation in the Labour Party during this period). However, in the early 1990s some constituency activists did begin to challenge the central party by publicizing their concerns about the rumoured slump in membership (to under half a million members, according to at least one estimate), and about Central Office indebtedness.[58] At the party's 1993 conference, some delegates opposed a proposal from the party chair to give the central party more oversight over local-party financing; instead of supporting this, they made their own counter-demand of more constituency control over Central Office budgets.[59] Yet, in 1994, as local-government and by-election results and public-opinion polls showed waning Conservative appeal, those who were dissatisfied with their party pinned their hopes on a change in leadership, or a change in party policies (particularly those concerning European integration)—in other words, they did not focus on organizational reform as a way to bolster party fortunes.

THE STRATEGIC ABANDONMENT OF MEMBERSHIP ORGANIZATION?

The preceding accounts give some initial hints about the ways in which organizers in each of these parties have broken from prevailing assumptions about how a party can profit from its membership. Most importantly, they have shown that party leaders have been willing to pay a price for their attempts to reorder relations between central parties and individual members. For instance, in the past two decades, all four national parties have channelled new resources into starting, or popularizing, magazines which aim to strengthen the direct ties between (at least some) individual members and their parties. These new magazines have provided three of the parties with excuses for collecting the addresses of individual party members—information that was gathered even in the face of outright opposition from leaders of local parties. In order to attract and retain members, national leaders in these three parties (all except the Conservative Party) have also been willing to expand members' opportunities for participation. (This theme will be examined in more detail in Chapter 6.)

In the past forty-five years, all four parties have indeed become more centralized and more computerized, two factors sometimes named as catalysts for parties' declining interest in membership. However, these initial portraits of the parties' efforts at organizational reform do not provide conclusive evidence that all of them steadily lost interest in assembling large memberships once they adopted new technologies. Indeed, the accounts suggest that at least in the German parties and the Labour Party, strategists have continued to find new ways to employ members profitably.

As a result, national organizers in all three parties have recently given attention to schemes for improving the effectiveness, and the attractiveness, of party membership. The Conservative Party represents a more ambiguous case. At this point the most that can be said is that its organizers have not actively attempted to discourage enrolment.

The membership figures reported in Tables 3.1 and 3.6 make clear how small a proportion of each country's population has enrolled in any of these parties. Since mid-century, the four parties have never enrolled *massive* memberships. Even in 1950, at the height of the British parties' boasts about membership, more than 90 per cent of potential voters did *not* belong to either the Conservative or the Labour Party. In the Bonn Republic the two big German parties together never enrolled as many as 5 per cent of voters. These figures point to one reason why membership evidence alone is inadequate to support the proposition that Germany and Britain in the 1990s are at the end of the era of membership parties and of party-based mass politics, because for decades only a small minority of each country's voters has taken advantage of the opportunities for participation which the parties have provided. Another reason why figures for party membership cannot be used as indicators of party strategy is that declining figures for membership are not, by themselves, proof that party organizers have ceased to attempt to recruit members. Changing figures on enrolment may be produced by one or more of three intertwined factors: changes in a party's interest in having members; changes in citizens' general and specific interest in joining parties; and changes in record-keeping methods. Of these factors, only the effects of the third type (record-keeping) can be separated with relative confidence as to accuracy. Yet incidents noted in the preceding organizational histories, such as the failures of recruiting drives, suggest that variations in the second factor (citizen interest) can also have an important impact on these numbers. In other words, membership figures alone are insufficient as evidence of changes in party organizers' aims. To discover the latter, it is necessary to examine more direct evidence of changes in party calculations about the value of membership resources.

The following two chapters take up the task of investigating changes in the ways that party organizers have portrayed the appropriate tasks for members. These chapters consider party organizers' changing answers to two questions: what are members supposed to do for their national parties during national election campaigns, and what are members supposed to do for their national parties between national campaigns? As will become clear, answers to these questions have been far from static.

4

Party Members and Electioneering

But because the organization is not, and cannot be, an end in itself, a vital organization also needs to have clear and guiding policies with the goal: *Winning political power in a democratic state*!

SPD Yearbook[1]

PARTIES' efforts to 'win political power in a democratic state' culminate most dramatically in the campaigns which precede national elections. Whenever and wherever there are competitive partisan elections, parties and party candidates compete for visibility and support using both novel and well-tried techniques. Because of this, analyses of changing electioneering styles have been central to diagnoses of trends in party organizational strategies, including trends affecting relations between parties and their members.

As the discussion in the first chapter suggested, many party observers have concluded that a key cause of organizational change in membership parties in the late twentieth century is that party organizers have ceased to value members as volunteer campaigners. According to one prevalent view, a principal reason why emerging parties originally valued members was that member-volunteers helped them when they could not afford to campaign in other ways; however, members ceased to represent such a useful asset once the parties gained access to new electioneering tools and to the means to purchase them. This scenario assumes that changes in campaign techniques have led party strategists to deflate their assessment of the advantages offered by members. Given the widespread acceptance of this view, the place to begin the current investigation of changing strategies in regard to party membership is with a consideration of changes in the roles which British and German parties have traditionally assigned to members during national election campaigns. First, however, it is worth reviewing the arguments about why and how changing electioneering styles are supposed to contribute to the obsolescence of membership parties.

THE IMPACT OF NEW TECHNOLOGIES

Analysts who were trying to explain post-1945 changes in party organizations in the United States were the first fully to develop arguments about how new communications technologies would transform parties' organizing styles. Even before the first televised presidential debates in the United States, V. O. Key was noting that in American campaigns 'the door-bell ringers have lost their function of mobilizing the vote to the public-relations experts, to the specialists in radio and television, and to others who deal in mass communications'.[2] Four presidential elections later, another observer was still delivering a similar verdict: 'The air waves and computer are performing many of the voter contact activities that campaign workers once undertook.'[3] Even a book from the mid-1980s whose title proclaimed, 'the party goes on', agreed that in the United States professional campaigners and new technologies had taken over campaign activities once performed by volunteers, and had made the efforts of local parties irrelevant for all but the lowest level of elections.[4]

Some—but not all—observers of British and German parties reached similar conclusions about the effects of new technologies on party organizations. Only a few years after the first televised British election analysts were already linking the centralization of British campaigns to the 'marginalization of mass membership'.[5] As one observer of the 1966 British elections noted

The growing centralization of campaigning means that it is the national, not the local propaganda which matters. Radio and television advertising and newspaper reports have largely displaced the more traditional forms of electioneering.[6]

A few years later, yet another pair of analysts suggested that

developments in the mass media, opinion polling and public relations have bypassed electioneering at the local level. They have been exploited by the national campaigners in a way that has undermined the constituency campaign.[7]

In the 1970s and 1980s, some analysts of West German elections also linked the use of new technologies in election campaigns with the marginalization of party membership organizations.[8] More recently, several multi-country studies which included British and German parties have also found broad trends towards reduced reliance on activists, and increased reliance on mass media, opinion polling, and professional advertisers.[9]

But not all observers have agreed that professional electioneering sounded the death-knell for parties outside legislatures—not even for American local parties. Thus, for instance, in the 1980s Samuel Eldersveld argued that there was insufficient evidence to conclude that local-party activism had really declined, because 'to dismiss the local organization as superseded by the mass media or scorned by the candidate-centered campaign or ignored by the incumbent congressman (or state legislator), *particularly as something which has happened recently*, is not supported by the evidence'.[10] Eldersveld's sceptical observation suggests that the relevant question for researchers is not whether parties and candidates have adopted new communications technologies; parties inside and outside the United States undoubtedly have made increasing use of these new channels. Instead, the pressing question is whether employing these technologies always transforms electioneering in similar ways. In particular, it has yet to be established whether the observation that technology marginalizes volunteer campaigners is as universally valid as the similar economic axiom that good money drives out bad, or whether other system-specific factors (such as rules of electoral competition) also play a role in determining the pace and extent of such a change.

Three plausible scenarios describe how party organizers might view members' efforts after national electioneering becomes primarily focused on national media: they could expect members' electioneering efforts to dwindle as they are replaced by new technologies; they could expect members to continue old electioneering customs, if only for the sake of party traditions; or they could hope that members would perform new tasks which would complement and perhaps enhance the new technologies.

The first of these scenarios has been discussed already: because of new technologies, national party campaigners deflate their expectations about the value of local campaigning, and may therefore attempt to limit the autonomy, or even the scope, of local campaigns. According to the second scenario, the power of party traditions limits technological determinism. National organizers who believe in the electoral value of showing the flag in time-honoured ways may continue to advocate the use of long-practised local campaign activities. National organizers might also continue to endorse 'old-fashioned' campaign methods because stasis is the path of least resistance, or because local electioneering is thought to produce non-electoral goods (such as preventing local activists from devoting their energies to potentially more embarrassing causes). According to the third scenario, the preferred mixture of members and new technologies depends both on the extent to which organizers see shortcomings in the new communications techniques, and on the relative availability of members and other resources. This third perspective suggests that complete marginalization of the membership is less likely where the use of new techniques is limited by environmental factors (for instance, where there are legal limits on television use, or where media markets are much larger than electoral districts). It also suggests that even in parties which whole-heartedly endorse mass media campaigning, party organizers may nevertheless devise new roles for members.[11]

Under all three scenarios, mass media electioneering becomes a primary tool of political communication. The difference between these accounts is in how they describe what happens to membership as a *secondary* tool. When all parties rely on appeals in the electronic media, will some parties attempt to distinguish themselves by also relying on members' supplemental campaign efforts? This is the question asked here about the German and British parties' changing electioneering strategies.

The current chapter begins by examining the extent to which the German and British national parties have actually adopted new communications technologies to perform campaign tasks. It then looks for corresponding changes in party organizers' ideal portraits of members' electioneering activities. This discussion considers whether any or all of the parties developed new roles for members as they adopted new technologies, or whether organizers came to view the party membership as an obsolete appendage to national electioneering efforts.

GERMANY: CHANGING CAMPAIGN STRATEGIES

The German parties usually begin their plans and preparations for national and local campaigns months—and even years—in advance. Elections to the German *Bundestag* are always held on Sundays, and are usually held four years apart. Because the constitution permits early dissolution of parliament only in exceptional circumstances, in most years campaign organizers can correctly anticipate the approximate date of the election. (Only in 1972 and 1983 have campaign planners been surprised by early elections.) As a result, German parties now begin their well-financed pre-campaigns many months in advance of the final 'hot phase' of the campaign, which lasts for about six weeks.

Changes at the National Level

Campaigning for the first *Bundestag* election was, by subsequent standards, very modest. In the wake of the 1948 currency reform all parties faced shortages of both money and paper. In addition, they had little time to prepare their 1949 campaigns, because the constitution of the new Federal Republic was ratified only three months before the first federal elections were held. Under these circumstances, it was not surprising that party campaigners returned to the more peaceful of the campaign methods which had been employed in the Weimar Republic.[12] The parties continued to rely on traditional techniques for mobilizing party supporters even after the relaxation of imposed and self-imposed restraints on campaign spending and rhetoric.

Print media of various sorts were the primary channels of communication for German campaigns as late as the early 1960s. In the 1950s the volume of campaign leaflets, letters, posters, and newspaper advertisements increased rapidly as paper shortages disappeared. The parties relied on local volunteers and professional delivery-firms to distribute most of their leaflets, and both parties sometimes even mailed millions of campaign letters. In the elections from 1953 to 1961, the CDU spent large sums renting almost all available billboard sites for the duration of the campaign, and it supplemented these large advertisements with, reportedly, millions of posters which volunteers hung on free sites.

In contrast, the SPD relied almost exclusively on volunteer poster-hangers and on non-commercial sites. Both parties, but particularly the better-financed CDU, made extensive use of newspaper advertising to publicize their campaign messages.[13]

However, even in the 1950s the national parties did not confine their campaigns to the print media, which party organizers already considered to be old-fashioned. In 1953, for instance, the SPD's department for press and propaganda boasted about its 'deliberate production of acoustical propaganda tools, in contrast to the early preference for written propaganda'.[14] More importantly, the parties made use of free advertising-time on public radio stations and even, starting in 1957, on the fledgling television networks. National campaigners arranged speaking-tours for top and middle-ranking party leaders. They also sent fleets of party 'film vans', and even an SPD political cabaret, touring the countryside during the campaigns of the 1950s.[15]

As German federal elections became increasingly competitive in the 1960s, they also became increasingly centralized. Centralization was fostered by the growing public subsidies which enabled the party headquarters to expand their permanent staffs, and it was also promoted by (central) campaign planners who argued that an effective party must speak with a single voice. In this spirit, SPD organizers chose 'the campaign forged in a single mould' (*Wahlkampf aus einem Guß*) as the slogan for their 1961 election preparations, and this motto continued to guide central campaign efforts throughout the 1960s. In the same decade the SPD's publicity department assumed increasing responsibility for the production of local campaign material, 'so that the unity of the total concept was preserved even in the smallest county or local newspaper'.[16] Campaign centralization was both accompanied, and propelled, by increasing reliance on the tools and advice of professional advertisers. CDU national organizers began consulting marketing-specialists and commissioning pre-election opinion-polls as early as 1953, but it was not until the 1960s that SPD campaigners began to rely heavily on the advice of market researchers and advertisers.[17] These trends of the 1950s and 1960s continued, so that one observer could describe the most prominent characteristics of German campaigns in the 1970s and 1980s as, 'centralization, intra-party professionalization, and commercialization'.[18]

Television provided another impulse for party planners to centralize their campaigns, because television gave parties direct and immediate access to a vast cross-section of potential voters. By the 1961 election, observers were already labelling television (news, interviews, and advertisements) as the most important medium of communications in German campaigns.[19] This importance only increased throughout the 1960s as television ownership expanded rapidly. The campaigns of the 1980s and 1990s were dominated by news shows featuring interviews with, or debates between, top party leaders, and by free advertisements on the public television stations. German campaigners looked to the United States for hints about how to generate images which would produce favourable coverage on television news programmes.[20]

On the other hand, the German parties were relatively slow to exploit opportunities for advertising on private radio and television stations. German parties have never been permitted to buy advertising-time on publicly owned stations, but this prohibition has not applied to private stations. However, until the end of the 1980s most such stations had small audiences. The CDU was the first party to venture into private advertising, in 1989, when it purchased advertising-spots on private television and radio for the European elections. By the 1990 *Bundestag* election both CDU and SPD local and national campaigners were experimenting with the use of paid advertising-time on private local radio stations and on private television networks.[21]

In Germany national party organizers have used new technologies to improve not only their direct communication with potential party voters, but also their communication with local campaigners. By 1987 teleprinters, fax machines, and computer networks linked many SPD and CDU local offices with federal headquarters, and both central parties continued to invest in improving local parties' communications equipment.[22] Such new technologies enabled the 1976 SPD campaign to introduce a new tool, 'television leaflets', and these became a standard part of subsequent campaigns. To produce these leaflets, federal organizers write an immediate response to questions raised during televised interviews or debates, then electronically transmit the text to regional headquarters. During the same night the regional parties use the text to print leaflets, and the next morning local volunteers distribute these topical leaflets to doorsteps and at factory gates. Such a quick response is thought to reinforce the advantage (or reduce the damage) of televised communications from the party to voters.

In addition to producing more standardized campaign leaflets, CDU and SPD campaigners in Bonn have assumed control over most other aspects of the production of campaign publicity. As in the past, the central parties still continue to dictate the schedules of speaking-engagements for many national campaigners, but now they also produce television and newspaper advertisements, and provide designs and text for most local campaign materials. Since the mid-1980s the parties have also been experimenting with direct mail in an effort further to centralize their contacts with individual supporters.[23]

As this suggests, even in the 1990s German campaigns were not confined to the airwaves. In part this is because party strategists have perceived television advertisements to be problematic instruments, since good advertisements take days or weeks to produce. Because they worried about quick response-time, the parties continued to make extensive use of newspaper advertisements even after their television publicity could reach the entire electorate. At the beginning of the 1990s, as in the 1950s, newspaper advertising remained one of the biggest items in parties' campaign budgets. This relative status may change in the near future, however, if German parties increase their purchases of television advertising.

In the last West German elections in 1987, and in the first post-unification elections, the national parties continued to employ traditional techniques such as holding large rallies and distributing leaflets. They also continued to co-ordinate extensive speaking-tours for large numbers of party campaigners, although party organizers now tended to judge the success of these tours more in terms of the publicity they generated than in terms of crowd size. In addition, by the 1980s the national parties had transformed their use of another traditional campaign tool, the 'election newspapers', which local parties were supposed to deliver on successive Sundays during the campaign. The parties printed millions of copies of these newspapers, which increasingly resembled popular tabloids.

Yet although traditional practices have not vanished, national electioneering in the Federal Republic has changed as party organizers have eagerly explored the new possibilities presented by emerging electioneering technologies. Campaign planners have focused on maximizing their parties' television exposure. They have used new techniques and technologies to improve communications with individual voters (direct mail) and with local campaigners (teleprinters, computer networks). They have hired market researchers and advertisers to help them design nationally co-ordinated election campaigns. The German parties have thus whole-heartedly adopted the technologies which are often associated with predictions about the obsolescence of membership strategies. The next section examines the extent to which the availability and use of these new communications technologies have actually altered party organizers' ideas about how local parties, and local members, can and should contribute to national electoral success.

Changing Expectations About Local Campaign Activity

The first thing to stress when seeking to establish the impact of new technologies is that national campaigners in the Federal Republic have never expected local parties to mobilize very large teams of volunteer campaigners. Now, as in the past, most local campaigning can be accomplished by small teams of activists.[24] However, party organizers have changed their advice about where these small teams should focus their efforts.

In the 1940s and 1950s, SPD publications urged local supporters to concentrate their campaign efforts on hanging posters, distributing leaflets, and staging public meetings. Local campaigners were expected to produce many of these posters and leaflets themselves. In addition to making banners and window displays, local branches were supposed to hold public demonstrations of support, for instance with party-organized fife-and-drum corps or, a 'must do', with parades and torchlight processions. Meetings for party members and for the general public were a standard part of all campaigns in the 1950s, though even then SPD advice urged local parties to enliven traditional political speeches with other entertainment, such as choirs or cabaret troupes.

Although local parties were supposed to increase their public visibility at campaign times, the tasks they were asked to perform were not labour-intensive. According to the SPD's main campaign guide from the 1950s, helpers were needed for the following jobs: 'Distributing propaganda materials; enlivening meetings; conducting propaganda conversations; speaking up in SPD and in opponents' meetings; operating technical equipment; preparing propaganda materials; collecting financial and in-kind donations; selling party literature.'[25] On election day, campaigners were supposed to tour the district with loudspeaker vans, drive voters to the polls, and staff information-booths in front of polling-stations. SPD branches were advised to enrol about 5 per cent of their members as 'volunteer publicists' (*Werbehelfer*) to help with these tasks.

Local parties were seldom asked to engage in such ambitious and labour-intensive efforts as making one or more personal calls to every household in the area (as were their British counterparts). Exceptionally, in 1957 SPD national organizers did urge local campaigners to use British-style systematic efforts to mobilize supporters on election day. However, these techniques apparently did not find much favour at the local level, and reference to such techniques had disappeared from SPD materials by the 1970s.

Organizers in the much smaller CDU probably held an even less labour-intensive vision of local campaigning in the 1950s, although there is not as much evidence on this, because in the 1950s the still-weak federal headquarters published little campaign advice. In 1957, the CDU members' newsletter highlighted only one type of contribution readers could make to that year's campaign: a financial one. But though the federal party did not outline specific campaign plans for the bulk of its membership, in 1957, and again in 1961, the federal CDU did try to build up a local network of interested and informed representatives (*Vertrauensleute*). These members received extra mailings from the central party so that they could represent CDU positions in local political discussions.[26]

As the preceding section explained, national-level campaigning began changing in the 1960s. These changes were only slowly reflected in party advice about local campaign efforts. Throughout the 1960s, such advice continued to emphasize preparations for local campaign meetings, even though national organizers often acknowledged the declining public interest in such events. A 1969 CDU pamphlet still advised local campaigners to use old standbys such as cinema advertising, roving film and loudspeaker vans, posters, leaflets, and automobile processions. But national organizers did add a few new tasks to their recommendations, and both parties' campaign advice began emphasizing the importance of work that local parties could do between elections. As a CDU party manager explained in this context in the mid-1960s, the growing population of floating voters and the overuse of advertising created a 'continuing imperative' for local parties' public-relations work.[27] (Chapter 5 evaluates the development and consequences of expanding views about campaigning as a continuous project.)

After 1957, SPD advice on campaigning began urging local parties more fully to exploit the party's comparatively large membership. Party pamphlets urged local campaigners to make sure that all members who wanted to help were actually given an individual assignment, even if this task was no more than talking about politics with non-enrolled friends.[28] Indeed, by 1969 the latter activity had been elevated to one of the central jobs for party members, and it continued to hold this status in both CDU and SPD publications in the next decades. SPD campaign analyses in the late 1960s began emphasizing the electoral utility of members' informal contacts. Party organizers placed a newly elevated value on members' street-corner discussions (with or without the candidate), conversations at work and with neighbours, and doorstep-visits to voters.[29] Meanwhile, CDU advice on campaigning began portraying members as valuable 'opinion carriers and multipliers'.[30]

Party strategists' views about the importance of mobilizing individual members were strengthened by a study which linked the CDU's poor results in the 1972 election to the widespread reluctance of CDU supporters to speak out during the 1972 campaign.[31] CDU organizers vowed that such 'spirals of silence' would not recur, and SPD organizers quickly picked up on this new orthodoxy about what mattered in election campaigns. A submission to the CDU's 1973 commission on party organization neatly summarized this change in perceptions about the utility of local campaigning:

Before, it seemed important to build up a distribution organization which could bring prepared publicity material into every last corner, and which could achieve the most equal possible scheduling of speakers in countless events. Now, however, concern about the effectiveness of mass media publicity, and the great attention given to mass rallies, make it necessary to concentrate professional 'campaign managers' in a tightly organized party headquarters. Even so, the importance of personal opinion leadership demands that the primary task of the 'base organization' must be this: to get party supporters to carry out more informal—but nevertheless systematic—propaganda work in the many local social organizations, and in neighbourhood and professional groups.[32]

The SPD's 1976 electioneering handbook gave a similar view of the new aims of local-level campaigning:

Campaigning means—increasing the audience for social-democratic arguments through personal conversations, civic initiatives, new information, and argumentative publicity in the constituency, in the home town, and in the neighbourhood; building up a small, active organization for the campaign.[33]

This position was reaffirmed before the 1990 campaign, when an SPD brochure explained:

Every party member must become a campaigner. For this to happen there needs to be information and mobilization long before the election. Every party member must know that even the most beautiful billboard does not have anything like the same power to convince as a personal conversation. The SPD in particular achieves its successes through the engaged activity of its members.[34]

This revised view of the purpose of local campaigning was reflected in new types of advice for local campaigners. Since 1976, pre-election editions of both parties' membership magazines have urged members independently to proclaim their political convictions by talking about politics with acquaintances and neighbours, by placing small advertisements in local newspapers, or by writing 'letters to the editor'. Members have been asked to display the party name or logo on a wide variety of merchandise: lapel pins, T-shirts, pens, notebooks, automobile stickers—in 1976 the CDU magazine even sold bikinis stamped with the party logo. Ever since the mid-1970s, parties' lists of suggested tasks for campaign helpers have placed such independent initiatives ahead of more traditional tasks (such as hanging posters, distributing leaflets, or staffing information-stands).

Thus, in the mid-1970s SPD and CDU visions of local campaigning expanded to incorporate a much larger role for members working in casual settings, independently of the local parties. Ideas about the proper work for local parties also changed at about the same time. In particular, national campaigners began urging local parties to concentrate on activities directed more towards convincing floating voters than towards mobilizing the party's core electorate. Although local parties were still expected to organize a few traditional public meetings to showcase visiting politicians, they were now urged to organize a greater number of campaign meetings with primarily social agendas. Before the 1976 and 1980 autumn elections, local campaigners were advised to enliven summer vacations by sponsoring non-political festivities (such as amateur theatricals or fairs) and community projects (such as playground renovations and tree-watering initiatives for public parks). Prior to the 1983 and 1987 winter campaigns, SPD and CDU advice highlighted the electoral value of sponsoring other social occasions, including pre-Christmas coffee-parties, theatre trips for senior citizens, sleigh-rides, ski-trips, and fireside political chats. Campaigners were reminded that outdoor information-stands were more inviting when citizens received free mulled wine or Christmas cake along with party leaflets.

Since the 1970s the German parties have urged their local campaigners to take advantage of other new techniques and technologies. Some of this advice merely 'modernized' traditional practices by relabelling them (market-place booths became 'info-stands', leaflet distribution became 'street actions' and 'factory actions'). But the national parties also developed genuinely new campaign tools, such as the video cassettes the SPD produced in 1983 to serve as discussion-openers for 'living-room meetings', or the computer games it developed to help educate members before the 1994 European elections. More importantly, in the 1980s national-party advice began recommending the selective use of telephone campaigning, even though court decisions guaranteeing privacy have set strict limits on how the telephone can be used.[35] For instance, a 1986 CDU brochure on 'new forms of campaigning' argued that 'massive telephoning projects' could be a 'normal component of political work', while the SPD's 1990 campaign brochure offered similar advice on 'telephone actions'.[36] Furthermore, both parties now encourage local campaigners to use personal computers for sending targeted campaign letters.[37]

In Germany most local campaigning ends before dawn on election day. During the night before the election, teams of volunteers may deliver the last issue of the party's election newspaper, or may distribute 'don't forget to vote' reminders. (The latter are sometimes wrapped around fresh breakfast-rolls.) But party advice has never set very difficult tasks for German campaigners on election day itself, perhaps because electoral participation in German federal elections has usually exceeded 80 per cent. Recent suggestions for activities on election day include such minor tasks as holding parties to thank campaign helpers, checking election posters, and even setting up refreshment stands near polling-stations. Local activists are also supposed to offer voters transportation to the polls, but delivering on this offer is not considered to be a demanding organizational task.

The preceding descriptions of the national parties' advice makes clear that German campaign strategies have relied on only small reserves of active members to conduct traditional local campaigns. Even when members were streaming into both parties in the late 1960s and early 1970s, CDU constituency candidates were advised to assemble teams of only five to ten helpers to visit voters, plus a few others to hang posters, distribute leaflets, produce publicity, and arrange meetings. SPD local campaigners were told that they needed only a 'small but active' organization.[38]

However, after the mid-1970s national organizers did try to develop a few new campaign tasks for volunteers inside the parties, tasks which would enable the parties to profit from their enlarged memberships. In the campaigns of the 1980s both parties attempted to enlist tens of thousands of members to deliver nationally produced campaign materials. Indeed, a report from CDU headquarters described recruiting these deliverers as the primary goal of the CDU's member mobilization before the 1987 election.[39] The national parties also tried to mobilize a large corps of volunteers to guarantee immediate delivery of their new 'television leaflets'. In employing these new outreach-tools, the national parties used members to provide cheap and rapid delivery of party messages.

In short, since the 1950s German national campaigns have indeed become increasingly reliant on mass media communication, increasingly centralized, and increasingly professionalized. As a result, some traditional local campaign jobs have disappeared. Yet despite this, neither SPD nor CDU national strategies entirely abandoned the idea that members can be organizational assets during elections. Not only did national organizers add new jobs to the repertory of tasks for local campaigners inside the local parties; they also began attaching new significance to the vote-winning contributions members can provide when acting independently of their local parties.

BRITAIN: CHANGING CAMPAIGN STRATEGIES

To many foreign observers, the most striking feature of a British parliamentary election may be the brevity of the official campaign. Although British general elections must be held at least once every five years, they can be called at any time, and with little advance warning. New parliamentary elections are held within five weeks after parliament's dissolution is announced. This uncertain scheduling has shaped campaign practices at both the local and national levels, not the least because campaigners hoard their resources until they can be sure that an election is imminent.[40]

Changes at the National Level

In Britain after the Second World War, as in Germany, campaigners revived many techniques of earlier decades. In the first elections Labour and Conservative national campaigns made extensive use of large public rallies to present their candidates and programmes. During the campaigns, each party's leader toured the country by train and car, and the national headquarters co-ordinated speaking-tours for other prominent representatives of the party.

In this period, as in the past, British organizers relied on newspaper accounts to spread party messages beyond rally audiences. But they also began to take advantage of a new outlet for party messages: free broadcasting-time. Since 1945 all British parties have received free slots for 'party election broadcasts' on public stations, first on radio alone, and then, starting in 1951, on television as well. Initially, the party broadcasts were the only reports about party politics which were aired immediately before elections. Until 1959, British television and radio newscasts completely ignored party politics during official campaign periods, because directors of the British Broadcasting Corporation (BBC) maintained that any other coverage would violate the BBC's mandate of political neutrality. BBC directors revised this interpretation in 1959, and by the time of the 1964 election, broadcasters felt relatively unrestricted in covering the parties and their leaders during campaigns.[41]

From this time onward, national organizers increasingly focused their efforts on capturing favourable publicity in nightly newscasts, while voters increasingly focused their attention on the television performances of a few party leaders. By the 1980s, television campaigning had become so important that the needs of television reporters dictated the timing and location of leaders' speeches, while 'photo opportunities' largely replaced leaders' less photogenic (and more dangerous) 'walkabouts'. Ticket-only political rallies became the norm, in part because campaign publicists could not risk admitting hecklers, who might spoil the free television-coverage; gaining this coverage was the main reason that the parties sponsored ever more elaborate, and ever more expensive, rallies.[42]

The expansion of election broadcasting is not the only reason why 1959 has been called a turning-point in the conduct of British parliamentary campaigns.[43] In that year the Labour Party also introduced the daily press conference as part of its campaign, and the innovation proved so successful that the Conservatives immediately imitated it.[44] All subsequent campaigns have included a daily round of news conferences, which are scheduled to accommodate newspaper and television production timetables.

A further novelty in 1959 was the Conservative Party's heavy reliance on professionals from the advertising business to design an extensive campaign of billboard and newspaper publicity, which ran prior to the official campaign.[45] Labour Party leaders decried their opponents' use of professional advertising techniques, but electoral defeat soon persuaded them, too, to consult professional advertisers. However, for both symbolic and financial reasons the Labour Party has mostly relied on volunteer advertising advisers.

Using the expertise and tools of the advertising profession increased the costs of both parties' 1964 campaigns. The Conservatives spent particularly heavily on what turned out to be a losing campaign for them.[46] This sobering experience helped dampen subsequent spending on national campaigns, and it was not until 1987 that inflation-adjusted campaign expenses reached 1964 levels.[47] The new jump in spending resulted in part from a renewed Conservative Party interest in using the expertise of professional advertising agencies. From 1978 through the early 1990s the Conservative Central Office relied heavily on a single advertising-firm (Saatchi & Saatchi), which designed not only party advertisements and posters, but also conference-platform backdrops and party leaflets. At times it even counselled the prime minister about which television shows to visit. These were all tasks which previously had been performed by the party's professional staff.[48] In turn, the success of Conservative Party advertising prompted the Labour Party to re-examine its own publicity needs. As a result, the Labour Party hired its own advertising firm for the first time in the 1983 campaign. This new commitment to the techniques of professional advertising apparently paid dividends in 1987, when the Labour Party was widely judged to have run the 'best' (though losing) campaign. In the 1990s both parties continued to employ professional advertisers during, and between, elections.

The parties' election budgets ballooned in the 1980s as they began sponsoring campaigns in national newspapers and on billboards. Until 1974, British organizers had assumed that the laws which strictly limited local spending on campaigns also prevented national parties from buying newspaper publicity during the official campaign period. But after the Liberal Party's unchallenged use of national newspaper advertisements in 1974, the other parties also began investing in such advertisements. In 1987, both the Conservative and Labour national campaigns sponsored extravagant series of full-page newspaper advertisements. Paying for these advertisements raised campaign spending to real levels which had not been seen since 1964. In 1992 party strategists were careful not to repeat this competition for paid newspaper-space, though the Conservatives opted instead for a costly series of billboard advertisements.[49]

Meanwhile, the parties' national headquarters continued to print and distribute other types of written campaign propaganda. Since the 1950s the national parties have produced large volumes of leaflets, posters, and windowbills for use by constituency campaigns. Although they now have access to alternative advertising techniques, the national parties have continued to produce an impressive volume of campaign materials for local use; indeed, the Labour Party headquarters claimed to have printed a record volume of campaign materials for the 1987 election.[50]

In addition, both national parties in Britain have experimented with direct mail as a method of campaigning. Conservative organizers tried out direct mail before the 1983 and 1987 elections, when the party headquarters sent out thousands of letters soliciting funds and new members. (For legal reasons, these efforts were halted once the elections were announced.[51]) Before the 1987 election the Labour Party also used direct mail to appeal for funds to finance the national campaigns. Both parties continue to develop their use of direct mail in the 1990s.

Finally, the British parties have recently developed technical capacities which allow them to maintain closer communications-links between national and local campaigns. Since the 1970s national parties have installed computer networks, teleprinters, and fax machines to link central, regional, and local campaigners. National campaigners now use these channels to try to ensure that local campaigners are aware of, and can echo, centrally determined responses to each campaign day's media headlines. However, even the best technology cannot alter the fact that once the official campaign begins, constituency campaigners have little time to read the messages sent by national organizers.

These accounts show that the British parties, like the German parties, have rapidly adjusted the style of national campaigns to take advantage of new technological possibilities. Despite legal limits on their use of broadcasting, and despite the lack of public subsidies to help them pay for professionally trained staffs, the British parties have not failed to embrace new possibilities for direct communication from party leaders to potential voters. The next section explores the extent to which the centralization and professionalization of British campaigns has prompted national organizers to play down the local campaigns of individual party members.

Changing Expectations About Local Campaign Activity

Constituency campaigns in contemporary Britain remain strongly marked by their nineteenth-century origins.[52] The weight of the past is most clearly evident in the stringent legislation which governs campaign spending by parliamentary candidates. Legislation on campaign spending, which was originally enacted in the nineteenth century to prevent bribery of voters, invalidates the election of candidates if they or their supporters exceed very low spending limits. (The allowable amounts are calculated using a formula that considers the number of eligible voters and the geographic compactness of the constituency. In 1992, the average expenditure for Conservative and Labour constituency campaigns was under £6,000, with most candidates spending close to the permitted maximum.)[53] Anti-corruption laws explicitly prohibit British campaigners from sponsoring German-style 'friendly' campaign events, events at which food, alcohol, or other small gifts are distributed.

For more than the past century, British local campaigning has revolved around the canvass, an activity once described as 'the one supreme instrument of electoral organisation'.[54] Doorstep canvassing and accurate record-keeping were essential in British campaigns before the First World War, because parties needed to ensure that all their eligible supporters were listed on electoral registers. When manhood suffrage was enacted in 1918, local governments took over the job of preparing accurate electoral registers, and one of the original reasons for party canvassing disappeared. Despite this, party organizers continued to view the canvass as a useful tool for mobilizing party supporters, and for ensuring that they could recognize the name of their party's candidate on the ballot. In turn, this second function became much less important after 1970, when British electoral legislation was amended to permit candidates to place their party affiliations (or other descriptive information) on the ballot.

Official party descriptions of how to conduct the ideal canvass have changed little since the 1950s, although justifications for conducting such exercises have altered. For both parties, the ideal canvass begins long before an election, when local campaigners visit every household in a constituency in order to compile a complete record of individual voting intentions. In theory this canvass record should be updated every year, as new electoral registers appear. Once an election is called, local campaigners can use their canvass information to target the distribution of election materials, to remind elderly supporters to apply for postal ballots, to arrange transportation to the polls for supporters, or to find supporters who are willing to display party posters in windows. But traditionally the main use of canvass records comes on election day itself. The best-run parties have volunteers at every polling-station recording the names of those who vote. Other volunteers combine this information with canvass records, and then attempt to mobilize supporters who have not yet voted. Thus, in stark contrast to German parties, British parties have viewed election day as the culmination of local campaigning, and as the day requiring the maximum number of volunteers.

Addressing envelopes used to be another traditionally labour-intensive campaign task for British local parties. These envelopes were once necessary for distributing the single free mailing which parliamentary candidates are permitted to send to all electors in their constituencies. Because elections have never been pre-scheduled, envelope addressing was usually done at the last minute, once it was clear which year's electoral register would be used. As soon as an election was announced, constituency campaigns marshalled volunteers to address envelopes as well as to canvass voters and deliver leaflets.

The campaign activities described above determined the jobs for which local volunteers were said to be needed in the 1950s and 1960s. Thus, one Labour Party publication from this period noted that during elections party members should canvass, should distribute literature, and should display party posters in the windows of their homes. A Conservative Party pamphlet from this era listed similar activities among its campaign tasks for members, but also expanded the list to include giving speeches, asking questions or acting as stewards at meetings, lending cars, lending rooms for 'cottage meetings', and acting as election-day poll-watchers or messengers.

For reasons already mentioned, 1959 may have marked a turning-point in the way the British parties fought campaigns at the national level. However, it did not mark a similar change in party organizers' ideas about the proper conduct of constituency campaigns. In the 1960s and 1970s national organizers in both British parties began expressing doubts about the effectiveness of traditional local campaigning, and about the ability of shrinking local memberships to conduct such campaigns. Yet their advice to local campaigners changed only slowly, perhaps because strict local spending-limits also reduced the scope for innovation in local campaigns. (Throughout the past four decades costs for printing have devoured most of candidates' budgets: the one-page leaflet which candidates mail to all voters can use up more than half of this limit.[55]) Thus, for example, a 1980 Conservative list of local electioneering jobs differed little from the party's 1950 list: 'Addressing Envelopes; Delivery of Leaflets; Postal and Proxy Votes; A Full Canvass; Maximum Display of Posters; Typing up NCRs ['No carbon required' canvass records]; Transport; Running Committee Rooms; Telling at Polling Stations; Calling up known supporters on polling day; Ensuring maximum exposure for the Candidate'.[56]

However, underneath this continuity, some changes did creep into national organizers' visions of local campaigning. For instance, by the end of the 1980s, the first of the tasks on the preceding Conservative list (the laborious task of hand-addressing envelopes to all constituency voters) was considered obsolete. By 1992 computers had become standard equipment in many constituency offices, where they were often used to print address labels from computerized electoral registers.[57] Even constituencies without computers could eliminate the task of hand-addressing envelopes, because from 1987 onward the post office has delivered *unaddressed* election leaflets. In addition the national parties have helped develop software designed to make it easier for local parties to employ personal computers in such traditional constituency tasks as recording canvass information, and in less traditional tasks such as using canvass information for direct-mail campaigning.[58]

In the 1980s, canvassing remained at the heart of the British parties' advice about how to conduct local electioneering activities. Yet such advice gradually redefined the purpose of canvassing, shifting the focus away from its utility in preparing for massive election-day mobilization, and placing greater stress on its role in reaching members of target groups (such as young or ethnic-minority voters). Computerization of canvass records did not alter the fact that local campaigners needed to gather information for their records by systematically contacting voters. But in the 1980s party publications began urging local campaigners to supplement doorstep visits with telephone canvassing. This technique began to be more widely adopted by the 1992 election, despite the risk that it could make candidates vulnerable to the very serious charge of exceeding their campaign budgets.

National organizers' expectations about one type of local campaigning—the public meeting—have changed markedly since the 1950s. Local campaigners were once urged to arrange a whole series of formal and informal public meetings throughout the constituency, meetings which were intended to give voters a chance to meet the local candidate. As a 1948 pamphlet for local Conservatives asserted

Public meetings remain, in spite of other methods of publicity such as the Press, the wireless and Party literature, one of the most useful and effective forms of propaganda.[59]

But in the following years attendance at campaign meetings declined, and party organizers began advising candidates to hold fewer meetings. By the 1980s both parties urged their local campaigners to replace general public meetings with a few smaller meetings, and to focus these on specific issues aimed at target groups. Local campaigners were advised to concentrate on arranging activities such as motorcades, street-stalls, or concerts; these are all activities which take advantage of ready-made audiences, and which showcase the party presence in the community without conveying detailed political messages.

Since the 1950s Labour and Conservative Party advice to constituency campaigners has changed only slightly. Unlike the German parties, the British parties developed relatively few new local tasks to replace those which fell out of favour as campaigning changed at the national level. The British parties did not develop elaborate theories of personal campaigning, nor did they encourage local campaigners to participate in co-ordinated publicity actions. They did, however, urge local parties to adopt new technologies to help in the performance of traditional tasks such as canvassing and leafleting. These new technologies may have been particularly important for constituencies where volunteers are in short supply; however, they have almost certainly increased local parties' dependence on one particular kind of volunteer: the computer expert. In short, because the tasks of British constituency campaigning are little changed, and because some of the methods for carrying out these tasks have been streamlined, the local campaigns envisaged by today's national organizers are almost certainly less labour-intensive than those outlined by their counterparts in the 1950s.

SUMMARY: INERTIA AND INNOVATIONS

These accounts of changing campaign styles have shown that British and German party strategists have sometimes enthusiastically, and sometimes reluctantly, embraced the tools and ideas of market researchers and professional advertisers. Since the 1950s all four parties' national campaigns have adopted television as their primary channel of election communication. Party organizers' expectations about local campaign efforts have changed along with their changing ideas about national electioneering. Yet the direction of these changes cannot be neatly summarized because, in the words of the three scenarios presented at the beginning of this chapter, party organizers' views about members' campaign roles have showed signs of stasis, decline, *and* innovation.

In some areas of campaigning, 'decline' best characterizes changes in expectations about members' electoral contributions. For instance, national organizers in all four parties have lowered their expectations about the extent to which local volunteers will arrange and attend public meetings, events that were once considered to be at the heart of local electioneering efforts. In Britain particularly, some traditional campaign jobs have also become less dependent on member-volunteers (for instance, addressing envelopes and pasting-up electoral registers). Furthermore, all four national parties have removed most editorial and design responsibility from local campaigners. Because national campaigners now place a premium on visually unified publicity, all four national parties now print, or at least design, most of the publicity materials used by local campaigns. This centralization of publicity efforts has relieved local campaigners of the need (and, to some extent, the opportunity) to summarize party aims visually or textually. These efforts to homogenize campaign messages by centralizing publicity seem to support Alan Ware's charge that in this age of new communications-technologies, party members will be left only with those campaign tasks which are routine and uncreative.[60]

But the label 'decline' does not apply to the whole range of local campaign activities. German and, to a lesser extent, British organizers have developed new visions about how local campaigning should change if it is better to complement televised campaigning. In the 1970s and 1980s, both German and British local campaigners were encouraged to respond to declining public interest in political meetings by seeking out potential voters in the places where they work and shop. German local campaigners were asked to participate in nationally co-ordinated campaign actions (such as delivering party newspapers). And finally, in the 1970s and 1980s German party organizers developed new ideas about how to profit from the support of those party members who would not participate in local campaigning. German parties' membership magazines now urge individual volunteers actively to participate in everyday political discussions in order to persuade undecided voters, and to strengthen wavering partisans.

In Britain, national organizers remained committed to the very traditional idea of doorstep canvassing, but in the 1980s they also began developing new ideas about the point of this exercise. They have come to view canvassing as a tool for figuring out how to target the delivery of campaign materials, instead of as a tool whose main use is for mobilizing pre-existing supporters. The national parties also began urging local campaigners to use telephones and computers in order to make canvassing less labour-intensive and more effective.

In short, in neither country did the centralized use of new communications technologies entirely extinguish the local component of national campaign strategies. On the contrary, party strategists agreed that new technologies should not be confined to the national level. The growing accessibility of new technologies (including microcomputers, photocopiers, teleprinters, and fax machines) prompted national organizers to devise new campaign tasks for local members.

Technological availability has not been the only fuel for innovation in expectations about how local efforts can contribute to national electoral success. Beginning in the 1970s national organizers, particularly those in Germany, voiced growing doubts about whether mass media communication is sufficient for shaping public opinion. German party organizers have responded to these doubts by emphasizing ways that local campaigners complement impersonal national campaigns. They have urged local parties to sponsor activities which are good-humoured and not particularly political, activities which will appeal to voters who find national campaigns too earnest, and national politicians too distant.

These changed ideas about members' electioneering tasks could be summarized by returning to the second chapter's discussion of different benefits which parties may reap from membership organization. In the words of that chapter's distinctions, changed campaign strategies have not led any of the parties to disavow the need for 'labour benefits' (members as volunteer workers inside the party). However, the German parties in particular have clearly acquired greater appreciation of members' potential provision of 'outreach benefits' (members as independent ambassadors to the community).

In both countries, the favoured local electioneering activities are still better conducted by formal members than by transient groups of party supporters. As Chapter 2 argued, when (as in Germany) national organizers recognize a value in having individual campaigners who independently represent the party in casual conversations, they have an incentive to educate supporters about party policies and personnel so that these supporters have the confidence to participate in informal political discussions. If party organizers want to have politically educated supporters, they have an incentive to recruit, because education for supporters is most easily transmitted to enrolled members in local and national meetings, or via party publications. Where campaigns are short and elections are not pre-scheduled (as in Britain) the need to assemble an election team at short notice creates another strong reason not to rely solely on *ad hoc* local organization.

The preceding accounts suggest that none of the contemporary parties entirely discount the value of the contributions members may make during national political campaigns. However, the next chapter introduces another and even stronger reason which explains why organizers in these four parties continue to value enrolled supporters, and to prefer standing memberships to *ad hoc* organizations: party strategists have increasingly come to think of local electioneering as a long-term effort. Organizers in all four parties now proclaim that local efforts to win votes can only be effective if they begin long before the date of the national election. As party organizers have changed their assessments about when and how potential voters are to be won, they have developed a wide range of new inter-election activities for local members.

5

Party Members and Inter-Election Activities

Success in winning elections will only come from continuous campaigning between elections. Increasing membership, raising more money and effective communication are all part of a successful programme of political campaigning.

Conservative Party pamphlet[1]

JUST as soon as election outcomes are announced, party organizers may relentlessly assert to tired party activists that 'the next campaign begins the moment that the last vote is counted'.[2] But not all parties make active inter-election agendas an integral component of their vote-winning strategies: some, like Duverger's cadre parties, allow their extra-parliamentary organizations largely to hibernate between elections. Moreover, even in those parties where permanent campaigning is valued, party organizers can hold very different ideas about the form and intensity inter-election campaign efforts should assume. They may urge local parties to focus inter-election energies on inward-oriented activities, such as member education, or they may exhort local parties to reach out to an audience far outside the inner circle of party supporters. Because of the potential importance of inter-election activities in parties' overall campaign strategies, and because of the diverse forms such activities may assume, assessments about party members' changing roles must consider the jobs which party organizers assign to members between, as well as during, the periods which immediately precede national elections.

The current chapter thus continues the investigation of British and German parties' organizing strategies by examining changing ideas about members' involvement in three types of inter-election activity: maintaining the local parties; participating in local government; and reaching out to the broader community. Whereas the previous chapter found signs of both increasing and decreasing expectations about what party members should do immediately prior to national elections, the present chapter finds that organizers in the four German and British parties have clearly raised their expectations about what is to be gained from members' inter-election activities.

ORGANIZATIONAL MAINTENANCE

Both the German and the British parties have traditionally sustained extra-parliamentary organizations consisting of central party bureaucracies and networks of branch-based membership associations. As the previous chapter made clear, organizers in all four national parties have long considered the efforts of these local associations to have at least a minor role to play in campaign efforts. Because of this, they have necessarily viewed work to maintain or expand the local associations as a fundamental prerequisite for more directly political work. However, in recent decades organizers in all four parties have developed new ideas about precisely what it is members need to do to keep the local organizations running, and to help sustain the parties' central bureaucracies.

Members and Party Funding

Under certain circumstances, party members' most important contributions to organizational maintenance may be the money they donate to the coffers of the local and national party. Indeed, financial pressures may have provided some parties with the initial impulse to organize their supporters.[3] Conversely, the importance of membership funding, and of membership itself, may well drop in parties which gain access to other revenue sources. According to one version of such predictions, parties—including those which were once primarily financed by membership dues—will be tempted to neglect fundraising from members just as soon as they gain access to potentially richer sources of financial support, such as public subsidies and corporate donations.[4] According to another version, parties may try to improve their financial situations by courting individual donors in ways that drop all distinctions between 'members' and other supporters. In seeking to emulate the fundraising successes of non-profit organizations such as Greenpeace or international medical charities, parties may dilute the meaning of membership until it becomes a direct-mail transaction lacking all non-financial implications (membership brings neither obligations nor privileges).[5] In either scenario, party organizers cease to view members as a valuable source of revenue. In the words of Chapter 2, they no longer esteem members for the financial benefits they provide. One way to determine whether either scenario accurately characterizes developments in the four British and German parties is to ask whether national party leaders have made any efforts to maintain or increase party revenues from membership.

Membership Dues and National Party Revenue

Party leaders can attempt to boost members' financial support for the central party by increasing the level of dues, improving the methods of dues collection, raising the central party's portion of dues, or expanding the size of the party membership. In addition, they can ask members voluntarily to support special fundraising initiatives. A glance at each of the countries shows that at various times, German and British party leaders have employed all these techniques.

Germany

Public subsidies have provided a very solid financial foundation for all the German parties since 1967, when the *Bundestag* passed legislation authorizing public compensation for parties' electioneering activities. The parliamentary parties (except the Greens) have regularly worked together to increase these subsidies. Almost as regularly, the constitutional court has intervened in these cross-party deals, and has forced the parties to modify the format and distribution of the subsidies. After initial passage of the federal legislation on political subsidies, all the German states also introduced similar subsidies for parties contesting state-level elections.

Until the introduction of public subsidies, membership dues had been by far the most important component of SPD finance. Ever since the party was founded in the nineteenth century, SPD organizers had expected individual party members to pay non-

trivial dues. The party's 1950 conference formalized these expectations when it adopted an income-related schedule of dues.
Subsequently the SPD has only infrequently raised its dues rates
(about once every decade; see Table 5.1). In 1990, the party
treasurer and other leaders persuaded the party conference to
accept a special three-year levy on top of regular dues, the
proceeds of which were to be divided among the federal and
regional parties in order to support efforts to build up the SPD
in eastern Germany. Some blamed this controversial increase for
the subsequent decline in party membership, and a year later the
party's business manager was still being forced to defend the
increase.[6] Thus, it was more than a routine matter when the new
SPD leader, Rudolf Scharping, successfully battled to get the 1993
party conference to accept an increase in dues rates. Though

TABLE 5.1. *CDU and SPD minimum yearly dues (DM)*

Year change implemented	Minimum yearly dues (for members in employment)	
	CDU	SPD
1950	n.a.[a]	12.00
1952	n.a.	14.40
1962	n.a.	18.00
1964	12.00	18.00
1971	36.00	18.00
1972	36.00	36.00
1975	36.00	48.00
1976	60.00	48.00
1979	60.00	60.00
1991	60.00	84.00[b]
1995	60.00	96.00

Note: n.a. = not applicable.

[a] No nationally set dues until 1964.
[b] Includes a three-year minimum solidarity-charge of DM2
per month to finance organizational reconstruction in the
east.

Sources: For the CDU: CDU, *Bundesparteitag*, various years.
For the SPD: SPD, *Jahrbuch*, various years, and *Parteitag*,
1990 and 1993.

Scharping lost his simultaneous attempt to institute automatic inflation-adjustment in dues levels, he did get the party conference to agree to routinely consider dues increases every second year.[7]

SPD fundraisers have used other tools to try to boost revenues from members. Because the party's minimum levels of dues have been relatively static, its treasurers have frequently exhorted members voluntarily to pay more as their incomes increased, and not merely to pay the minimum rates. Treasurers have stressed the great potential for 'honesty in dues assessments' to boost party revenues; as the SPD's 1979–81 Yearbook noted with (mock?) astonishment, 70 per cent of SPD members placed themselves in the lowest two income-brackets on the party's dues schedule.[8] However, national party efforts to encourage increases in voluntary payment have apparently met with only limited success.

In contrast, SPD initiatives to improve the rates of dues collection have been much more successful. In the 1970s and 1980s, national organizers began urging local parties to replace the traditional weekly or monthly doorstep collection of dues with the more reliable and predictable method of monthly deduction from bank accounts. National organizers endorsed bank collection of dues despite charges that the party was needlessly abandoning house-to-house collection, one of the institutions that had traditionally played an important role in strengthening ties between individual party members. By the end of the 1980s, two thirds of SPD members had their dues automatically deducted from their bank accounts.[9]

In stark contrast to the SPD, the federal CDU initially relied primarily on big donations from industry. Local and regional parties were free to set their own level of dues and dues-collection procedures, and the federal party received no income from membership dues. It was not until 1959 that the CDU party conference formally approved the idea that local parties should be required to contribute something to federal-party coffers. This conference approved a scheme whereby local parties were expected to forward DM0.10 per member per month to the national party (the equivalent of a 'membership tax'). The party's 1964 conference adopted the first national schedule of recommended dues, which, like those in the SPD, were income-related. CDU party organizers urged local parties to collect the newly established dues by bank transfer. Finally, in 1967 the party conference followed leadership advice to encourage local parties to pay their fair shares to the federal party. It did this by changing its statutes so that delegates to future conferences would be allocated to local parties according to the number of members for which they forwarded the yearly 'membership tax'.

These changes reflected a new recognition of the potential importance of members as a source of national income. Subsequently, however, the CDU has only rarely attempted to use increases in either the dues rate or the 'membership tax' to boost party income (see Table 5.1). As a result, by the end of the 1980s some in party headquarters were complaining that membership did not generate sufficient income for the federal party. Indeed, some even argued that membership represented a financial liability, because membership dues were low and stagnant, while costs of communicating with members were high and rising.[10] In 1989 CDU leaders used such arguments to persuade a reluctant party conference to increase the portion of membership dues channelled to the federal party.[11]

For both parties, membership dues have been the major instrument for raising funds from individual supporters, but both parties have also called upon members and other supporters to provide additional revenues for the central party. Above all, the national parties have tended to appeal for help in times of financial crisis. For instance, when the SPD was trying to reduce its debts in the mid-1970s, party organizers published an appeal for special donations and put a bank deposit slip on the cover of the party's membership magazine; this ensured that even inactive members would be reached by the request.[12] Similarly, in the 1990s the CDU did not copy the SPD's tactic of temporarily raising dues to benefit its branches in the new eastern states; instead, CDU leaders appealed to members to make voluntary contributions for this purpose.[13]

Thus, despite their generous levels of public funding, the German parties have not neglected to cultivate their membership as a source of funds. One reason for this is that a provision of the 1967 Parties Law prohibits extra-parliamentary parties from receiving more than half of their overall (local, state, and national) funding from public subsidies. Another reason for parties to look for private funds is that the subsidized parties are obliged to publish annual accounts showing the proportion of party income provided by members, by public sources, and by corporations and large individual donors. Furthermore, since 1993 court-ordered revisions to legislation on party subsidies have increased the incentives for parties to rely on private funds.

In setting guidelines for the new legislation on party finance, the courts took account of public criticism of 'self-service' financing practices.[14] As a result, the new legislation permanently froze overall funding to extra-parliamentary party organizations at an inflation-adjusted equivalent of the 1989–92 average annual rate of subsidy. Like previous arrangements, the new legislation distributed much of the subsidy money to parties according to their electoral success (although the new legislation considered party performance in state as well as in federal elections). However, the new system was based on parties' absolute success in mobilizing supporters, not, as before, on their relative success in winning a share of the vote. As a result, starting in the mid-1990s, overall levels of public subsidies reflected election turn-out, and parties were given new incentives to maximize that turn-out, not just to increase their share of the vote. The new formula for distributing public funds also rewarded parties for raising private funds, because it gave them partial matching grants for political contributions from individuals (a category which included membership dues), and because it withheld vote-based subsidies from parties unless they raised at least an equal sum through private donations. At the same time that the new legislation made the payment of public subsidies more dependent on parties' private fundraising efforts, it also lowered individuals' incentives for making large contributions by sharply reducing deductibility for political contributions. It also abolished the tax deductibility of corporate political contributions.[15]

The cumulative and deliberate result of these changes was to give the German parties (especially the smallest ones) increased incentives to seek funds outside the public purse, particularly from their members. But even before the new legislation was adopted, German party leaders had taken the risk of confronting party conferences in order to demand increased membership-funding for the federal party. In short, in the 1990s German party leaders seemed to retain a vital interest in raising money from members.

Britain

In Britain, in contrast to Germany, public subsidies to political parties have always been parsimonious, being largely confined to the free postage for one election mailing which is given to all parliamentary candidates, and to support for the parliamentary parties' comparatively modest staffs. Parliament has occasionally considered expanding public funding for parties, but the idea has never found cross-party support. Conservative MPs have generally opposed it, at least in part because their party has comparatively good access to other sources of funds. In 1994 they once again blocked increased political subsidies when the subject was investigated by a parliamentary committee.[16] Yet although the British parties have not been able to rely on large public subsidies, they certainly have not relied solely on members' contributions.

Trade-union contributions have always provided the bulk of Labour Party funds. Because of this, Labour Party organizers have been able to view individual members merely as a supplemental source of party revenue. Nevertheless, in the 1980s, Labour leaders began to reassess the advantages of membership-based financing. As a result, they initiated frequent changes in the level of dues while trying to strike a good balance between boosting party revenues and attracting and retaining members. Accordingly, proposals to change the level of dues and constituency-party affiliation fees remained controversial topics at party conferences well into the 1990s (see Table 5.2).

Like their German counterparts, Labour Party organizers also endorsed new methods of dues collection as a way to regularize the flow of revenue from this source. Stabilizing income was one of the goals named by party leaders in the late 1980s when they persuaded constituencies to adopt membership procedures which virtually eliminated the time-honoured but labour-intensive job of collecting local dues. Members of the party executive pushed for this change even in the face of arguments that the elimination of dues collectors would weaken solidary ties. Under the new scheme, members were encouraged to pay annual dues either by cheque or by bank debit. In 1988 party headquarters demonstrated its preference for the latter by rewarding members who bought their party membership using a bank debit: all who did so were automatically entered into a draw to win a trip to Venice.[17]

TABLE 5.2. *Labour Party minimum yearly dues* (£)

Year change implemented	Minimum yearly dues (for members in employment)	Year change implemented	Minimum yearly dues (for members in employment)
1945[a]	0.30	1986	8.60
1965	0.60	1987	10.00
1971	1.20	1988	10.60
1980	3.00	1989	10.00
1981	5.00	1992	15.00
1982	6.00	1993	18.00
1984	7.00	1994	15.00
1985	8.00		

Note: All amounts in new pence

[a] 1945 level continues previous rates.

Sources: Labour Party, *NEC Reports to Conference*, various years.

Since 1945, Labour Party headquarters has regularly experimented with other ways of raising money from members, including distributing fundraising appeals and organizing party lotteries. In the late 1980s, the party began supplementing these methods with new techniques. For instance, in 1989 it began offering members the party's own credit card (sporting a hologram of the Houses of Parliament), for which the party receives both a per-card payment and a small commission on most purchases made with the card.[18] During recent party conferences and before general elections, the Labour Party has also placed front-page advertisements in national newspapers, inviting readers to call a free phone number if they wanted to contribute to the party, or if they wanted to enrol as party members.[19] The most effective new scheme for raising funds from members has probably been the party's establishment of a club for 'Labour Supporters'. These supporters are party members who pay £5 per week to the central party. In 1993 about 28,000 such 'Supporters' contributed over £2 million to the party, a sum which reportedly made them the largest single source of party funds that year.[20]

Whereas the Labour Party has relied on trade-union backing, the work of the national Conservative Party has always been heavily supported by large donations from firms and individuals. The party's real and symbolic reliance on membership contributions has been much lower, because the Conservative Party (like the CDU of the 1950s) has neither a national schedule of dues nor a system to coerce local associations into forwarding a portion of individual dues to support the work of the national party. However, the national party does ask for voluntary contributions from the local parties. The Conservative Party introduced a formal system for soliciting these contributions as early as 1948, when the party conference gave its approval to a formula for calculating recommended levels of constituency contributions to the national party; these voluntary 'quotas' were based on each constituency's proportion of Conservative voters. Adoption of the quota scheme provided a big initial boost in local payments to the party's Central Office. However, subsequent revisions of quota levels have barely kept pace with inflation, and national leaders have not been very successful in convincing constituencies to meet even these modest targets. (For instance, in 1984, one year after a strong Conservative general-election victory, ninety-five Conservative constituency associations paid nothing to Conservative Central Office, among them sixty-one constituencies with Conservative MPs).[21] In the 1980s Central Office organizers experimented with new schemes to help constituencies increase the revenues they were receiving from members (such as providing those who paid higher annual subscriptions with cards which gave them discounts at certain stores); however, the monies raised by these schemes mostly stayed within the local associations.[22]

The national Conservative Party has benefited from occasional special fundraising appeals. In 1947 party leaders successfully appealed for members and supporters to raise £1 million for the central party (although much of the resulting money probably came from a few big contributions).[23] A similar attempt in 1967 exceeded its target of £2 million, with over two-thirds of this money said to have come from constituency sources.[24] In the 1980s, Conservative Central Office conducted less publicized mass appeals when it began making limited use of direct-mail fundraising, sending letters which combined calls for contributions with invitations to join the party (as in a 1987 appeal mailed to shareholders in the newly privatized British Telecom).[25] In 1993 the Conservative Party followed the examples of the Labour Party and Liberal Democrats when it introduced its own fundraising credit card for party members.[26]

Thus, in Britain in recent years it has been the Labour Party in particular which has experimented with ways to cultivate membership as a financial resource for the central party. In contrast, the Conservative Central Office has taken few steps to try to force Conservative constituency associations to share more of their wealth. Instead, the Conservative Party has looked for revenues beyond its membership, and has focused on developing a network of direct-mail financial backers beyond the party membership.

Membership and Local-Party Fundraising

So far, the discussion has focused on ways in which party organizers have sought to profit from members as a direct source of revenue for the central parties. Through their dues, members also help fund parties' local organizations. But at the local level, members' financial value may far exceed their own direct capacity to contribute, because members may also boost party funds by working as volunteer fundraisers. Particularly in Britain, constituency parties have often relied heavily on the proceeds of local activities to finance the salaries of their employees ('agents'), and to pay the rents for their premises. Fundraising has been less crucial to the German local parties. Today the publicly subsidized state and federal parties can offer local parties high levels of support in the form of personnel and materials. Yet even before public subsidies were introduced, German party organizers did not expect that members would devote much attention to fundraising.

Germany

Local parties in Germany get much of their revenues from the portion of membership dues which remains at the local level. These monies cover most local expenses, which are kept relatively low because the state and federal parties pay for personnel, equipment, and even some campaign materials. As a result, local parties have spent little time raising funds, and national organizers have apparently felt little need to issue fundraising advice for local activists. Such advice as they have given has emphasized ways that local parties can generate more money from within their memberships. For instance, one SPD article advised local parties to increase revenues by encouraging members to pay dues at higher levels, by collecting a 'thirteenth month' of dues from existing members, by collecting special contributions from SPD office-holders, or by selling 'election-fund tokens' to party members. In 1990, the SPD's pre-election fundraising advice for local campaigners stressed the advantages of sending personalized letters of appeal to members and other known supporters; it also suggested that parties might raise money by recruiting new members, and by selling refreshments at party events. As this advice makes clear, German organizers have not viewed local-party fundraising as a labour-intensive task.[27]

Britain

In Britain, party organizers have always taken quite a different attitude towards local fundraising. At least since the late 1940s, when the Conservative Party introduced constituency quotas and limits on candidate contributions to constituency parties, organizers in this party have considered fundraising to be a primary, and time-consuming, task for local Conservative associations. According to the party's model rules, raising funds for national and local purposes is one of the explicit aims of local associations.[28] Indeed, in 1974 the leader of the Conservative Party's extra-parliamentary organization gave a revealing insight into how Conservative organizers have considered fundraising to be closely intertwined with the party's wider campaigning goals; during a House of Lords debate he defended Conservative opposition to public subsidies for political parties by declaring that, 'if we were to take away any real need to raise funds, a great deal of local political work might well collapse'.[29]

In the Conservative Party, active party members are supposed to organize fundraising activities, and less active members and other sympathizers are expected to attend these events in order to ensure their financial success. In this party, local fundraising is supposed to yield more than financial dividends. It is also supposed to keep local parties in the public eye, and to keep party workers united, 'exercising them between elections, and holding the interest of supporters less inclined to take part in more serious day to day political activities'.[30]

Conservative Party recommendations on fundraising have changed little over the past sixty years. Favoured activities include social gatherings (fêtes, garden parties, parties in the home), sales (of produce, crafts, second-hand items), and entertainments and games (whist drives, contests, films).[31] Such events provide a wide range of jobs for member volunteers. In the 1980s central organizers expanded their lists of recommended fundraisers when they began encouraging local parties to take advantage of the fundraising potential of new computer technology, for instance for mailing fundraising letters, or for running lotteries by mail.[32]

Fundraising advice has been much less prominent in Labour Party discussions of constituency organization, perhaps because many constituency Labour Parties have relied heavily on local trade-union support. Nevertheless, such advice as has been given by Labour Party organizers has not differed much from that dispensed by their Conservative counterparts. They have encouraged local Labour parties to generate money using events such as rummage sales, theatre visits, and dances—events which are expected to produce social as well as financial rewards. Handbooks produced by the Labour Party have also highlighted the fundraising utility of local- and national-party lotteries and other games of chance, although in the 1950s one national organizer found such schemes to be so over-used that she felt compelled to warn constituency parties not to rely exclusively on competitions, but also to raise funds with social activities and bazaars.[33] In addition, more recent Labour Party advice on fundraising, like Conservative Party advice, has urged local parties to supplement traditional fundraising practices with mailed appeals.[34]

The preceding discussion of party fundraising suggests that leaders in all four parties continue to view direct and indirect monetary contributions as a fundamental obligation of members, and as a prime reason to enrol members. This is true even in the German parties, which have gained access to very large public subsidies. In the 1990s party leaders still appreciate the benefits of members' financial support, and as a result leaders of the three parties which have national schedules of dues have risked confrontations with dissatisfied delegates to party conferences in order to win increases in dues. In all four parties, organizers have also invested in other schemes to increase the contributions members make to national and local parties. On the other hand, up to now the parties' quests for funds have not led them to take many steps to blur further the distinctions between enrolled and non-enrolled supporters. So far, the British and German parties have made only tentative efforts to gather small donations from non-member supporters, though organizers in all four parties are clearly intrigued by the fundraising success of direct-mail and media appeals in the United States. By the mid-1990s it was the British Conservative Party—which already had the loosest definition of membership and which was least aggressive in channeling members' dues to the central party—which had probably gone the furthest in exploring new avenues of fundraising. Yet, even in this party such efforts remained at relatively low levels.

Thus, none of these parties' fundraising strategies conforms to the scenario in which parties gain access to new sources of funds and consequently lose interest in members' financial contributions. Whatever the actual proportion of party revenue contributed by party members (a question explored in Chapter 7), party organizers apparently continue to place a high marginal value on these contributions. However, the following sections suggest that party organizers have been less steadfast in relying on members to perform other tasks relating to organizational maintenance.

Recruiting Members

Before parties can take advantage of members as organizational resources, they must first be able recruit and to retain them. Chapter 3 has already described how organizers in all four national parties regularly staged party-wide recruiting drives during the past half-century. What it did not describe was organizers' ideas about what local supporters should do during, and between, these drives in order to win and to retain party members. Changing ideas about optimal recruiting techniques, like changing ideas about electioneering, have shifted the emphasis from big meetings to targeted personal contacts.

Germany

SPD pamphlets from the 1950s advised local parties to recruit using a combination of events designed to attract attention (lectures, films, dances, parades) and personal approaches (letters, visits), but to keep the emphasis on the former. Local parties were supposed to conduct such membership drives every two years.[35] In the 1960s SPD organizational advice gave increasing attention to personal recruitment, and by the 1970s the party's brochures had ceased to advocate large-scale recruiting events; instead, they urged local parties to assemble a small corps of recruiters to contact a handful of known sympathizers. Local parties were advised to reinforce these personal contacts with publicity, and with political and social events intended primarily to integrate new members after they were recruited.[36]

As the CDU adjusted to its more precarious political position in the 1960s and 1970s, the party headquarters issued reams of recruitment advice for local parties. As in the SPD's advice, the emphasis in the CDU pamphlets also shifted away from large recruitment meetings towards personal visits by a few trained local 'contacters'. According to the recruitment model elaborated by CDU organizers in this period, local parties were supposed to reinforce personal recruiting visits with a programme of publicity and special events. In the 1990s, CDU pamphlets continued to promote an updated version of this 'contacter model' for recruiting, with the newer model adding telephone and direct-mail contacts to personal visits.[37]

Britain

Labour Party advice on recruitment from the 1940s until the 1970s urged the use of short recruiting campaigns which combined public meetings with doorstep visits.[38] In the 1980s, targeted visits and other types of personal contacts still remained at the core of the party's recommendations about recruiting. Other former stand-bys, including public recruiting meetings and door-to-door sales of party literature, disappeared from party advice about how to find new members.[39] Meanwhile, from the 1950s to the 1990s, Conservative Party advice on recruitment favoured doorstep canvassing and the delivery of leaflets as ways to reach out to potential members.[40]

The recruiting techniques recommended by today's British and German parties can function only if local parties have a corps of dedicated members who are willing to proselytize during face-to-face discussions. For such recruiting efforts to be successful, local parties must have at least a few members with sufficient political education and enthusiasm to be able to conduct persuasive discussions about the advantages of party membership.

Retaining Members

Of course, it is not enough to recruit members in order to maintain the organization; parties must also be able to retain their new recruits. In all four parties, collecting annual dues is the central administrative task of membership retention. In the 1950s, the SPD, the Labour and Conservative Parties, and to a lesser extent the CDU, all relied on the time-honoured practice of doorstep dues-collecting to keep members in good standing with the party. This was a labour-intensive process, but organizers favoured it because it guaranteed that even inactive members would receive regular visits from party representatives. However, by the end of the 1980s national organizers in all four parties had become convinced of the need for more efficient, albeit more impersonal, methods of collecting dues. As a result, the national parties either urged or forced local parties to introduce new collection-procedures. These changes made membership renewal a much less labour-intensive task.

Germany

SPD branches were traditionally expected to organize networks of 'house collectors' (*Hauskassierer*) to maintain weekly or monthly contact with members in specific streets or apartment buildings, and some organizers viewed this system of dues-collection as an essential feature of the party's organization.[41] This perspective was embodied in the 1950s and 1960s by long-time party treasurer Alfred Nau, who regularly used his speeches at the party conference to praise house collectors as the 'living ligament' connecting party members with the party leadership.[42] Yet, even when Nau was treasurer, it was difficult for local parties to find sufficient numbers of house collectors. This problem became acute in the 1970s, as SPD membership expanded just when many veteran collectors retired. Because this shortage coincided with serious financial difficulties for the national party, it persuaded SPD organizers that timely and predictable payment was more important than the regular contact with members which personal dues-collection provided.[43] As a result, by the 1980s SPD leaders repeatedly used conference speeches and party publications to urge local parties to collect dues by bank transfer.

CDU organizers endorsed dues collection by bank transfer at least as early as 1967, when changed party regulations gave local parties greater incentives to institute the regular collection of dues.[44] By 1980 CDU associations had used these procedures for so long that one party publication even noted a long-term drawback of this method of collection: once members signed bank-deduction agreements, they tended not to increase their contributions from year to year.[45] The method reduced membership attrition, but it also held back the growth of revenue from party dues.

Britain

As in the SPD, doorstep dues-collection was also a long and honoured tradition in the Labour Party, whose publications described monthly collectors as a vital 'link between the member and the machine'.[46] Although in the 1970s and 1980s Labour Party branches had serious difficulties in finding sufficient collectors for this labour-intensive task, until the mid-1980s Labour publications continued to portray doorstep collection as the principal method of membership retention. (Party advice did change to favour quarterly or annual collection over weekly or monthly visits.)[47] However, when the Labour Party introduced its new system of national membership in 1988, it practically abolished the job of local dues-collector. Under the new system, party members pay their dues directly to the national party, and local collectors call only on those who do not respond to renewal-notices sent by the national office.

The Conservative Party differs from the other three because its dues revenue, and its dues collection, have remained entirely in the hands of the local associations. Nevertheless, even in this party, national organizers have changed their advice about how local parties ought to collect annual subscriptions. In the 1940s and 1950s Conservative Party publications repeatedly urged constituencies to establish networks of subscription collectors to call on members and deliver leaflets to neighbours.[48] At a minimum, Conservative associations were supposed to have sufficient volunteers to make yearly visits asking members to renew their subscriptions. More recently, however, national organizers have urged constituencies to adopt less labour-intensive methods of collection; instead of initially calling on all members, they are now advised to send printed (though perhaps computer-personalized) renewal letters. National organizers favour renewal letters both because they require fewer volunteers, and because they are said to increase overall donations (because members may be more generous when they write cheques than when they merely pull out spare change for a doorstep collector).[49]

This discussion of the various tasks which local parties perform in order to maintain the organization has shown that since the 1950s strategists in all four parties have generally lowered their expectations about how many active members are needed to sustain the local and national organizations. For instance, in all four parties organizers have reduced their expectations about how much volunteer labour is needed to retain members (to collect dues). In addition, the German parties' newer recruiting techniques require fewer volunteers. However, this is not the whole story about changes in the extent to which parties rely on members to provide crucial inter-election support. Even as some basic maintenance tasks have become less labour-intensive, national organizers have thought up new inter-election jobs for party members.

LOCAL POLITICS

During the past decades, organizers in the parties being studied here have increasingly emphasized connections between success in local-government contests and national-party prospects. Even in the Conservative Party and the CDU, both of which used to have many strong advocates of non-partisan local government, political advisers now urge party members to be active partisan participants in local government, and in local-government campaigns.

Germany

In the SPD there is a long tradition of viewing success in local politics as a key ingredient in party strategy; as a result, members have been expected to contest local-government elections whenever possible. In contrast, Christian Democrats initially favoured non-partisan local government, and party strategists only became concerned about maximizing CDU representation at the local level once the party's national position weakened.[50] In the 1960s, the party's growing concern with local government was reflected in resolutions of party conferences which endorsed greater CDU participation in local politics, and which urged parties to field CDU candidates for even the smallest local councils.[51] After 1969, when the CDU became an opposition party in the *Bundestag*, party organizers began putting even more emphasis on participation in local politics. As one party publication from the mid-1970s explained, 'If the party does not succeed in winning and holding on to majorities in the cities and towns, it will not be successful in the long-term at the Federal and state level.'[52] Even once the CDU returned to government in Bonn, party publications continued to describe campaigning for local-government seats as one of the most consequential and substantive tasks for local parties.[53]

The German parties' advice on local-government campaigning has differed little from their advice about local efforts for federal elections. The similarities between recommended local tasks for both levels of elections increased in the 1970s, when both CDU and SPD state parties started producing greater amounts of campaign materials for local elections.[54] After this, local campaigners were relieved of most responsibility for the design of local as well as federal campaign publicity. Now the primary local task during campaigns is to disseminate, not create, political materials.

Britain

Before 1945, leading Conservatives opposed partisan local government outside urban areas, and they criticized the Labour Party for contributing to its spread. However, after the Conservative Party found itself in opposition in 1945, its organizers started preaching the virtues of partisan participation in local politics. As an editorial in the party's new local-government magazine explained at this time, party involvement in local government could bring organizational rewards while simultaneously generating good will for the Conservative Party:

There is more support to be gained for the party by a Council with a Conservative majority providing a much needed playing field than by the distribution of countless leaflets. A canvasser may give a householder ten good reasons for joining the Conservative Party but fail to convince, where a Conservative councillor who sees the drains are put right, or the dustbins emptied, will succeed. . . . Every election keeps the local organization on its toes, and prepares it for a General Election. . .[55]

The Conservative Party's national organizers continued to affirm the importance of local-government work even after the party returned to the government benches in Westminster. In the 1980s and 1990s, however, Conservatives had a hard time holding on to local-government seats during their long period in control of the national government. During this time, Liberal (and later Social Democratic and Liberal Democratic) challengers ran successful 'community-politics' campaigns in former Tory strongholds. The Conservative government responded to the spread of Labour- and Liberal/Labour–controlled local councils by restricting the competencies of local governments. This reduced the scope of local policy-making, but it gave journalists even more reason to portray the annual batch of local elections as referenda on the national government. Conservative Party organizers responded to these losses by urging supporters to stay involved in local politics in order to implement Conservative ideas about governance, strengthen local-party organization, and maintain Conservative credibility.

At the beginning of the twentieth century the Labour Party gained its earliest electoral successes in local-government contests. Even after the party proved its ability to win national elections, the national party still urged constituency parties to make careful preparations for local elections. This was partly because the elections were considered to be important in their own right, but it also reflected the view that local-government campaigning was 'part of an exercise to improve our election machinery'.[56] In the 1980s, as the opposition party faced a strong Conservative government, Labour Party pamphlets described success in local government as more important than ever, arguing that the party's 'values and its philosophy, will be judged not only by its performance nationally as an opposition party, but also by its actions as the party with a majority in local authorities up and down the country'.[57]

Because organizers in both British parties have viewed competition and success in local-government elections as crucial to party success at the national level, they have expected constituency parties and individual members to contest as many seats as possible in all local-government elections. Although neither of the two largest parties has candidates everywhere, both contest a much higher proportion of seats than they did in the 1940s and 1950s.[58] This expansion has been possible only because local parties have continued to be able to find many members who are willing and qualified to stand as candidates.

Over the past decades, the two British parties have given advice about the conduct of local-government campaigning that has consistently mirrored their recommendations for parliamentary campaigns. In other words, in the past, the emphasis of these campaigns was supposed to be on canvassing, leafleting, public meetings, and voter mobilization. The latter was particularly important because of traditionally low turn-out in local elections.[59] In the 1980s, however, both parties started issuing new advice about how to win local-government seats through year-round campaign efforts. This move towards year-round campaigning will be discussed more fully in the following section.

In sum, in both Germany and Britain, national parties now expect their locally organized members to contest several rounds of elections in addition to those for the national parliaments. At the local level, these campaigns can be at least as labour-intensive as those for national political offices. For the parties which have increased their involvement in local government (the Conservatives and the CDU), the commitment to local government has meant that local parties are now expected to find more candidates who are willing and qualified to compete for public office under the party label. Although local parties may find such candidates outside the party membership, political recruitment is certainly much easier for parties when they can draw upon a roster of members who have already proven their understanding of, and commitment to, party policies. Thus, the parties' ongoing or increased commitment to maintain visibility through participation in local government provides all four parties with reasons to value their reservoirs of enrolled supporters.

POLITICAL OUTREACH AND PUBLICITY

So far, the current chapter has presented a picture of local parties making year-round contributions to national party prospects by recruiting members, raising funds, and contesting local-government elections. In addition to this, organizers in all four parties have traditionally expected local parties to sponsor at least a few meetings and social events for party members between elections. However, it is in another area that party organizers have most changed their views about how members can help their parties. During the 1970s and 1980s party strategists broadened their ideas about how members' outreach activities between elections could contribute to long-term electoral support for the party. One result of this was a reassessment of the value of apparently 'inactive' members. Such changes were particularly important in Germany.

In Germany in the 1950s and early 1960s, when the parties issued advice about inter-election activities, it generally focused on ways to improve internal organization at the local level. Although SPD pamphlets did not overlook such outward-oriented activities as holding regular public meetings and delivering leaflets, they certainly did not depict them as central inter-election occupations for local parties.[60] (For instance, in 1955, one SPD pamphlet suggested that the work of most local organizations could be improved by holding a meeting for the public 'at least once a year'.[61]) Even in the 1950s, SPD organizers recognized that public meetings were a commodity for which the demand was limited, and they issued strict warnings that parties should not bore their audiences when they did organize public events.[62]

The generational shift which helped bring about the Bad Godesberg transformation of the SPD's programme also fostered new ways of looking at party members' inter-election contributions. This change was already evident in 1958, when one party official argued that

The willingness trustingly to accept the arguments of a party does not just awake during an election. This willingness arises during the many preceding months. . . . The pertinent argument made by the almost 700,000 Social Democrats when talking with their friends, colleagues and relatives is the most important weapon of the SPD . . .[63]

Twenty-five years later SPD organizers were still repeating the argument about the importance of members' informal oral propaganda:

People's political opinions are most deeply shaped by conversations with those around them, whether in the family, at work, in the neighbourhood, or among friends. This is where the large capital of the social-democratic movement should be brought in: the members who are convinced of the correctness of the social-democratic programme.[64]

The few organizing handbooks issued by the national CDU in the 1950s neither urged local parties to participate in national inter-election publicity campaigns, nor advised local parties to sponsor frequent publicity events. It was not until the 1960s, when CDU leaders tried to inject new vigour into the life of local parties, that national organizers began to try to stimulate local publicity efforts.

In both the CDU and SPD in the 1960s, party organizers were spurred to develop new types of local outreach by the suspicion, already voiced by a CDU reformer in 1962, that

Voters' opinion formation can barely be influenced by isolated advertisements during the campaign. Instead, it can only be decisively influenced by continuous public-relations work.[65]

Echoing academic studies of political communications, in this decade organizers in both parties began describing members as vote 'multipliers', who aided the party through their impact in everyday conversations.[66] This perspective continued to be influential in both parties, and it led national organizers to promote a series of specific ways in which local branches and individual members could increase their contacts with potential supporters. By the 1980s, some German party strategists were even arguing that local parties and individual members make their biggest contributions merely by visibly embodying party commitment and community involvement—virtues which national advertising alone cannot easily convey.

In Germany (as in Britain), it was the success of established parties' political competitors which did the most to convince national organizers that local parties should increase their outreach activities. CDU and SPD strategists responded to the success of German 'citizens' initiatives' (*Bürgerinitiativen*) by adopting these groups as models for inter-election activity by local parties. Citizens' initiatives have usually been single-issue groups organized around such concerns as creating more pre-school places, cleaning up local nature areas, or closing nuclear power plants. These initiatives proliferated in the 1970s and 1980s, nurtured in part by widespread disenchantment with the traditional political parties.[67] Though CDU and SPD leaders often rejected the political aims of these groups, they could not overlook the evident appeal of their organizational mode. Instead, organizers in the established parties fought back by urging their members to emulate, and even to join, the originally *anti-party* citizens' initiatives.

In Britain until the 1980s, the primary inter-election outreach-activities for British local parties continued to be leaflet delivery, canvassing, public meetings, fundraising events, and, for the Labour Party, door-to-door sales of party literature. Organizers in both parties considered doorstep contact with voters to be essential for training election-time canvassers and for improving canvassing records prior to campaigns. In addition, local parties were expected to support national inter-election publicity campaigns with their own local publicity and events.[68] However, these traditions began to change in recent years. As early as the 1960s both parties' publications began shifting the focus away from public meetings. By the end of the 1970s, new party pamphlets were urging local branches to adopt other ways of maintaining regular contacts with voters between elections.

Liberal Party victories in local-government elections of the 1970s and early 1980s were the strongest catalyst for such changes in Conservative and Labour Party inter-election strategies. These victories provided evidence of the growing appeal of the Liberal Party's 'community-politics' approach, and thereby prompted changes in long-held ideas about appropriate activities for local parties.[69] Key components of the community-politics approach included organizing initiatives dealing with specific local problems (school closings, changes in zoning), and producing and distributing local newsletters to promote these causes and advertise the successes of Liberal (later Liberal Democrat) local councillors in aiding constituents. Labour and Conservative publications initially derided the Liberals for these efforts, dismissing them as trivial 'pavement politics'. But these methods began to command more respect once they started translating into local-government victories in traditional Labour and Conservative strongholds. Soon Conservative and Labour national organizers were urging their branch parties and local-government councillors to emulate the Liberals' formula of constituent service and newsletter publicity.

In both Germany and Britain the success of political competitors prompted party organizers to shift their recommendations for local inter-election activity to favour more community-centred tasks. As a result, new advice urged local parties to change the nature and style of their outreach efforts, to re-examine the purpose of party newsletters, and to provide more tangible help for individuals through offices providing services to constituents. Each of these areas will be examined in turn.

Community Involvement

One of the biggest changes in the organizing tactics of the German parties and of the Labour Party came in the 1970s and 1980s, when party organizers began looking beyond contributions made by active members within the party. At this point they began to see so-called 'inactive members' as potentially valuable resources. According to the new perception, party members are ambassadors to the community who can and should represent their parties in diverse spheres of life.

Germany

For the German parties, emulating citizens' initiatives meant expanding the role of local parties and party members in projects to improve the community. As early as 1973 CDU organizers were already urging local parties to increase their community involvement by sponsoring such sympathy-winning projects as starting 'meals-on-wheels' services, providing television sets for elderly citizens, cleaning up parks, or raising funds for charity. Some subsequent CDU recommendations for local activities were more issue-oriented, though still seemingly non-partisan; these included supporting projects to promote environmental protection, human rights, or third-world development. CDU organizers also urged local parties to strengthen their contacts with citizens' initiatives and other non-party groups, and they encouraged individual members to assume leading roles within these groups.[70] Such efforts were expected to produce long-term electoral rewards, because, as the CDU's 1976 campaign manager argued

Citizens only allow themselves to be *persuaded* during a campaign—not to be steamrollered. Whoever was not in contact with them before the election, whoever did not speak beforehand with associations and clubs, whoever cannot listen—that party does not have a single chance of persuading voters during the short, hot, phase of the campaign.[71]

Local associations did not adapt to the new vision as readily as some in the party headquarters would have liked. Thus, in 1988 a top aide in the CDU bureaucracy complained

In a society with countless citizens' initiatives, with well-informed, self-confident, and active citizens, a people's party like the CDU must frequently and systematically seek out direct conversation with citizens, with groups in society, with associations, etc. Party conferences which are open, even for non-members, open work-groups, targeted approaches to the most important groups and organizations—these must all be normal types of party work. In fact, the opposite is the case.[72]

A subsequent document on party reform reaffirmed the position that the party would benefit 'from having as many members as possible who are ready and willing convincingly to represent the goals of the CDU in conversation and through other forms of participation'. This report concluded, 'The engagement of CDU members in churches, clubs, and associations must be increased. This important work for society wins respect that can also aid the CDU.'[73] Another pamphlet on 'addressing target groups' urged local parties to use videos, music, and informal discussions to reach out to citizens. Parties should use 'forms of meetings which are suited for activating members and citizens and for acquainting target groups with CDU policies', forms which included CDU-inspired citizens' initiatives.[74]

   SPD organizers began promoting similar ideas in the 1970s and 1980s. Though it has become common to view the SPD as a party which foundered in the 1970s partly because it did not respond creatively to the challenges of citizen politics,[75] this failure cannot be blamed on organizers' inability to sense the appeal of the new outlets for political participation. As early as 1975 SPD national organizers, like their CDU counterparts, were urging local parties to co-operate with citizens' initiatives and with other non-party groups.[76] As the handbook of an SPD state party noted at the time, 'Co-operation with, and also, in special cases, the foundation or initial support of, a citizens' initiative, is a tool of modern branch-party work for achieving social-democratic policies.'[77] National SPD organizers chided local parties for not heeding this advice, and in 1981 they introduced a (still extant) national prize to recognize local projects 'which exemplify how the party should converse with politically non-aligned citizens; which further the manifold co-operation between social democrats and other social forces—with associations, with churches, with clubs, with citizens' initiatives, etc.'.[78] After the first contest, the party published a follow-up booklet giving details about how local parties could imitate successful projects, including schemes with such titles as 'Hello Neighbour', 'Leisure, Sport, and Games', 'Search for Historical Clues', and 'Solidarity with Workers and the Unemployed'.[79]

As SPD organizing advice began emphasizing community-outreach activities, it began to lay less stress on the member-only meetings which once had been central to the party's local life. In the 1950s, SPD organizers distinguished between meetings for members (which should be held at least six times a year, and where party solidarity should be nurtured with comradely greetings and songs), and less frequent public meetings (which aimed to educate a broader audience).[80] By the mid-1970s, party organizers regularly urged local parties to make all meetings open and welcoming to non-party members, and to replace traditional formats with more interesting civic visits, social occasions, or topical debates.[81] Advice from the national party also increasingly portrayed community outreach as something which individual members could and should do on their own.

Britain

In the 1970s and early 1980s British party organizers also began encouraging their local activists to increase outreach efforts.[82] For a time during the 1970s a new 'Community Affairs Department' in Conservative Central Office supported local parties' attempts to strengthen ties with particular groups in the population (for example, Asians or trade-union members). In the 1980s, as Liberal and

Social Democratic candidates captured an increasing number of formerly Tory seats on local councils, Conservative organizers advised local activists to improve their own 'community-politics' profile by devoting more energy to inter-election survey canvassing, an activity in which canvassers ask residents to talk about local problems and about political complaints. Survey canvassing was said to be useful because, 'All too often our opponents produce successful campaigns on issues ignored by our local organization. This is particularly true of Local Government elections.'[83] Conservative Party organizers also advised members to emulate Liberal tactics by becoming more involved outside the party, for instance by working in community organizations such as parent-teacher associations.[84]

The Labour Party also became receptive to such ideas. Even before this party saw itself almost pushed into third place in the contest for the popular vote in the 1983 general election, Labour Party organizers had begun calling for local parties to compete with community-politics campaigns. At the time, the party's assistant national agent argued that local-party work had to change because society had changed. The break-up of traditional party loyalties meant that '[d]iscussion and persuasion on the doorstep now form an important part of our election work, which means that our election campaigns must start earlier, and that there must be a great deal more activity between elections'. The agent further urged that this inter-election activity should specifically be aimed at increasing party contact with other groups:

A strategy should be devised for our approach to target groups and community groups. 'Community Politics' is really a term for good politics—political parties and their representatives involving themselves in local issues which are important to many people.[85]

After the Labour Party's defeat in 1987, the party's national headquarters launched a new initiative ('Labour Listens') to encourage constituency activists to form more 'accurate' views of voters' concerns. To do this, local parties were supposed to sponsor survey canvassing, telephone canvassing, and meetings with non-party groups—'from the local small businesses community, pre-school groups and local churches and other religious communities to the residents of a particular [housing] estate'.[86] The stated aim of this inter-election campaigning was to make the party 'part of the community rather than some strange separate entity'.[87] What was most novel about this publicity exercise was that national organizers openly described attainment of this goal as a two-sided process: what was needed was to bring voters into contact with the party, but also to make local activists more aware of the diverse views held by potential supporters.[88] In the 1990s, Labour strategists continued to argue that, in areas where the party was weak, local campaigning could only be successful if local activists emulated Liberal Democrat approaches to politics because, as one campaign manager explained, 'Pavement politics treats people as individuals (or at least as small communities and interest groups), and not as homogenous groups of voters with natural allegiances.'[89]

Constituency Service

At the same time that German and British party organizers began urging party members to increase inter-election contacts with non-party groups, they also began encouraging local parties to increase the intensity and the visibility of their aid to local constituents. In both countries, party pamphlets portrayed constituent service as a task for party activists as well as for elected officials.

Germany

In the 1970s and 1980s the German parties began promoting the 'citizens' office' (*Bürgerbüro*) as the ideal channel through which active members could offer service to local communities. The citizens' office was not a new idea in the SPD, but the party's organizers began highlighting it as part of their efforts to help the party compete with citizens' initiatives. According to party pamphlets, citizens' offices were supposed to be sponsored by several branch parties, and they were supposed to be identified with the local party, and not merely with the local *Bundestag* representative.[90] In the mid-1970s the CDU likewise began urging its local councillors and party officials to become more accessible to constituents by establishing regular times to meet individual citizens—something that might take place within the citizens' offices which local CDU associations were encouraged to open.[91]

Britain

Constituency service was not a new activity in Britain. At least since the 1950s members of parliament had been advised to hold consultation sessions ('surgeries') to help constituents. However, in recent years both parties have begun to encourage local-government councillors to schedule their own open sessions. As one Conservative brochure explained in 1986:

Helping people with individual problems is an essential part of a Councillor's job. A surgery or advice centre is a useful way of inviting electors to come along and tell you their problems. It is important that the public perceive you as an acceptable person, someone willing to listen and help.[92]

Labour Party advice from the 1980s also recommended that local councillors should hold regular surgeries. Scheduling periodic opportunities to meet individual constituents was described as a crucial campaign-tool, because they helped the party to 'maintain a high and popular profile within the community'.[93] According to advice issued by both the Labour and Conservative parties, increased service to constituents primarily meant increased work for elected officials. However, such work at least marginally increased the demands placed on other local activists, because non-elected volunteers (especially party officers) were supposed to help elected representatives by co-ordinating surgeries and addressing constituents' problems.

Community Newsletters

Community involvement and constituency service form one side of the British and German parties' new approach to using inter-election efforts to win sympathy for the entire party. Publicity for these outreach efforts forms the other side. Starting in the 1970s, changing printing technologies made it progressively easier for amateurs to produce their own local publications. Since then, organizers in all four parties have promoted the production of local newsletters. They have endorsed newsletters as the ideal channel for spreading the word about activities organized by the local party, and have advised local parties to use these newsletters as channels for two-way communication. To achieve the latter purpose, parties are supposed to incorporate complaint- and request-forms into the newsletter as a way of stimulating requests for constituency-service work.

Party newsletters were not a new idea in either country in the 1970s. In earlier years many German and British branch and constituency associations had produced publications for their members. But in the 1970s and early 1980s national organizers in all four parties began encouraging local activists to produce newsletters with a larger circulation, and with a format aimed at the entire community. Such regular newsletters were to be delivered by a team of member-volunteers. By the 1980s, all four national headquarters were supporting publishers of local newsletters by offering production advice and copy-ready graphics and articles.

Germany

German party organizers began promoting the use of community newsletters in the mid-1970s as part of their efforts to make local associations appear more involved in their communities.[94] One CDU document from this period described the manifold benefits to be expected from such publications:

CDU newspapers promote dialogue with citizens and nurture party members' sense of belonging. They encourage meaningful participation in the CDU's local parties. They present local problems from a CDU perspective, and, with a well-functioning delivery system, they arrive in every household. Not least of all, they are an outstanding tool in election campaigns.[95]

Subsequent CDU organizing advice has continued to encourage local parties to view the production of community newsletters as an important year-round task.[96]

SPD organizers have depicted local newsletters as tools for combating those 'barriers in the media' which allegedly disadvantage the SPD.[97] They have argued that centralization in the regular newspaper market provides producers of party newsletters with an ideal opportunity, because 'large newspapers cannot be as close to citizens nor as full of information about the neighbourhood'.[98] One party publication even claimed that the regular production of a community newsletter benefited a local party by producing an electoral bonus of up to 2 per cent.[99] In the 1980s the SPD emphasized its support for local newsletters by establishing an office in its party headquarters to help local producers of news-papers. Although one director of this office emphasized the natural limits for such centralized aid (because local papers would lose some of their impact if their content and style looked too profes-sional), the central office subsequently boosted its support for newsletter producers by distributing articles and graphics on com-puter disks.[100]

Britain

In Britain, Liberal Party constituency newsletters proliferated in the 1970s and early 1980s when some of the party's organizers began promoting them as an essential part of the community-politics approach. Because of the success of Liberal local-govern-ment candidates in the 1980s, both Labour and Conservative organizers started urging their branch activists and local council-lors to emulate the techniques of their Liberal challengers, includ-ing the production of newsletters to communicate with local voters. As one 1984 Conservative publication proclaimed in praise of the party's constituency newsletters, 'We are back to communicating regularly with electors—and communicating about our local actions on their behalf. Community politics is Conservative politics.'[101] Other Conservative publications from this period described local newsletters in similar terms, portraying them, for example, as 'the foundation of our constituency cam-paigns' between elections.[102] In the 1980s Labour Party organizers also began urging branch parties to produce newsletters in order to increase party visibility. A resolution adopted by the 1985 Labour Party conference encouraged constituency parties to 'ensure more effort and energy is put into outward campaigning with regular newssheets being produced by every party, taking up community as well as national issues'.[103]

ACTIVE AND INACTIVE MEMBERS

The preceding sections have shown how organizers in all four parties have re-evaluated the nature and importance of members' political work and their contributions to inter-election maintenance. Most importantly, by the end of the 1980s, organizing strategies in all four parties had shifted towards placing a much higher value on the ways that local supporters could engage in year-round political-outreach activities.

At the local level, party maintenance became less labour-intensive in recent years as all the parties introduced new methods of collecting dues (and, in Germany, of recruiting members). In Britain, this coincided with a similar trend in the area of campaign activities. At the same time, however, party organizers were expanding their ideas about the ways in which members could contribute to party success. As a result, they began to encourage local parties to concentrate on the slow and cumulative task of building political visibility and support. To fulfil their new roles as party representatives to the wider community, party members needed to redirect their energies away from maintaining local associations and providing activities for the inner circle of active members, towards courting potential political supporters who traditionally had little contact with the local face of party politics.

In order for local parties to fill these new roles, some members who had been active inside the local parties needed to redirect their efforts into outward-looking projects such as newsletter production and constituency service. Party organizers began to urge members to work as party ambassadors in non-party groups. They also began to expect that more local members would devote time to local-government work and to local-government campaigning. In short, in all four parties, organizers' increased expectations about local inter-election outreach seem to have at least counterbalanced their diminished expectations about members' activities in certain areas of campaigning and organizational maintenance.

As organizers in all four parties began to see greater electoral rewards in members' inter-election activities, they also altered their views about what type of membership the party should strive to assemble. According to these new ideas, national parties relied on local branches and individual members to bolster party legitimacy through both their formal and their informal contacts in neighbourhoods, work-places, and schools. In response, national organizers reassessed the value of members who never participate in the activities of local parties. As party strategists gained a greater appreciation for the vote-winning ability of declared supporters who were engaged outside the universe of party affairs, they also became more aware of the help even the so-called 'inactive' members could provide.

This shift in party ideas about what constitutes a useful member is clearly visible in the materials which the national parties have prepared for recruitment campaigns. For example, a 1985 CDU pamphlet urged recruiters to reassure potential members that they were welcome even if they never intended to participate to any greater extent than by paying dues.[104] This was a big change from the mid-1960s, when the CDU's business manager had argued, 'You can't succeed in politics with members who are just corpses in the file, nor with people who are just sympathizers. We need active and working members.'[105] SPD organizers' attitudes had undergone a similar change as early as the mid-1970s, when an SPD federal manager reminded conference delegates not to under-estimate the 'inactive' two-thirds of the party membership: 'We need to appreciate the big factor of mere support—"membership as an affirmation of faith".'[106] By the 1990s, leaders of both parties were also urging local parties to consider new ways of making themselves open to supporters who were not prepared to make a commitment to full membership. Such schemes were supposed to make party membership appealing to wider segments of the electorate, and thereby increase party outreach in diverse spheres. (See Chapter 6 for more details.)

In the 1980s a similar shift in attitudes was visible in the Labour Party. This spirit was evident, for instance, when the party's chief organizer reminded recruiters that new members helped the party whether or not they regularly attended meetings: 'Many [new members] will want to help, but only at election time. And many will just want to get on with their lives, and also—as democratic socialists who share our vision and values—to be members of the party; and there is nothing wrong with that.'[107] In the late 1980s, the party's head office produced a special training-video for recruiters which underscored the point that potential members might be scared away by the misperception that membership meant attending meetings.[108] This attitude stood in sharp contrast to attitudes expressed in the party's 1944 membership campaign, the stated goal of which was to 'enrol *live* members [because] [i]t is the working membership that is important'.[109] Only Conserva-tive Party materials do not show this shift towards welcoming 'inactive' members; however, this lack is undoubtedly due to the fact that the party's very inclusive rules for enrolment have always promoted membership quantity, not activist quality.

SUMMARY: CHANGING INTER-ELECTION TASKS FOR MEMBERS

Looking beyond formal campaign activities to examine members' assigned inter-election functions thus gives a very different picture of how roles for members have developed in a mass media era. This is not a picture of the technology-driven obsolescence of membership organization as an electoral tool. On the contrary, in all four parties organizers have assigned members an increased, not a diminished, role in year-round campaign strategies. Instead of finding the 'decline' of parties as would-be membership organizations, the investigations so far have revealed the transformation of party strategists' prevailing ideas about the benefits (and costs) of maintaining membership organizations. Ever since the introduction of television, party planners have become interested in new and very specific types of support which members can provide during and between elections, and by working both inside and outside the local parties. In particular, to use the language of the second chapter's model, they have come to place a much higher value on members' ability to multiply votes by everyday contacts (outreach benefits). Today, personal contact is at the core of much of the activity parties assign to members, because national organizers view the membership organization as a resource for supplementing impersonal mass media messages with more personal contacts.

Up to now, this consideration of the development of German and British parties' organizing strategies has aimed to assess the validity of 'demand-side' predictions about the organizational decline of membership parties. Central to such predictions is the assumption that for some reason or reasons, party leaders have come to view members as superfluous. As a result, they have ceased to channel resources into recruiting or maintaining the party membership. The evidence presented so far argues against accepting such an interpretation of developments in the German and British parties. Instead, the accounts have shown that each of the contemporary parties has retained roles for members precisely because party organizers have adapted their ideas and arguments about what it is that members are good for.

Such findings help to validate the model of party change which was presented in Chapter 2. The fundamental premise of this model is that new tools for electioneering, and new circumstances of electoral competition, are not the only catalysts which lead to top-down changes in the organization of membership parties. In addition, new understandings of the tasks which labour or capital must accomplish, and new interpretations of what constitutes useful 'labour', may be equally important in precipitating organizational change. According to the second chapter's model, party leaders will initiate organizational changes if they alter their assessments about the costs and benefits generated by party membership, or if they determine that some membership incentives have become more or less effective. The discussions up to this point have demonstrated the plausibility of this perspective, by showing that party organizers in four established membership parties have not held static ideas about the proper tasks for enrolled supporters.

In this context, it is worth noting the role of social-science research in shaping, and even precipitating, some of the new interpretations about how to influence voters and win elections. Each of the parties has employed trained social scientists as consultants or as full-time staff members. Many recent initiatives on party reform (including those discussed in more detail in Chapter 6) have been buttressed, if not inspired, by the latest public-opinion research on voters, and even on party members. (Perhaps the most notable example of this described in the preceding pages was the influence of Noelle-Neumann's 'spiral of silence' hypothesis on German parties' campaign tactics in the mid-1970s.) Party organizers are consumers of data on public opinion, and their discussions of election strategies suggest that many of them keep abreast of current research on the formation of political attitudes and on the long-term implications of social changes. This awareness may even offer a partial explanation of why parties appear to act in ways that social science predicts— because party leaders and organizers do not make their decisions in a vacuum of ignorance about theories of organizational and human behaviour.

By showing that parties have demanded new support from

members in order to complement their use of new technologies, these investigations have provided support for the notion that studies of parties should take account of qualitative, as well as quantitative, shifts in parties' labour–capital ratios. They have also made clear that such ratios alone are inadequate to describe changes in membership parties' organizing strategies, because, taken in isolation, they reveal nothing about the level of overall demand. Capital intensive professionalization may reduce a party's relative reliance on volunteer support, but it does not necessarily diminish the party's absolute demand for membership labour.

Finally, the preceding accounts have shown that party organizers' attitudes towards members' activities have shifted at about the same time that parties have redesigned some of their membership structures. However, what has not yet been done is to try to provide more evidence that party organizers actually make the kind of calculations described in Chapter 2, or to try to demonstrate that specific organizational changes can be linked to identifiable shifts in party leaders' assessments about the utility of membership. This task is taken up in the following chapter, which attempts to explain three very recent organizational changes in terms of party leaders' strategic calculations about the costs and benefits of adjusting the inducements for enrolling.

6

Linking Party Strategies with Organizational Change

> What counts is to develop our work structures and our communications capabilities so that in the future the SPD can win members and motivate them, and also so that it can win elections.
>
> SPD discussion paper[1]

AT least since Michels presented his 'iron law of oligarchy', observers of political parties have considered transfer of power from party leaders to party members to be the least likely direction for organizational change within parties.[2] Yet, in this same period three of the four parties studied here changed in precisely this way. In 1993 both the British Labour Party and the German SPD altered their national statutes in order to give individual members the right to participate directly in the selection of party leaders. In the same year, a similar change in statutes was made by the CDU in North Rhine-Westphalia (which enrolled almost one third of the CDU's total membership), and other CDU state associations considered following suit. These unanticipated procedural changes, which transfer important decision-making power from delegate assemblies to individual party members, provide valuable opportunities to test and refine existing interpretations of organizational behaviour within parties. Here, the main purpose in examining these cases is to ask whether they provide direct evidence that changing ideas about membership utility actually help shape specific organizational reforms.

The resource model of strategic change introduced in Chapter 2 argued that top-down changes in parties' structures and procedures can usefully be interpreted as reflections of party leaders' changing calculations about the costs, and the benefits, of enrolling members. From this perspective it is not implausible to posit that the iron law of oligarchy could bend, or at least begin to rust from within, particularly if party leaders calculate that the transfer of decision-making to members is an electorally profitable trade-off. However, the search here is for more than plausibility; what is sought is sufficient evidence to conclude that specific changes in statutes resulted, in whole or in part, from party leaders' strategic calculations about the potential utility of enrolling party members. The following accounts try to find such evidence of the motors of change by examining the debates and struggles that paved the way for alterations in each of the party's formal channels of power.

GERMANY: REMODELLING THE 'MODERN' PARTY

At the beginning of the 1990s, Germany's two largest parties were struggling to identify and adopt more marketable programmatic and organizational identities. Organizers in these parties had begun publicly acknowledging the erosion of various traditional bases of party support even before German unification and its consequences created unforeseen political challenges. Support for the parties dropped further in the early 1990s as Germans in both east and west faced high unemployment, rising taxes, and relatively high inflation. Although the CDU-led government rapidly lost popularity after its 1990 victory, the SPD did not automatically profit from the declining support for its traditional rival. Instead, voters who objected to the government were just as likely to find fault with *all* established parties.[3] Such erosion of support for traditional political alternatives seemed to account for the declining electoral turn-out, and for the declining share of the vote won by the two largest parties. Several protest parties temporarily profited from this popular political discontent, including the 'Instead Party' (*Stattpartei*: the ultimate anti-party party, which won seats in Hamburg state elections in 1993), and parties of the far right (including the *Republikaner* and the German People's Union (*Deutsche Volksunion*: DVU), which won seats in European and/ or municipal elections in the late 1980s and early 1990s).

Political observers both inside and outside the CDU and SPD argued that initiatives on party organization were a necessary response to Germany's new political conditions. It was not that anyone claimed that organizational reform could single-handedly cure German political malaise or secure future election victories; however, some did portray such reform as a necessary therapy for Germany's ageing parties. Views like these were expressed within both parties in the late 1980s and early 1990s in the course of discussions triggered by the preparation of official party reports concerning pending organizational challenges.

These reports—the CDU's *Modern People's Parties in the 1990s*, and the SPD's *SPD 2000*—were commissioned at the urging of national organizers, who argued that their parties were failing to benefit sufficiently from enrolled members. The reports and their reform proposals reflected organizers' discontent with the contributions of individual party members, and with patterns of political activity within local parties. In turn, the parties' headquarters gave prominent publicity to these reports, because national organizers knew that the recommendations they contained would only be implemented if party élites at all levels could be persuaded to accept their diagnoses and prescriptions.

Identifying the Problems

In 1988, when the CDU was suffering a slump in popularity, its conference endorsed the request of the party executive to commission a report about how to reform the party's extra-parliamentary organization. The report was written by a group of social scientists, party organizers, and party officers, who buttressed their conclusions with evidence gathered by a specially commissioned survey of the CDU's local associations. In this report, and in the debates it inspired, there is rich evidence of party élites discussing organizational strategies in terms of explicit calculations about the uses of membership, and about the necessity of adjusting membership incentives in order to appeal to supporters who fit particular profiles.

After the SPD lost its third consecutive *Bundestag* election, in 1990, SPD leaders likewise commissioned their own investigation into appropriate modes of organizational work within the party. As in the slightly earlier organizational debates in the CDU, the SPD's re-examination of its extra-parliamentary organization was shaped by perceptions that the party must improve its efforts to adjust to changes in society. In this period, an assistant to the party manager summarized the prevailing attitude in party headquarters when he noted that the SPD, like all the 'decimated people's parties', must learn that 'social change, with its new values, life-styles, and increased mobility, has also created new conditions for party work'.[4] In fact, SPD organizers thought that the party was adapting poorly to such social changes. Thus, when the party executive asked the 1991 party conference to authorize the organizational report, the motion it presented characterized the SPD as a collection of self-preoccupied local associations which spent time on boring activities and discussions, which were unwelcoming to casual supporters, and which did very little to communicate with voters.[5]

The impetus for both the CDU and SPD reports on organizational reform thus came from the parties' national leaders and top-level professional organizers. In both parties, those who were responsible for setting organizational strategies believed that the extra-parliamentary organizations were not responding adequately to rapid changes in politics and society. Because they were prompted by similar concerns, each of the reports presented similar diagnoses of the problems which were confronting their parties. Furthermore, each of them testified to the need for parties to adapt their organizations in order successfully to tackle changes in society in general, and in their own electorates in particular.

The reports discussed two types of social and political change which demanded immediate responses. First, they considered the causes and implications of the increasing appeal of 'new' parties (particularly the *Republikaner* and other right-wing parties). Second, they looked for ways to explain, and then diminish, the apparently growing distance between German citizens and all parties. This political malaise was labelled *Politik- und Parteienverdrossenheit* (disaffection with politics and with parties) in the jargon of the 1990s. The preamble to the CDU report drew particular attention to the gravity of *Parteienverdrossenheit*, and it noted that '[i]t is especially important to overcome citizens' loss of trust in their parties, which has been visible since the beginning of the 1980s'.[6]

The longer SPD report presented a fuller explanation of why parties needed new organizational ideas. It argued that changes in society had altered the conditions under which parties communicate with undecided voters. According to the SPD report, most citizens could be placed in one of two groups of mass-media consumers: those who were politically engaged, and those who were politically unengaged. Although both groups were said to gather most or all of their political information from the mass media, it was only the politically unengaged whose views were said to be swayed by emotional reports in the media. In contrast, the politically engaged were said to form their opinions by participating in discussions, in which they were most likely to be influenced by those who could confront them with appealing arguments and examples of concrete accomplishments. The SPD report concluded that this division among voters presented a problem for the party's organizational strategy, because the latter group (the politically engaged) was growing, and was beyond the reach of centrally directed media campaigns.[7]

The parties' reports did more than identify external social and technological changes to which party organizations needed to respond. They also drew attention to internal problems which were reducing the potential benefits that might be won from the membership organizations. Each report explained why having low levels of young members, and of female members, might undermine party support from young, and from female, voters. For the CDU, the perceived problem lay in the fact that the party was becoming an organization composed of older males. The survey commissioned for the report revealed that more than half the CDU's members were over 50, that fewer than 7 per cent of its members were under 30, and that there were even some local parties which had neither female members *nor* male members younger than 30.[8] The authors of the CDU report emphasized that such 'deficits in the membership structure'[9] made it difficult for the party successfully to portray itself as a party for all people. The report pointed out that this problem was further exacerbated by the fact that the unbalanced composition of the membership deprived the party of reservoirs from which to recruit young, or female, candidates—and candidates constituted the most visible face of the party's politics. The SPD report also noted similar problems in attracting younger members, and it warned that

[t]he fact that it is not going any better for other parties is not much consolation. Without the younger generation, the SPD cannot remain a large membership party.[10]

It is clear that party organizers' newly heightened concern about the lack of young and female members arose at least as much from a change in their perceptions as from a change in either the age- or gender-distributions of party memberships. The predominant maleness of party memberships was nothing new in the 1980s, while the ageing of the party membership was to some extent the inevitable price paid for the parties' tremendous enrolment successes in the 1970s. What was new was the heightened importance attributed to membership composition as a resource that would generate electoral support.

Thus, both reports presented arguments about why even a 'modern' party must continue to rely on its membership base. But another subtext ran through both the CDU and SPD reports: that locally organized membership is only one leg of a party's organizational strategy. The reports reminded readers of the need for a professionally run party headquarters which must be staffed by people trained to use the latest communications technologies and techniques. However, both reports rejected the notion that a party must be *either* a party of amateurs or a party of technocrats; they argued instead that modern parties can and must rely on professionals *and* volunteers in order to win public support.

It is important to point out the areas of activity which were almost wholly omitted in these discussions of the purposes of organizational reform. Most telling was the failure to discuss members' contributions as volunteer workers within the party. Also absent were portraits of members as a source of ideas for party leaders, or as an institutionalized check for keeping party élites in touch with popular opinion. These latter omissions are all the more significant because, as will be shown, both reports recommended ways of strengthening party channels of bottom-up communication and influence even though party leaders maintained that the party was already offering voters good ideas and good candidates.

On the other hand, reformers recognized that potential voters were evidently not equally impressed with parties' ideas and candidates. They therefore viewed the activities of local members as a valuable resource which could be used to help bridge the apparently growing gap between the national-level parties and the citizens who had been their traditional supporters. Both parties' reports reflected the hopes of party organizers that the contacts and activities of individual members outside the party sphere could break down hostility towards professional politicians and established parties. Such was the conclusion of the previously discussed SPD theory of communications, which described why contemporary parties needed active and articulate members to capture the attention and interest of politically engaged citizens. CDU organizers likewise concluded that '[i]t is essential for modern party work [that we] have the greatest possible number of members who are willing and able to represent the political goals of the CDU in conversation, and in other forms of involvement'.[11] For these reasons, organizers in both parties attached increased value to members who could provide outreach benefits, in other words, who could boost party support through their community contacts.

In addition, the reports gave evidence of a growing interest in boosting individual members' contributions in the area of symbolic politics. The documents portrayed members as assets who could enhance a party's public image by improving its membership statistics; in other words, members could provide legitimacy benefits merely by enlisting. Both reports made clear that some individuals (for example, women and young people) were more valuable than others when it came to improving statistics about membership, or about the composition of candidate slates.

The reports also commented on how social changes had diminished the value of the membership benefits offered by the parties. The SPD's analysis was particularly explicit in explaining why parties would find it more difficult to recruit in the 1990s. According to its report, people had previously joined a party to get information about politics, but they no longer needed to do this, because information was now amply provided by mass media. As a result, other possible reasons for joining a party had become more important: individuals now valued party membership because it provided opportunities for clarifying personal political opinions (for instance, by participating in discussions), for exerting political influence, and for assuming party or public office.[12] The SPD report (like the CDU report) therefore concluded that parties must increase their offerings of such expressive benefits in order to increase their chances of recruiting and retaining members.

Thus, at the end of the 1980s and the beginning of the 1990s, organizers in both the CDU and SPD were presenting very similar analyses of their parties' new organizational challenges. They argued that changes outside the parties made it necessary to experiment with new methods of winning the support of increasingly independent voters. Further, they contended that some traditional features of extra-parliamentary party organization were decreasingly useful in attracting voters or members. Given the similarities of the diagnoses, it is not surprising that the reports presented somewhat similar remedies for improving the health and effectiveness of the respective party organizations.

The Prescribed Organizational Cures

The reports' proposals for increasing membership benefits fell into two categories. The first sort argued that parties should consciously compete with other leisure-time alternatives by offering more solidary and purposive incentives, including one which other organizations cannot provide, namely, direct influence in selecting candidates and determining party policies. The second sort argued that parties should lower some of their membership barriers in order to reduce the costs of enrolment. Each of these sets of recommendations can be considered separately.

The two reports argued that making party life more enjoyable and more personally fulfilling would combat declining membership levels, and would reverse trends towards declining participation in party activities. As the SPD's 1993 discussion paper asserted, 'We want to encourage the motivation of members for doing party work: involvement in the SPD should be fun and appealing.'[13] The 1989 CDU report wrote, 'Today, party offerings must deliberately compete with other free-time activities, and therefore cannot refrain from strengthening feelings of togetherness.'[14] This was the same message that CDU general secretary Volker Rühe delivered to the party's 1991 conference:

Political interest and political engagement cannot be taken for granted in a leisure society. The CDU must be modern and attractive if it wants to prevail in the competition for citizens' attention and approval.[15]

Recent calls to make party life more entertaining may have been particularly urgent, but they are certainly not novel. At least since the 1960s, national organizers have been telling local leaders that they must stop holding boring meetings if they want to compete with television and other forms of entertainment. Of course, these calls do not necessarily produce great changes, because national organizers have few tools other than exhortation with which to change the atmosphere of local meetings. Perhaps because they cannot control what goes on in such meetings, ever since the 1970s organizers in both parties have made some top-down efforts to produce collective solidary incentives. Thus, when both national parties began sending membership magazines to all members in the 1970s, they were not only trying to provide new channels of communications from leaders to party members. They were also trying to boost what German party organizers refer to as the 'we feeling' (*Das Wir-Gefühl*)—the sense of group identity. More recently, it is the national SPD which has been most imaginative in its attempts to create centrally provided solidary benefits. For instance, since 1985 the SPD has sponsored vacation study-tours for members; these compete with other tour companies, not on price but on group atmosphere.[16]

These examples show that even before they issued their reports on party work in the 1990s, both national parties had already made some efforts to make membership more attractive by increasing solidary rewards for party members. The reports on organizational reform argued that local parties could and should do more to increase the attractiveness of membership by appealing to members' desire to make a positive difference in the wider community. In other words, they needed to offer members more purposive incentives. The SPD and CDU reports both endorsed two main strategies for doing this. One was to increase the extent to which individual members felt involved in the process of selecting party personnel and policies. The other was to offer members more opportunities to make direct, though perhaps non-partisan, contributions to their local communities.

Writers of both parties' reports favoured new decision-making rules which could provide members with a greater sense of involvement in party policies. The CDU report was more cautious in this regard, and it began its discussion of the subject by noting how well delegate democracy had worked in the past. However, it then argued that local and regional parties should nevertheless experiment with redesigning their procedure for selecting candidates, 'so that party members can be given the strongest possibilities for participation, for instance through meetings of the whole membership, through membership surveys, and through open meetings of delegates'.[17] The SPD report drew on the party's 1991 membership survey to buttress its call for the creation of greater opportunities for membership participation. According to the report, the survey showed that many members were strongly attracted by purposive incentives; indeed 'the desire for political participation, and interest in getting more political information, were the most important reasons for joining the SPD'.[18] The authors concluded that expanding opportunities for direct participation could significantly enhance the attractiveness of party membership. Like its CDU counterpart, the SPD report did not recommend imposing direct democratic decision-making on all levels of the party organization; however it did assert that

in order to improve links between the members and the party, it is necessary to offer . . . improved opportunities to influence decisions. . . . Selecting candidates for local, state, and federal parliaments with a membership primary [*Urwahl*] is one possibility for increasing the decision-making opportunities for members.[19]

Both reports also urged local parties to increase their offerings of another kind of purposive incentive: those generated by participation in community-service activities. As Chapter 5 showed, party organizers had begun to promote such activities in the 1970s, and the later reports reaffirmed earlier arguments about the desirability of local service-projects. They noted that local parties can make enrolment more attractive by offering members opportunities to participate in the kinds of service activities which produce direct, visible results. In the vivid words of one summary of the CDU report, 'Television makes people passive, party work makes them active. You can also look at it from a psychological viewpoint: television frustrates, party work creates hope. That is our chance as a peoples' party to win new members.'[20]

In arguing in favour of expanding opportunities for political participation, both reports were arguing in favour of providing more of the sort of membership incentive which would appeal to the most politically committed supporters. As has been shown in earlier chapters, party organizers in the late 1980s and early 1990s considered this type of supporter to be especially useful, because those who joined because of political convictions were the members who were most likely to share their political views with friends and colleagues.

The reports also recommended changes that would make membership more appealing to other groups who were perceived to be in particularly short supply—namely, female and younger members. One way party organizers hoped to attract members of this kind was by giving them easier access to party and public offices. Throughout the 1980s, many CDU leaders had resisted calls for quotas to get more women on the party's candidate slates. The party's 1989 report also refrained from calling for quotas, but it did urge state and local CDU parties to make greater efforts voluntarily to increase the proportion of female, young, retired, and blue-collar candidates for party and public office.[21] By the time of the SPD report, this party had already adopted (in 1985) quotas guaranteeing female members greater access to party and public office, and the effects of these quotas began to be felt in the 1990s. Yet SPD organizers were still distressed by the party's ageing public face. Thus, the 1993 SPD report proposed that local parties should try to attract young members by reserving 10 per cent of places on local-government candidate slates (including *good* places) for party members who were younger than 30.[22]

In addition to endorsing ways to make membership more attractive by increasing membership benefits, both reports argued in favour of changes intended to reduce the costs of enrolment. The reports gave special attention to the problem of how to lower supposed psychological barriers to membership. As the CDU report explained, the party must develop more opportunities for short-term participation, because 'this can help reduce the inhibitions of those who are interested, but who (still) shy away from commitment'.[23] Another way to reduce these inhibitions was by lowering the barriers separating members from non-members—for instance, by encouraging non-enrolled supporters to participate in party activities. Both reports encouraged local parties to take steps in this direction, although voting privileges were to remain strictly reserved for party members. Two years after the CDU report was issued, party organizers were still calling for greater openness towards non-members. In answer to a question about how the CDU could combat disaffection with political parties (*Parteienverdrossenheit*), the general secretary of the time, Rühe, replied that his party must respond to new demands from citizens by developing new forms of party work:

This includes better political communication and a stronger dialogue with citizens. For instance, if a young mother wants to work with the CDU for a while, without becoming a member—that should happen more often. A good example is also opening party meetings to [all] interested citizens. . . . [24]

The 1993 SPD report endorsed the same sentiment in its recommendations: 'The SPD will need to open itself to participation by interested and engagement-ready citizens who are not members, by offering new forms of party work, including projects that last for a limited time.'[25]

In addition, both reports recommended that local parties should take a further step towards reducing the distinction between members and non-members by deliberately recruiting candidates outside the existing ranks of the local party. The CDU report argued that one of the advantages of candidates who had been engaged in church groups or sports clubs but who had not found time for party work, was that these people did not conform to the unpopular stereotype of politicians as careerists who had accomplished little outside the political realm.[26] The SPD report echoed this recommendation that local parties could profit by making more use of non-member candidates: 'Opening the party to non-members should also have a [good] effect on the distribution of political offices. In the future there will still be local-government ballots which include non-member candidates.'[27]

Such support for opening even the most fundamental of party activities to non-members makes clear what it is that today's party organizers value about members: above all, they value them because they bring the party message into the community. In order to attract supporters who can unobtrusively advertise their partisan loyalties, party organizers have tinkered both with the price and with the privileges of party 'membership products'. If non-member supporters can be activated for party work merely by lowering participation barriers and by offering solidary incentives, so much the better. However, if this is insufficient, then party leaders have also been willing to back changes which aim to appeal to potential members by offering them meaningful decision-making roles within the party.

The Consequences

The proposals endorsed in the party reports met with different fates. The opposition SPD quickly enacted many of the advocated changes. On the other hand, at the national level the CDU responded only slowly to its own experts' recommendations.

The CDU's limited response resulted in part from the circumstances of the report's preparation and publication. The document bore the clear hand of those associated with the party's long-serving general secretary, Heiner Geißler. However, Helmut Kohl had ousted Geißler from his job even before the report was formally presented to the 1989 party conference. Geißler's immediate successors were not particularly interested in the unglamorous work of organizational reform. Furthermore, within a month of the CDU's 1989 conference the agenda of German politics had been radically changed by developments in East Germany. CDU leaders found little time to worry about problems of party organization as they confronted the much more complex issues which the country faced as it travelled rapidly towards unification. In addition, at the federal level organizational reform seemed much less pressing after Kohl and his party had won a solid victory in the 1990 federal elections. Yet despite these unfavourable circumstances, the arguments of the 1989 CDU report were not entirely ignored. The CDU lost ground in a string of state-level elections in the early 1990s, and some state CDU parties responded by adopting ideas advocated in the report. For instance, in 1993 state parties in Schleswig-Holstein and North Rhine-Westphalia adopted one of the report's ideas about lowering membership barriers when they introduced free 'trial-year' memberships for those between the ages of 18 and 25.[28] Additionally, as will be discussed below, a few state parties responded to the call for greater participation by members in party decision-making.

In contrast, circumstances surrounding the SPD's 1993 report helped to hasten the enactment of its recommendations. In the spring of 1993 the SPD's chair and presumed future chancellor-candidate, Björn Engholm, unexpectedly resigned.[29] This sudden vacancy left the SPD with at least three claimants to the title of heir-apparent, and it thus raised the spectre of a messy and very public fight for succession only eighteen months before scheduled federal elections. Yet within a few weeks of Engholm's resignation, members of the SPD executive had united behind a novel idea about how intra-party rivalries might be settled, and perhaps even used to the party's advantage. They decided to ballot party members in order to determine whom the party conference should select as the new chair.

The idea of using party primaries to select parliamentary or party officials was not entirely new in the SPD, but it was not until the end of the 1980s that it found a prominent advocate.[30] Karlheinz Blessing, Engholm's party manager, used his position to promote the adoption of this device, though even then it did not meet with universal approval.[31] Crucially, however, the 1993 report on party modernization (written under Blessing's direction) endorsed party primaries as a way to attract new party members by expanding members' opportunities for participation. This report was already circulating before Engholm's resignation produced the succession crisis, and the existence of such official recommendations served as justification for the party executive to experiment with membership ballots even before the report had been debated, or the party statutes had been amended to authorize primary procedures.

However, this sequence of events does not demonstrate that SPD leaders turned to party primaries for the reason stated in the report—namely, in order to make membership more attractive by increasing opportunities for participation. Closer inspection reveals that some members of the party executive may have advocated the initial use of a primary for reasons other than, or in addition to, the desire to expand member-democracy. At least some supporters of the experiment were probably motivated by calculations about how the new procedure might affect the outcome of the contest. Not coincidentally, the strongest advocates of the membership primary included the strongest opponents of the leadership bid made by Gerhard Schröder (minister-president of Lower Saxony), who was the candidate considered most likely to win if the leadership contest were to be decided by delegates to the party conference.[32] An intra-party dispute over the membership ballot was avoided only because Schröder endorsed the new procedure after it had received favourable news-coverage.

Once the party executive had decided to employ this new method of selecting the party chair, SPD leaders tried to gain maximum benefits from this risky experiment in expanded intra-party democracy. In press accounts they portrayed use of the membership ballot as an indicator of the SPD's responsiveness to its members, and as proof that parties did not have to be élite-dominated associations. Meanwhile, party leaders could only hope that participation levels would not be so low as to make these claims look ridiculous. In the event, the ballot was a double success for the party: the outcome clearly settled the contest for succession in favour of Rudolf Scharping (minister-president of Rhineland-Palatinate), and the high rate of participation convinced even the most sceptical of journalists that such procedures were good for the polity.[33] Because of the success of these *ad hoc* procedures, an SPD conference in late 1993 followed the recommendations of the *SPD 2000* report and amended party statutes to create permanent procedures for party primaries. This same conference rejected the report's recommendation to permit consultative membership ballots on policy questions before they were debated by party conferences, but it authorized regional parties to call binding intra-party plebiscites on policies after they have been officially adopted.[34]

CDU leaders could not fail to notice the tremendous boost in publicity which the SPD gained from its use of a membership primary. Within weeks of the ballot for the SPD leadership, the CDU in North Rhine-Westphalia had changed its statutes to permit party-internal primaries and party-internal 'referenda' on policy questions. The SPD's positive experience with a membership ballot certainly helped to strengthen the arguments which leaders of the state party put forward in favour of the changes; however, these changes originally grew out of the CDU's own debates about reform, and they were on the conference agenda long before the SPD primary was scheduled. It is no coincidence that it was the CDU in North Rhine-Westphalia which led the way in this, for this state party had long stood in the shadow of the SPD. In the early 1990s, CDU leaders in this state promoted intra-party ballots, as well as changes such as the introduction of directly elected mayors, because democratization seemed to be an electorally popular issue. It was not only in North Rhine-Westphalia that leaders recognized the electoral attractiveness of expanding opportunities for participation within the party. Later in 1993, members of some other state-level CDU parties advocated similar changes for their parties.[35]

An examination of the parties' debates about organizational reform thus shows that the adoption of new decision-making procedures in 1993 was neither a simple nor an isolated change. Instead, this change was preceded by leadership-initiated discussions about ways of using members to boost the flagging fortunes of the parties. New procedures were then enacted as part of a set of measures with which party leaders sought simultaneously to boost the attractiveness of party membership, and increase the legitimacy and outreach benefits provided by the members.

BRITAIN: 'MODERNIZERS' IN THE LABOUR PARTY

In Britain in the late 1980s and 1990s, leaders of the opposition Labour Party were also considering the question of how the structures of the party's membership organization could make electoral victories more—or less—likely. Notable results of this process were the 1993 changes in the party's statutes which gave individual members direct votes in the selection of leaders and candidates. These changes followed in the wake of a whole decade of top-down efforts to increase the party's net benefits from its membership. Labour Party organizers had used this period not only to reflect on how members could aid party efforts, but also to consider how the process of party enrolment, and the experience of party life, might encourage or discourage potential members. Unlike their German counterparts, the Labour Party's organizers never summarized their justifications for organizational reform in a single authoritative report. Nevertheless, it is possible to discern some of the calculations that lay behind the organizational initiatives by looking at the period's intra-party debates.

Identifying the Problem

In 1983 the new party leader, Neil Kinnock, and his supporters in the party executive and party bureaucracy, began considering proposals for intra-party reform. In doing so they were responding both to the party's disastrous defeats in the 1979 and 1983 general elections and to the factional divisions which had plagued the party in the early years of the Thatcher government. Organizational reform found continued support under John Smith, who replaced Kinnock as party leader in the wake of the party's narrow defeat in the 1992 general election. Tony Blair, another Labour 'modernizer', became party leader in 1994, after Smith's untimely death. All three leaders, and their supporters on the party executive and among the party's professional employees, used party-commissioned opinion-polls and focus-group assessments as ammunition in intra-party struggles to persuade constituency parties and party-affiliated trade unions for their ambitious organizational reforms.[36]

Labour's modernizers blamed party decision-making processes for saddling the party with vote-losing personnel and policies. Kinnock and his allies were particularly concerned to halt the bad publicity generated by the selection of parliamentary candidates in some constituencies, and by the very controversial policies of some extremist Labour-controlled local authorities. Local parties' radical decisions could strongly shape public perceptions of the Labour Party as a whole, but they were largely beyond the direct control of the national executive. In the mid-1980s the party's central organizers argued that newly expanded channels of party democracy were partly responsible for producing these extreme decisions, because only small, self-selected, segments of the membership were taking advantage of decision-making opportunities. Party organizers contended that it was because party activists were unrepresentative, and ideologically extreme, that the programmatic costs of party membership had increased following the 1979 changes in the procedures for the selection of candidates and leaders.

These debates continued throughout the late 1980s and early 1990s. Party modernizers consistently argued that the Labour Party could only win a general election if it successfully shed two negative images: that of the party as the lap-dog of trade unions; and that of the party as the hostage of leftist extremists. The programmatic and organizational reforms endorsed by party modernizers were designed to erase both these images. In the terms of Chapter 2's discussion they can be described as attempts simultaneously to reduce the programmatic costs of the party's membership (members are policy extremists who impose vote-losing policies on leaders) and to increase the linkage and programmatic benefits provided by the membership (members keep leaders informed of public opinion and also contribute vote-winning ideas). For over a decade, Labour Party leaders worked to achieve these seemingly contradictory goals by attempting to expand the party membership, and by trying to increase the proportion of members involved in party decision-making.

The Cures and their Consequences

Labour Party organizers who despaired about the extremism of party activists concluded that a good way to decrease the costs imposed by membership, and to increase the linkage benefits provided by enrolled supporters, was to expand participation in party decision-making beyond the inner core of ideologically inspired activists. Influenced by this interpretation, leaders of the national party took up the cause of expanded member-democracy as a weapon which could be used against those on the party's left who had originally promoted the idea.

The leadership's new interest in member democracy was initially manifest in its support for greater participation by members in the selection of parliamentary candidates. Traditionally, the process of candidate selection had been controlled by the executive committees of constituency parties; these committees were usually composed of representatives from local trade unions and branch parties.[37] However, the 1988 Labour Party conference accepted leadership-backed proposals to change party statutes in order to give ordinary members a greater opportunity to influence selection. Under the new system, which was used before the 1992 elections, candidates were chosen by local 'electoral colleges'. This system limited the control of local trade-union representatives, who could now cast no more than 40 per cent of the votes of local electoral colleges. The rest were allocated by a selection meeting at which all members of the local party (not just the executive committee) could vote. The new rules further encouraged participation by those outside the small circle of party activists because they made provisions to give absentee ballots to members who were prevented from attending selection meetings by work schedules, poor health, or child-care responsibilities. (Indeed, in practice there was nothing to stop those who merely *disliked* such meetings from taking advantage of these provisions.)[38]

Labour Party leaders soon backed other steps to expand participation by individual members in party decision-making. After the Labour Party's 1992 defeat, John Smith used the full force of his new position as party leader to win trade-union and constituency support for these kinds of proposals. Both the 1990 and 1991 party conferences had endorsed the idea of mandatory one-member, one-vote procedures for the selection of candidates, but the proposal had still not been translated into party statutes by 1992.[39] Indeed, on the face of it, a proposal to increase the influence of direct members seemed unlikely to win conference support, because such a change would necessarily come at the expense of the same affiliated members (trade unions) who dominated the voting at party conferences. Yet because of Smith's strong support for the proposals, and because many trade-union leaders agreed that existing relations between unions and the party were becoming anachronistic and harmful to both sides, the Labour Party's 1993 conference did indeed accept an amendment entirely excluding local trade-union delegates from candidate selection by constituency parties, and stipulating that constituency parties should use a ballot of all individual members (rather than an electoral college) to select candidates.[40]

A second change approved by the 1993 conference gave individual party members a bigger role in selecting the party leader. Under the new rules, a postal ballot of all members determines how constituency votes will be allocated in the party's national electoral college. (Previously they had been distributed on the basis of decisions by the executive committees of constituency parties.) In this latter change it is particularly easy to see how democratization could appeal to party leaders not only because of its presumed attractiveness to party supporters, but also because of its presumed influence on party outcomes. In the 1988 leadership election, constituencies had been given the option of using a membership ballot as a way of deciding how to cast the local party vote. Evidence from this contest later showed that it was constituencies with full opportunities for member participation which had been most likely to support the centrist candidate (Neil Kinnock).[41]

However, even if democratization was a cause that served several ends, party leaders did seem to hope that these increased benefits to members would encourage supporters to enrol. This impression is strengthened by the fact that in the same period they also backed several changes designed to encourage affiliated members to become direct members. Thus, Labour Party leaders explicitly linked their support for a reduction in the voting-privileges of trade unions with their support for increased opportunities for direct members to contribute to decisions about party policies and personnel. They also connected it with support for reforms which made it easier for affiliated members directly to enrol in the party.[42]

Expanding the party's direct membership was a central components of plans for the Labour Party to change its public image into that of a party which was more dependent on 'ordinary' members than on radical activists or trade unions. Indeed, the party's national organizers argued that this image of a radical grassroots culture accounted for some of the party's difficulties with recruitment. They argued that party supporters were unwilling to enrol in an organization which was widely seen as consisting entirely of activists, many of whom were, moreover, thought to be both intolerant and unwelcoming. In response, the Labour Party's general secretary tried to bolster recruiting efforts by persuading local recruiters of the need to welcome even potentially inactive members: 'We need to get the message across that in order to be a member of the party you do not have to attend three meetings a week, three meetings a night in some cases.'[43]

Top-down efforts to reduce the costs incurred by individual members were not confined to exhortations. In this same period, the national party initiated or endorsed several steps designed to lower barriers to membership. In the mid-1980s the NEC persuaded the party conference to give the national party primary administrative responsibility for membership enrolment. The new procedures adopted at this time were supposed to make it easier for would-be members to join the party, to make it more efficient for the party to collect membership dues and renewals, and to make it more effective for the party to run national recruiting advertisements. Although in practice the national membership system initially increased the barriers to entry (because inexperience with running it generated great backlogs in processing records), it still may have served at the least one of its intended purposes, that of attracting the sort of supporter who might be deterred by initial contacts with party activists.[44]

The party leadership also endorsed other steps to lower membership barriers in order to aid recruiting efforts. Increased accessibility to membership was the reason given for reducing annual membership dues in 1993 (a change which reversed the trend of more than a decade of increases). More importantly, in 1988 the NEC backed an initiative to lower enrolment barriers by temporarily reducing membership fees for those who were already affiliated to the party through a trade union (the indirect members).[45] Though the lower fees initially attracted few new members, and though it risked producing substantial losses in revenue if existing members were the only ones to join at a lower rate, the 1992 party conference approved an NEC proposal permanently to reduce individual dues for those who were already indirect members.[46] Finally, as Labour Party membership reached precariously low levels in the early 1990s, party leaders took another step to reduce barriers to membership when the party authorized individuals to enrol as members without paying any dues, as long as their constituency parties paid the national party's portion on their behalf. This meant that local parties which were good fundraisers could afford to offer supporters free, or cut-price, memberships. In 1993 Tony Blair, Labour's future leader, summed up the interlinked ideas that underlay all these efforts to reduce membership barriers:

This plan for a mass membership is not a glorified recruitment drive to me—it's about transforming the way the Labour Party works, operates, and thinks. If we start to roll back the ludicrous idea that you have an ever larger membership fee and extract ever larger sums of money from an ever smaller membership and instead start to go in the opposite direction and start to have a large mass membership, the Labour Party can be transformed.[47]

In practice, transforming the way the party works has meant reducing enrolment costs, and increasing benefits for direct members (as well as restricting some benefits to affiliated members). These steps have been taken in order to entice affiliated members and other supporters into enrolling as individual members.

Thus, the recent measures adopted by the Labour Party conference to expand the rights of individual members can be seen as part of a top-down strategy which reflects changing perceptions about both the utility of membership and the effectiveness of membership incentives (and disincentives). To counteract negative images of the party generated by more radical activists,

Labour Party leaders adopted a strategy of increasing the size, visibility, and the influence of 'inactive' members. In order to win benefits that could result from membership expansion, party leaders were even willing to forgo some of the immediate financial dividends provided by members, though they hoped that expansion would eventually offset the revenue losses caused by cutting dues.

In the German parties, one of the prime arguments for extending voting rights to all members was that these opportunities would appeal to what had come to be seen as the most useful kind of members—those who were interested in politics and would talk about politics outside the party sphere. Organizers in the British Labour Party endorsed a similar set of changes, but apparently for somewhat different reasons. In the Labour Party, reallocating decision-making to individual members, and reducing enrolment costs, were primarily designed to increase the appeal of party membership and reduce the power wielded by radical activists. Party leaders hoped that expanding the membership would directly and indirectly boost the membership's generation of legitimacy benefits, and that it would reduce the programmatic costs imposed by members.

ORGANIZATIONAL CHANGE AND STRATEGIC CALCULATIONS

The purpose of these examinations has been to attempt to link specific organizational changes with leaders' changing views of membership incentives and party structures as tools for enhancing a party's electoral prospects. The cases described in this chapter do indeed seem to provide examples of how calculations about the electoral costs and benefits of enrolling members can prompt leaders to channel organizational change even in otherwise unexpected directions. Although these calculations were clearly not the only factors which influenced the timing or consequences of reform proposals, it is clear that the recommended reforms represented deliberate responses to what party leaders and organizers considered to be the prevailing preferences of potential party members, and of the broader party electorates.

The model set out in Chapter 2 posits that party leaders are likely to initiate organizational changes if they alter their ideas about the costs and benefits associated with enrolling party members, or if they perceive a change in the effectiveness of particular membership incentives. Leaders' changing assessments about the relative value of organizational resources and techniques do seem to have played a prominent role in the events that led the Labour Party, the SPD, and some state-level CDU associations to enhance the formal status of individual members. In all three parties, these changes were promoted as methods that could directly and indirectly improve the parties' electoral appeal: they would directly increase party legitimacy by strengthening the appearance of popular control, and they would attract members who would indirectly help by contributing moderate ideas (in the Labour Party) or by making new contacts in the community (in the German parties). In short, party leaders supported reforms that devolved formal powers because they calculated that their own immediate electoral prospects would be boosted by party commitment to participatory democracy at a time of what was perceived to be strong popular reaction against established party practices.

In the cases described above, changing perceptions about membership utility, and changing perceptions about the priorities of potential members, played important roles in determining the *direction* of organizational change. However, as already acknowledged in Chapter 2, changing assessments about the costs and benefits of membership are insufficient to explain the outcome or speed of these organizational reforms. Electoral circumstances and idiosyncratic events seem to have influenced the timing of changes, while struggles within the parties may have been decisive for the success and extent of these reforms. However, what has been shown in this chapter is that party leaders do sponsor research to find out what potential party members and voters want from their party. They then make efforts to tailor and retailor their party's 'membership product' in order to make membership a more attractive proposition for certain supporters. The organizational changes which result from perceived electoral crises are not random, nor are they necessarily scatter-shot efforts to attract any or all possible members. Instead, they can be carefully designed to appeal to a particular (large or small) audience among those who might be enticed into paying the costs of enrolling in a party.

Throughout the account so far the focus has been on assessing the validity of 'demand-side' predictions about the role of leadership strategies in hastening the organizational decline of member-ship parties. These predictions rest on models which argue that in a mass media age, party leaders necessarily come to view members as superfluous, and that they therefore cease to channel resources into recruiting or retaining them. The preceding chapters have argued against such simple models, and have shown, instead, how parties' adoption of new communications technologies can spur party strategists to develop new roles for party members.

Yet showing that party organizers have placed new responsibil-ities on party members reveals little about the extent of changes in the actual character of parties as membership organizations, because this character is shaped by both demand-side and sup-ply-side forces. The next chapter therefore continues the foregoing consideration of organizational decline by examining how changes in incentives to party enrolment have corresponded with changes in the extent to which parties have been able to rely on the support of their members.

7

Membership Support for Political Parties: How Much Has Really Changed?

> The victory of ideals must be organized.
>
> Keir Hardie[1]

WHAT have members done for membership parties in the second half of the twentieth century? This question cannot be answered merely by looking at what party organizers have hoped that members will contribute; instead, it must be answered by also looking at whether members have satisfied party organizers' expectations. Up to now this study has focused only on the former aspect, looking at how party leaders have changed their ideas about the ways in which members might be useful, and at the organizational reforms precipitated by these changed strategies and tactics. Evidence from party publications and party conferences has shown that in recent decades organizers in all four parties have modified their ideas about what members can contribute to parties' electoral successes. However, this sort of information does not reveal the extent to which party leaders have actually been able to count on the support of their members when trying to carry out their old and new organizing strategies.

The willingness of members to render aid is crucial to the success of many organizational initiatives. Of course, party leaders may be able to implement some tactics on their own. For instance, in countries where political parties can purchase television time, party reliance on mass media communication may be constrained only by leaders' fundraising abilities. In countries where legislation limits parties' access to television, party leaders may be able to boost their television exposure merely by co-operating with leaders of rival parties to increase allocated transmission time. Alternatively, if party leaders want to rely more on party employees, and less on the labour of member volunteers, they may be able to achieve this by instituting or increasing public subsidies for political parties (again, probably in concert with leaders of other parties). However, party leaders cannot successfully implement any strategy that demands members' support unless citizens are willing to enrol in parties, and they cannot profit from proposed new forms of membership activity unless enrolled members are willing to participate in these activities. Thus, party strategies alone do not provide an adequate indicator of the extent to which parties rely on their members; to understand how parties are changing, it is also necessary to look at more direct indicators of fluctuations in the support they receive from their members.

This chapter examines evidence about the extent to which German and British party members have provided their parties with the benefits listed in the second chapter. The discussion first considers the extent to which recent losses in membership may have undermined the legitimacy benefits which the remaining members provide. The chapter then examines evidence of the extent to which the parties have been financially dependent on their members. Finally, an account is offered of changes in members' active contributions to local party efforts. These sections give a clear picture of how much—and how little—has changed in the extent to which these four membership parties have been able to rely on the contributions of their enrolled supporters.

MEMBERSHIP SIZE AND LEGITIMACY BENEFITS

The legitimacy benefits conferred by membership statistics may be a function more of membership trends than of absolute size. Members can boost their party's political credibility merely by enrolling, because fluctuations in membership size provide an easy indicator of voluntary partisan support. Conversely, loss of membership may generate unfavourable publicity. This is precisely what has happened in recent years for the four German and British parties, all of which have suffered from declining enrolment. The parties have—fairly or unfairly—reaped only small or negative legitimacy-benefits from their remaining members, because the membership losses have been widely depicted as signs of dwindling electoral appeal.

As the numbers in Tables 3.1 and 3.6 showed, in the late 1980s and early 1990s membership declined in three of the parties. In the fourth party, the Labour Party, membership stabilized at historically low levels after experiencing an earlier decline (possibly in the 1970s). Even so, it was not until the 1980s that membership figures became an embarrassment to the party, because only then did more accurate accounts reveal that individual enrolment had fallen to levels not seen since the 1920s, at the dawn of the radio age. Estimates of Conservative Party membership also plunged to shockingly low levels by the mid-1990s. Both parties found that their declining memberships provided fodder for negative press reports. In Germany, too, press reports depicted the big parties' recruitment difficulties as signs of general disaffection with political parties, and as part of a possibly unstoppable trend. Such negative reports predominated, even though both parties retained relatively strong memberships in this period, with neither of their western memberships dropping below the levels of the mid-1960s, the dawn of the era of near-universal television ownership.

As the example of the German parties makes clear, marginal shifts in membership statistics may be more important than sheer size for determining the net legitimacy-benefits brought by membership enrolment. Membership growth is thus a double-edged sword, because even a slackening of this trend can be presented as a sign of dissatisfaction. Thus, paradoxically, in the mid-1990s it was the Labour Party which had the most to gain from even a modest increase in membership enrolment, because in this party stagnating membership had already established new, low expectations about 'normal' levels of membership.

MEMBERSHIP CONTRIBUTIONS AND FINANCIAL BENEFITS

Chapter 5 showed that in recent years leaders of the three parties which set party-wide levels for dues (the German parties and the Labour Party) have all risked grassroots hostility in order to win increases in members' contributions to central revenues. Examining the national parties' financial records helps to explain why party leaders have continued to treat members as an important component of party fundraising strategies even when they have gained increased access to other sources of revenue. It is easiest to draw conclusions about the financial importance of members for the German parties, because German parties which receive public subsidies must publish audited accounts.[2] Yet even the rougher British figures can provide some clues about trends in party financing.

The first thing to note is that the German parties have been much richer than their British counterparts, a difference which has much to do with the availability of public subsidies. One good year for illustrating this difference is 1987, a year in which both Germany and Britain held national parliamentary elections, and in which they both had similarly sized electorates. In 1987, the CDU's federal revenues were the equivalent of about £20 million and federal SPD revenues were about £23 million,[3] compared with about £15 million received by the Conservative Party and about £10 million received by the Labour Party.[4] The differences in total revenues were even greater than these national figures suggest, because the German parties also had more extensively developed, and much better-funded, regional parties. Yet despite the high public subsidies that helped to make them so well funded, at least until very recently the German central parties have been more

TABLE 7.1. *Membership dues as a percentage of federal-party incomes 1970–1990*

Electoral period	SPD	CDU
1970–1972	14	21
1973–1976	18	23
1977–1980	14	20
1981–1983	17	18
1984–1987	29	20
1988–1990	22	13

Note: After 1983, dues and other regular payments are reported jointly.

Sources: Deutscher Bundestag, *Rechenschaftsberichte der Parteien* (1967–83 in *Bundesanzeiger*; 1984–92 in *Bundestag Drucksachen*), various years.

dependent on members' contributions than their British counter-parts.

Because public subsidies for German parties are paid out in unequal yearly amounts, with the sums increasing along with the anticipated proximity of elections, the best way to evaluate party accounts is by calculating the average importance of members' contributions during each electoral period. Table 7.1 presents these calculations. It shows that members and other regular contributors have provided roughly one seventh to one third of the SPD and CDU federal budgets since the introduction of federal subsidies. These figures fluctuated, but they showed no clear downward trend before 1987, despite the fact that levels of public subsidies were rising quickly in these years. The relative importance of member-ship financing dropped in the period 1988–1990, particularly for the CDU; however, a large part of this decline occurred because German unification suddenly expanded the electorate, and thereby increased party subsidies. The figures in Table 7.1 show the continuing importance of member-based funding for the German parties at the federal level. These proportions would be even greater if funding for all levels of parties were taken into account (local and state as well as federal), because members consistently provide at least 30 to 40 per cent of the total income of the CDU and SPD.[5]

The introduction of public subsidies thus did not lead to an immediate, steady decline in parties' reliance on membership funding. However, the accounts do not show whether the parties were significantly more dependent on members' contributions before they could rely on public funds. The question is difficult to answer, because there are no public data on CDU financing before 1967, but it is clear that in the 1950s the federal CDU benefited very little from member financing. It was only in 1964 that this party began requiring local associations to forward a portion of members' dues to the central party. Thus, in the 1990s the federal CDU relied more on members' financial con-tributions than it had in the 1950s. In contrast, accounts published in SPD Yearbooks suggest that the SPD's central operations were much more dependent on members' contributions in the 1950s than they later became.

The extent to which each of the British parties has relied on membership contributions has fluctuated according to whether it was in government or in opposition. Calculations made by Michael Pinto-Duschinsky show that in the mid-1980s between 10 and 20 per cent of the budget for Conservative Central Office came from constituency contributions. This figure made the central party about as dependent on constituency party ('quota') contributions as it had been in the 1950s (another decade of Tory government), but it made it somewhat less dependent on locally generated revenue than it had been when the party was in opposition.[6] Pinto-Duschinsky did not make similar calculations concerning the Labour Party's reliance on the affiliation fees of local parties. However, comparing figures from the Labour Party's published accounts with Pinto-Duschinsky's revenue calculations indicates that in the 1980s Labour's headquarters received 10 to 15 per cent of its annual budget from constituencies' membership-linked affiliation-fees. This proportion was higher than it had been in the 1970s, when the Labour Party held office, but it was similar to figures from the late 1950s, when the party was also confined to the opposition benches.

Thus, only the SPD experienced a clear long-term drop in the proportion of its financial support coming from members' regular contributions, and even for the SPD this proportion stabilized after the introduction of subsidies. Furthermore, within each country there has apparently been considerable convergence in the extent to which the two big parties rely on members for revenues. In Germany, the CDU's income from membership increased sharply in the 1970s, while the SPD's relative reliance on members decreased as it began receiving subsidies. As a result, by the 1990s dues provided a comparable proportion of both German parties' incomes. In Britain in the late 1970s and early 1980s, the Labour Party raised dues frequently and increased its income from local-party affiliation fees. At the same time, Conservative Party central revenue from constituency quotas stagnated. Together, these factors helped to equalize the percentage of income both parties derived as a by-product of regular contributions from members.

In the early 1980s all four national-level parties were receiving between one tenth and one quarter of their incomes for the legislative period from organized memberships. These were certainly not startlingly high proportions, but they were also not insignificant sums. Furthermore, as Chapter 5 made clear, the parties' current reliance on funds from members is not just an accidental legacy, because party leaders have actively worked to raise or maintain levels of members' contributions.

Why have party leaders continued to try to collect small contributions from many members, when the parties have access to much richer sources of funds (public finance in Germany, corporate donations for the Conservative and Christian Democratic Parties, trade-union contributions for the Labour Party)? To begin with, none of the parties seems to have reached the point at which the marginal value of additional funds drops below zero. This became strikingly clear in the 1980s and 1990s, when all four parties amassed embarrassingly high debts after running expensive campaigns. (The German parties had already started having such problems in the 1970s.) Financial difficulties forced all four parties to reduce their central staffs and curtail their inter-election publicity. The German parties were further squeezed in 1993 by the new legislation on party finance, which limited overall levels of public funding for parties (as described in Chapter 5). Meanwhile, the British Conservative Party saw a big drop in individual and corporate donations both before and after its narrow 1992 election victory.[7] Parties which are in debt are in no position to ignore such proven sources of funds as member contributions. In addition, membership dues provide a comparatively stable source of funds, because, in contrast to business contributions, they are less tied to the immediate prospect of electoral success.

Finally, it has become increasingly clear that members' contributions provide legitimacy benefits as well as monetary rewards. As previously noted, the German parties have been under pressure from the courts and from public opinion to maximize the proportion of their revenues provided by private sources, and especially by party members. In the 1980s and 1990s Labour Party leaders, too, felt popular pressure to make their party relatively more dependent on membership dues, and less dependent on trade-union contributions. Similarly, after the 1992 elections, Conservatives were plagued with a rash of bad publicity about wealthy (and, in some cases, disreputable) donors receiving privileged access to ministers in return for very large contributions to party funds. This publicity cast a shadow over all Conservative funding practices, and it gave the party greater incentives to try to reap new benefits from constituency fundraising efforts.[8]

All these factors help to explain why the parties have made such evident efforts to maintain levels of membership funding even when members are not the single largest source of party funds. When factors like the regularity and perceived legitimacy of membership contributions are taken into account, members' financial support remained at least as important in the 1990s as it had been for the parties in the 1960s, and in most cases even earlier.

LABOUR BENEFITS AND OUTREACH BENEFITS

What has been the extent of change in the amount of political activity which members perform for their parties? This question is difficult to answer because there is so little systematic information on the subject. Recent studies of local parties have revealed much about the activities and attitudes of British and German party members in the 1980s and 1990s, but there are no comparable baselines against which to measure these findings. In lieu of this, the best that can be done is to piece together a picture of the past using the sources that are available. These include general historical accounts, which may overstate past virtues or past failings in order to make points about the present, and case-studies, which describe practices which may or may not have been representative of their period. Indeed, case-studies are quite likely to err on the side of exaggerating the activity of local parties, because few scholars will devote their attentions to documenting the (in)activities of moribund local parties.

Yet, even without making allowances for any possible exaggeration, what is striking about the case-study records of the British and German parties is that they show so little local political activity in the 1950s and 1960s. A comparison of these records with contemporary studies suggests that levels of participation in parties' campaign and inter-election activities may be higher today than they were before the spread of television-based political communication. Furthermore, these studies suggest that many of today's active members are engaged in tasks which are very different from those performed by their predecessors forty years ago; in other words, current activity cannot be described merely as the repetition of past rituals.

These changes can best be demonstrated by considering how, in each country, levels of member activity have changed in three areas for which the most evidence is available: national election campaigns; local-government work; and community outreach.

Germany

A comparison of reports from the 1980s and 1990s with those from the 1950s suggests that German party members' overtly political activities may actually have increased during this period. However, at least in the SPD, members' community-building activities have almost certainly decreased.

The *Bundestag* campaigns of the 1980s and 1990s reportedly drew on the services of a relatively high proportion of party members, though much of this increase merely reflects the traditionally low demands of previous German campaigns. Case-studies from federal elections of the 1950s and 1960s show that only a small proportion of party members were active in these campaigns. For instance, in the hard-fought 1969 parliamentary elections, some well-organized constituencies relied on fewer than fifty campaign helpers (in areas where party membership ranged between 1,000 and 2,000 people).[9] The 1969 verdict of a disappointed CDU supporter was probably more broadly applicable to local parliamentary campaigns from the 1950s until at least the early 1970s:

The election period clearly shows that most CDU/CSU members are fellow-travellers, not team members [*Mitläufer*, not *Mitstreiter*]. Although there are, of course, many exceptions, it is still clearly the case that those members who do not hold a party or public office do not help in campaigns.[10]

Because the baseline for local campaigning is so low, reports from elections in the 1980s and 1990s cannot support the diagnosis of a long-term decline in the extent of party members' campaign participation in Germany. If anything, they suggest that a greater number of members may have become involved in local campaigning once the national parties began recruiting local volunteers to deliver 'television leaflets' and weekend newspapers. For instance, CDU headquarters reported that about 90,000 CDU members delivered the CDU election paper in 1987 (the equivalent of more than 350 volunteers per constituency, or 13 per cent of the party membership). The SPD reportedly relied on over 100,000 volunteer deliverers for its election paper in 1980 (the equivalent of about 400 volunteers per constituency, or 11 per cent of the party membership).[11] Even allowing for the undoubted exaggeration in these numbers, they are still considerably higher than the 20–50 helpers reported for the constituency campaigns of the 1960s.

Between elections, German party members are now spending less time on inward-oriented activities, but are devoting more effort to inter-election outreach. Accounts from the 1950s imply that neither CDU nor SPD branch parties could expect a very large proportion of members to attend regular meetings. In West Berlin in the 1950s and 1960s between one fifth and one third of SPD and CDU members were attending party meetings. Studies from other areas in the same period gave slightly lower estimates. Furthermore, in many smaller towns and villages there were no regular meetings for members to visit, because party groups were either inactive (particularly for the CDU) or non-existent (particularly for the SPD).[12] In the 1970s and 1980s, even though both parties rapidly expanded, estimates of the proportion of members who attended meetings or were active in other ways stayed at about the same levels as in earlier years; if accurate, these figures mean that the actual number of active members increased.[13] On the other hand, particularly in the SPD, there was declining involvement in the inward-oriented activity of the door-to-door collection of dues. According to SPD estimates, over 5 per cent of the party's members worked as dues collectors in the 1950s and 1960s.[14] By the 1990s, most of these jobs had been eliminated because of the party's new bank-transfer arrangements.

Accounts from the 1950s do not present very detailed pictures of German local parties' inter-election outreach-work; however, it is not clear whether this scholarly inattention should be taken as proof of party inactivity. What is clearer is that by the 1970s and 1980s many local parties were devoting significant, and probably increasing, time to projects intended to keep them in touch with a broader public between federal elections. Thus, in one state-level study from 1981, 60 per cent of local SPD leaders named political outreach (including public meetings, information stands, and street festivals) as a focal point of their parties' public-oriented activities.[15] A somewhat smaller portion (38 per cent) of SPD leaders in a different German region named public meetings as one focus of the work of their local parties.[16]

There is no information on whether individual party members or local-party associations have followed the advice of the national party to become more active in local citizens' initiatives. However, there is evidence that members expanded their work in another area of party outreach—namely, producing community newspapers. By the early 1980s, the number of SPD community and factory newspapers had more than doubled from the 1,000 which was reported to exist in 1975. Less than a decade later the 1991–2 SPD Yearbook claimed that party members had published 20,000 neighbourhood and factory newspapers in 1990![17] The number of CDU local newspapers also grew, though at a slower pace. In 1977 local CDU associations produced an estimated 630 community newspapers, and in 1983 there were an estimated 800 regularly published local CDU newspapers. By 1986, another observer estimated that there were several thousand such CDU papers.[18] In short, local parties in many areas were clearly receptive to encouragement from the national party to expand this type of community contact.

On the other hand, even if local parties did increase their outreach efforts, they were not necessarily mobilizing many more members to accomplish the new tasks. For instance, one profile of an SPD community newspaper showed that such efforts depended on the energies of only a small but dedicated group of members; in this party, thirty (out of 378) members produced and delivered the paper to 7,000 households.[19] In other words, fewer than one tenth of this party's members were involved in newspaper production; this figure is well within the traditional range of estimates of 'active' members.

Local government is one area in which the work of German local parties, and of individual party members, has almost certainly increased since the 1950s. The consolidation of local government in the 1960s and early 1970s roughly halved the number of local-government seats.[20] However, in the same period leaders of local and national parties, particularly in the CDU, became more interested in having party representatives (not independents) contest all local-government seats. As a result, whereas in 1960 the combined number of CDU, CSU, and SPD local councillors was 67,000, by

1982, even after the consolidation of local government, there were 53,763 CDU and 40,283 SPD local-government representatives.[21] The 1982 figures for the two parties' local officials were equivalent to 7 per cent of CDU members and about 4 per cent of SPD members, though these figures slightly overstate the case, because it is not uncommon for individuals to hold office in both town and county parliaments. The proportion of members who stand (successfully or unsuccessfully) as candidates for local government is obviously much larger. Indeed, finding candidates to fill local-government slates can easily overtax the membership of a local party. This problem was apparent in West Germany even at the peak of membership recruitment, and after 1990 finding candidates became a grave problem for all the tiny local parties in the eastern German states.[22] As a result, in the west, and particularly in the east, by the 1990s the parties were coming to resemble associations of local councillors.[23] This does not support the complaint that parties now have largely inactive memberships; instead, it suggests a picture of parties without sufficient reserves of *inactive* members.

In Germany, selecting candidates for local government and contesting local elections has been called the 'high point of local-party work'.[24] Campaign tasks for municipal elections are similar to those for federal elections: party activists and individual candidates distribute leaflets, hang posters, and hold a few public meetings. Yet, despite the potentially high demands campaigning could put on those members of the party who are willing to be active, there is no evidence to suggest that local-government elections, either recently or in the more distant past, have generated particularly high levels of local activity. Indeed, a regional study from 1984 found that fewer than one quarter of local parties could mobilize more people as campaigners than were otherwise active in local parties throughout the year. The same study also found that more than three-quarters of the local parties conducted their local-government campaigns with twenty or fewer member-volunteers, while the median number of people in the local campaign-teams was only twelve. In real terms the number of campaigners varied only slightly according to the size of party memberships.[25]

Thus, the available evidence certainly does not point to an unbroken decline in all types of membership activity in the two

German parties during the past four decades. Some types of activities, such as dues collection, now require less effort by members than in the past; on the other hand, activities such as campaigning for federal elections have become somewhat more labour-intensive. Member involvement in federal campaigns increased once the national parties enlisted members to distribute party publications. Involvement in local-government campaigning may also have increased as parties contested more seats, but even so, only a low proportion of members participated in it. Local parties have apparently also increased their inter-election outreach-efforts (as shown by the proliferation of community newspapers). Even if the recent surge in anti-party rhetoric in Germany has contributed to a reduction in levels of political participation within the German parties, it seems unlikely to have brought members' political (as opposed to purely social) activities down to the levels of the 1950s.

Britain

Accounts of British membership parties in the 1950s suggest that some of the lamentations for formerly active constituency parties may be inspired by a nostalgic misperception of what members used to do. This is precisely the trap Ralph Miliband warned against when he cautioned Labour Party members against believing in the 'myth of Labour's golden past'.[26] When Miliband wrote this in 1964 he was trying to debunk notions of the *1930s* as the time of ideal organizational strength. Today it is perhaps more appropriate to warn observers of British parties against mythologizing the early *1950s* as a golden age of party-based political participation.

Chapter 4 described how Conservative and Labour Party organizing advice throughout the past half-century has stressed that local parties should put their greatest efforts into campaign canvassing. In recent years, party organizers have begun to redefine the stated purposes of canvassing. They now urge local activists to pay more attention to the targeted delivery of the party message and less to mobilization on election day. Changes in the activity of local parties seem to parallel (and may even precede) this changing advice. There is some evidence that local parties are no longer canvassing as much as they used to, and there is much stronger evidence of a decline in parties' efforts to boost turn-out on election day.

Ever since 1952 British post-election surveys have asked respondents whether they were called upon by party representatives during the campaign (see Table 7.2). These surveys show that the pre-television elections were indeed different from those that followed: in the 1950s, Conservative and Labour canvassers each contacted about one third of voters at some point during the campaign (a little more for the Conservatives, a little less for Labour). In 1964, the year of the first election with full television coverage, there was a big decline in each party's rates of contacting citizens and these rates never again returned to 1950 levels. On the other hand, after this initial drop, the figures did not show any further long-term decline, even though other changes since 1964 (including greater personal mobility, an expanded electorate, increased leisure-opportunities, and an increase in participation by women in the labour force) have all made it more difficult for parties to find voters in their homes.[27] The same surveys suggest that local parties' efforts at election-day mobilization

TABLE 7.2. *Voters canvassed during election campaigns 1951–1987 (%)*

Year	Visited by any party	Visited by Conservative Party	Visited by Labour Party
1951	53	44	37
1955	44	34	28
1959	50	39	32
1964	38	25	23
1966	31	20	15
1970	40	28	18
1974 (Feb.)	17	—	—
1979	44	28	23
1983	(29)	(14)	(12)
1987	39	19	20

Source: Kevin Swaddle, 'Coping with a Mass Electorate' (doctoral dissertation, Oxford University, 1990). Swaddle notes that the figures for 1951 may be artificially high, and that the figures for 1983 were taken a week before polling-day instead of after the election, so that figures for this year are not strictly comparable with others in the table.

also declined abruptly in the 1960s. In 1987, for instance, when three parties campaigned actively, 85 per cent of respondents reported that no party representative had visited their households on election day, compared with 70 per cent in the basically two-party race of 1959 (see Table 7.3). Again, however, rates of campaigning seemed to have stabilized by the 1980s.

Direct indicators of members' campaign input, as well as more indirect indicators of campaign outputs, also warn against exaggerating the magnitude or the persistence of a decline in party members' activity during electoral campaigns. Post-election surveys from 1966 to 1992 consistently found the same small proportion of respondents reporting that they had canvassed or done other work for a candidate during the campaign (about 2 per cent; see Table 7.4). While the 1959 survey found a somewhat higher level of activity, it is not clear whether this single result should really be accepted as evidence that citizens were more active partisans in the 1950s, particularly since a 1963 survey found that only 3 per cent of respondents reported *ever* having participated in a general-election campaign. As early as 1951 one observer labelled as 'exaggerations' parties' claims that between 3 and 5 per cent of voters were active canvassers.[28] Conversely, surveys of party

TABLE 7.3. *Households visited by party representative on election day 1959–1987 (%)*

Year	Visited by Conservatives	Visited by Labour	Not visited
1959	18	18	70
1964	16	13	76
1974 (Feb.)	10	9	83
1974 (Oct.)	10	10	81
1979	8	7	86
1983	6	8	85
1987	6	7	85

Sources: For 1959–74, George Gallup (ed.), *The Gallup International Public Opinion Polls: Great Britain 1937–1975* (New York: Random House, 1976), 542, 764, 856, 1099, 1315, 1374; for 1979, Elizabeth Hann Hastings and Philip K. Hastings (eds.), *Index to International Public Opinion 1983–84* (Westport, Conn.: Greenwood Press, 1985), 321; for 1983–7, eid. (eds.), *Index to International Public Opinion 1987–88* (Westport, Conn.: Greenwood Press, 1989), 312.

TABLE 7.4. *Participation in election campaigns 1959–1992 (%)*

Year	Canvassing for candidate	Doing other work for candidate
1959	5	6
1964	3	8
1970	2	2
1974 (Feb.)	1	2
1974 (Oct.)	2	2
1979	2	3
1983	2	4
1987	2	2
1992	2	2

Sources: For 1959–74, George Gallup (ed.), *The Gallup International Public Opinion Polls: Great Britain 1937–1975* (New York: Random House, 1976), 542, 764, 856, 1099, 1315, 1374; for 1979, Elizabeth Hann Hastings and Philip K. Hastings (eds.), *Index to International Public Opinion 1983–84* (Westport, Conn.: Greenwood Press, 1985), 321; for 1983–7, eid. (eds.), *Index to International Public Opinion 1987–88* (Westport, Conn.: Greenwood Press, 1989), 312.

members in the late 1980s and early 1990s suggested that in this period local parties were neither hibernating nor fully mobilized at election times. About one third of Labour members and about one tenth of Conservative members claimed to have 'frequently' canvassed for their parties. Slightly more than half of the Labour Party members, and one fifth of the Conservative Party members, claimed to be 'frequent' deliverers of election leaflets.[29]

The early survey results are buttressed by case-studies which suggest that most British constituency parties have never been able to call on the services of more than a minority of party members during parliamentary campaigns. Reports from the 1950s usually show well-organized local campaigns enlisting between 10 and 20 per cent of constituency-party members as helpers, though a few places reported figures well above or below this average.[30] Rates of participation in contemporary constituency campaigns are strikingly similar. For instance, Conservative and Labour party campaigners from both 'marginal' and 'safe' seats estimated that between 10 and 30 per cent of members had helped in their local campaigns before the 1987 general election.[31] In addition, there have been recent suggestions that efforts by national parties to target resources on marginal seats may have produced something of a resurgence of campaigning in specific areas.[32]

This closer inspection of case-study and survey evidence thus suggests that analysts who emphasize declining membership activity in British constituency campaigning may actually be overstating the average amount of campaigning in the past, and may be understating the amount of local effort invested in recent constituency campaigns. In contrast, there is stronger evidence of a decline in members' involvement in certain areas of inter-election activity, particularly organizational maintenance and inward-oriented events. However, this decline seems to represent a small, rather than a dramatic, drop in parties' ability to mobilize members for political activity.

The biggest change in parties' inter-election activity has almost certainly been in the extent to which local parties provide a centre for members' social lives. A 1952 description of the Manchester Labour Party conveys some sense of the former social importance of party events:

Labour's local organization is built on its ward parties, which hold meetings each month, generally in a school, a community centre or a church hall. Most wards have many other activities, too: summer outings, a Labour League of Youth, a Women's Group, and social evenings, perhaps twice a week, with music, dancing and refreshments: Labour Party pamphlets are often on sale at meetings and many wards print a news-sheet which is distributed to members each month when their subscriptions are collected.[33]

A generation later one analyst was already lamenting the disappearance of this world:

In the not too distant past, where Labour was strong, the ward and constituency parties used to enter fully into the lives of ordinary people. The social functions once provided by Labour parties, and which were so important in binding people to the party, have now all but disappeared.[34]

However, a word of caution is in order regarding both these views of party life in the 'golden past'. Even the author who painted the rosy picture of Manchester's Labour Party in its post-1945 heyday did not suggest that most members took advantage of these activities; instead, he noted that only between five and thirty-five of the 'several hundred' subscribing members in each ward attended monthly ward meetings.[35] Other evidence suggests that this was not an isolated occurrence; although in the past many more members may have been touched by local parties' social networks, the number of members participating in explicitly political activities between elections may have been relatively low throughout the post-1945 period.

Case-studies of Labour and Conservative branches in the 1950s suggest that the proportion of politically active members has changed little since this time. In the 1950s both Conservative and Labour parties could apparently expect between 5 and 15 per cent of their members to attend the regular (usually monthly) branch-party meetings.[36] Indeed, McKenzie estimated in 1955 that only 1 to 5 per cent of Labour Party members were 'continually active in party affairs between elections', although he believed that the portion was higher in the Conservative Party.[37]

Given these figures, it is not surprising to learn that complaints about shortages of active members are not new. McKenzie commented in the mid-1950s that few Labour constituencies had enough volunteers to organize a complete network of 'street collectors'; similarly, a 1967 Labour Party report confirmed his observation when it declared '[t]he truth is that there were always difficulties in finding sufficient collectors and it is becoming increasingly difficult to do so'.[38] Surveys conducted by Conservative Central Office in 1950 and 1951 did find that nearly all of this party's constituency associations in three southern counties maintained good networks of subscription collectors and leaflet deliverers. However, only a few years later a broader survey concluded that very few Conservative constituencies had sufficient volunteers actually to operate collection and delivery networks.[39] The situation for local parties did not improve, and many accounts of British politics from the 1960s emphasized the very small proportion of Conservative or Labour Party members who actually attended meetings or helped with party tasks.[40]

These low figures on membership participation in party activities put a different perspective on reports of limited local activism in the 1980s and 1990s. A survey of Labour Party members in 1989 found that 50 per cent of them gave no time to the party each month, but that 30 per cent did indeed devote a few hours a month to the party, and that 18 per cent devoted more than five hours; the latter figure was slightly higher than the proportion who held an elected position within the party. Furthermore, as many as half of the respondents to this survey noted that they 'occasionally' or 'frequently' attended Labour Party meetings.[41] In other interviews conducted in the late 1980s, leaders of local Labour Party branches estimated that between 5 and 20 per cent of members attended regular branch-party meetings; if anything, this was higher than the range reported in case-studies from the 1950s.[42] Of course, the proportion of active members may have increased as a result of declining membership, particularly because changes in the Labour Party's enrolment procedures may have reduced the number of members who are enrolled as a by-product of their membership in a social club or lottery scheme.[43] But this may not be the entire story, because some observers of the Labour Party had identified a trend towards increased activity by members even before the change in membership rules.[44] Whatever the explanation, in 1988 the Labour Party's director of organization optimistically claimed to find just such an increase in activity: 'It used to be supposed that only 10% of Party members were activists [but] the impression is that the level has increased. It would now appear that less people are being more active'.[45]

Even in the mid-1990s the Conservative Party could still claim roughly three times as many members as the Labour Party, but this party did not gain a proportionate boost in labour benefits. Given the lower barriers to Conservative Party membership, it is perhaps not surprising to find that members of this party are much less active than their Labour counterparts. In a 1992 survey of Conservative party members more than three-quarters of respondents reported that they usually gave no time whatsoever to party activities; only 8 per cent reported spending more than five hours a month on party business. The survey even revealed a slight decline in the activities of the ageing Conservative membership, which was a reduction from already very low levels.[46]

In the British parties the introduction of new methods of collecting dues may have coincided with, and hastened, the decline in the numbers of members who are involved in inward-oriented inter-election activities. In contrast, the proportion, and perhaps even the number, of British party members involved in outward-oriented political activity may actually have increased since the 1950s. Such a change seems particularly clear in the Conservative Party, which fielded an increasing number of party candidates for local-government seats. In the early 1970s local-government reorganization and the Conservative Party's more partisan commitment to local government, both helped reduce the number of uncontested local-government seats from more than one half to under one tenth of available seats. This change was only possible because more party members became involved in local-government work, both as candidates and as campaigners.[47] To contest these seats, local parties usually recruited from an inner core of existing activists; however, nomination as a local-government candidate also frequently drew less active members into assuming bigger roles in party and community life. In 1989 6 per cent of Labour Party members held seats on local councils, and 13 per cent of members described themselves as having occasionally or frequently stood for some level of public office. (In addition, 15 per cent said they had served as appointed members of policy advisory boards, such as school boards or health authorities.)[48] In the larger Conservative Party, 5 per cent of members had 'occasionally' or 'frequently' stood for public office.[49]

There are few clues about whether British local parties have increased other types of community-outreach work between parliamentary elections. As noted in Chapter 5, in the 1980s the national parties began urging local-party activists to produce newsletters, contact non-partisan groups, and increase constituency-service work. However, it is hard to judge the extent to which local parties heeded this advice. The British national parties do not disclose (and probably do not have) figures on newsletter production. One study of local councillors in eighteen areas in the early 1980s found that only 6 per cent of the Conservative councillors, and only 9 per cent of the Labour councillors, were sending regular newsletters to constituents; in contrast, 88 per cent of their Liberal counterparts were distributing newsletters.[50] On the other hand, interviews conducted in the late 1980s suggested that by the end of the decade such newsletters had become much more common, and were indeed almost standard in the most active Conservative and Labour branches.[51] In any case, for the Conservative and Labour Parties these newsletters were a new tool of year-round campaigning; as a result, even low levels of production represent an increase in this type of activity.

All the indicators show that today only a minority of British party members participate in either the campaign or inter-election activities of their local parties. What is less clear is whether these low levels of political activity represent a decline in member activity. This section has emphasized studies from the 1950s and early 1960s which show that rates of political participation in British parties were already very low before television became a principal channel of politics and a main competitor for citizens' leisure time. Such findings suggest that a 1961 description of post-war politics in Newcastle-under-Lyme might well be generally valid for Britain as a whole:

[I]f there is any evidence for the belief that Newcastle politics has been conducted by 'mass parties' it must spring from the period between 1943 and 1951, though in retrospect these years may seem an episode brought about by exceptional causes rather than as a stage in party development.[52]

Or, as another commentator wrote in 1975:

In all political parties, the decline since the extraordinary postwar peak should be seen in the context of participation levels in the twenties and thirties which were surprisingly low. Today, most local parties are indeed run by a handful of activists. Mass participation in electoral politics in Britain was something of a nine-year wonder (1944 to 1953, to be precise).[53]

THE MYTH OF THE BLIGHTED PRESENT?

A closer look at the British and German parties in the 1950s and early 1960s thus casts some doubts on the proposition that party members provide drastically reduced benefits for their parties in the contemporary era of televised politics and publicly subsidized campaigns. For all four parties, eroding levels of membership have recently devalued the legitimacy dividends that figures on party enrolment once provided. This is true even in the German parties, where membership levels are still far above historic lows. On the other hand, however, all four debt-plagued parties continue to rely on their members' financial contributions because they provide a stable source of income and an untainted source of party revenue. Furthermore, the parties continue to profit from their members' volunteer efforts both inside and outside the sphere of the local party. In all four parties, members' involvement in inward-oriented party activities has almost certainly declined in this period, but it seems likely that a higher proportion of members are now involved in local government and in community-outreach activities.

Such a conclusion about the continuing contributions of locally organized members suggests that national organizers' attempts to shift the focus of local parties' activity have not all been in vain. Changing strategies have helped to produce visible changes in what local parties and members of local parties are actually doing. While new campaign and communications techniques may have made members' efforts relatively less important in some fields, these innovations have not significantly diminished members' absolute contributions of energy and money, and they have not replaced party members as a source of democratic legitimacy. For all the above-named reasons, the preceding accounts of changing practices in the British and German local parties suggest that assessments of organizational change within parties may need to begin by accepting that it is fruitless to search for a 'golden past' of membership parties within the second half of the twentieth century.

8

The Changing Nature of Membership Parties

> The miscellaneous facts which hitherto have been disdain-
> fully thrown into the rubbish-heap of history and of the
> political news of the day have enabled me to rise step by
> step into the highest generalizations of political speculation
> and of the political art.
>
> Mosei Ostrogorski[1]

OSTROGORSKI'S immodest preferatory claim inaugurated a tradition of analysis of party organization which is now more than a
century old. Since Ostrogorski gathered his observations about
British and American parties, succeeding generations of scholars
have repeatedly validated his claim that studying the organizational development of parties provides a solid basis for 'the highest generalizations' about broader political trends. Many such
studies, including Ostrogorski's own, continue to provide useful
insights into past political practices even if their broadest conclusions have not always stood the test of time.

The present book clearly follows down the path marked by
Ostrogorski. Through the careful examination of the 'miscella-
neous facts' which reveal party organizers' plans, this study has
shown how it is possible to enrich current debates about 'party
decline' and 'party transformation' by adding a better understanding of why parties have enrolled members. Instead of merely
attributing motives to party planners, the preceding chapters have
taken seriously leaders' own interpretations of the challenges they
face, and of the tasks their organizations must master. As a result,
these accounts have been able to show how calculations about the
costs and benefits of membership enrolment have led party
leaders to endorse the structural and procedural reform of membership organizations. By providing an accurate picture of the
earlier organizational characteristics of four membership parties

in previous eras, and by carefully observing alterations in the parties' definitions and uses of membership, these chapters have been able to give a nuanced depiction of how and why relations between parties and members have been changing in the present.

Now, in this concluding chapter, it is time to redeem an earlier pledge to show how the dimensions introduced in the second chapter can be used as tools for describing and comparing patterns of organizational change within parties. After first using the three dimensions to assess developments within the German and British parties, the chapter will then re-examine some recent predictions about the future(s) of democratic party organizations in light of experiences within these parties.

ORGANIZATIONAL CONVERGENCE IN GERMANY AND BRITAIN?

The organizational dimensions introduced in Chapter 2 (inclusiveness, centralization, and mediation) were chosen in part because they describe aspects of relations between parties and members which are completely or mostly within the control of the parties themselves. This property makes it easier to ask whether, despite their different organizational traditions and environmental constraints, the four German and British parties have moved in similar directions as they seek to increase the benefits they gain, or minimize the costs they incur, from enrolling party members. Focusing on the direction of change makes it possible to draw some preliminary conclusions about patterns of development without the need precisely to locate each party's initial position.

The CDU, the SPD, and the Labour Party

Figures 8.1–8.4 depict the direction of movement along each of the dimensions by showing the parties' approximate positions at three points in time. These times—1953, 1973, and 1993—span the four decades of organizational development which were discussed in previous chapters. The schematic summaries of organizational changes in the German and British parties show clear similarities between three of the four parties. During the most recent period the two German parties and the British Labour Party each became

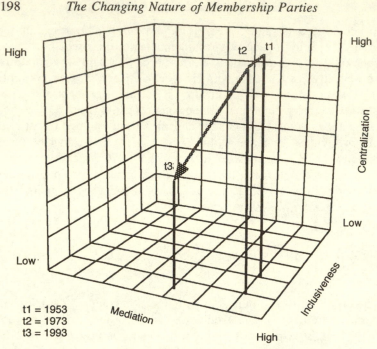

FIG. 8.1. SPD: Organizational change 1953–1993

more inclusive, less centralized, and less mediated in terms of relations between national party leaders and individual party members. This pattern raises the obvious question, to be discussed in a moment, of why the Conservative Party was different. First, however, it is necessary to explain the placement of the parties along the three dimensions.

Inclusiveness

The dimension of inclusiveness refers to the extent to which parties use privileges and obligations to distinguish members from other supporters. Placement along this dimension shows how widely a party extends the privileges that are within its control: are they given only to party officials or party activists, are they available to all enrolled party members, or does the party offer its privileges even to those who are outside the circle of party members? Figures 8.1–8.3 show that the two German parties and the Labour Party all

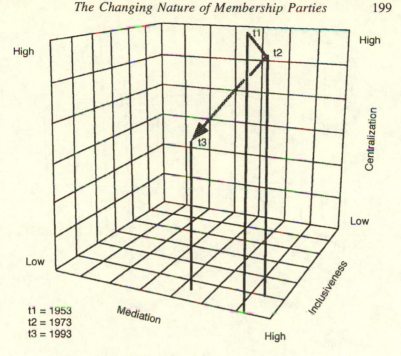

F<small>IG</small>. 8.2. CDU: Organizational change 1953–1993

became more inclusive after 1973. Much of this change occurred after the beginning of the 1980s, when national organizers in all three parties began urging party activists to make the local parties more open to participation by non-members, and when they introduced new procedures which made membership much easier to obtain. In Germany, CDU and SPD organizers further encouraged local parties to make the boundaries between members and non-members more porous with respect to recruiting candidates. In the Labour Party, reducing perceived barriers to membership was one of the avowed reasons for establishing the party's new system of national membership in the late 1980s. This commitment to making individual membership more accessible also led the party to make it less expensive, and less procedurally difficult, for indirect members to enrol as direct members. This trend of increasing inclusiveness was strong, but it also had clear limits; most importantly, all three parties continued to exclude non-members from participating in intra-party votes.

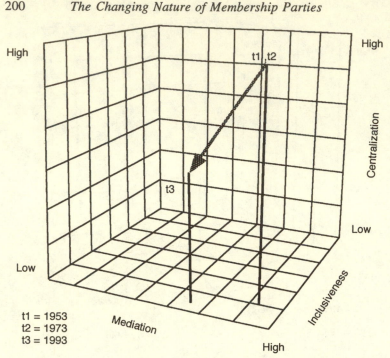

Fig. 8.3. Labour Party: Organizational change 1953–1993

From 1973 to 1993 all three parties moved towards greater inclusiveness. Looking back to the 1950s, however, one sees a slightly different picture. In the 1980s the CDU was moving in the direction of some of the practices of its first decades, when local parties routinely called upon non-members to stand as local-government candidates, and when requirements for CDU membership were much looser. Recent moves towards greater inclusiveness in the CDU represent a reversal of the party's 1960s trend towards more strictly defined membership.

As was discussed in Chapter 6, the parties' efforts to lower their membership barriers were prompted by two complementary assessments of the primary organizational challenges facing parties at the end of the century. First, they reflected party organizers' increased appreciation of the legitimacy and outreach benefits provided by what were formerly thought of as 'inactive' members. Second, they reflected party organizers' conviction that it was

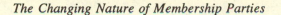

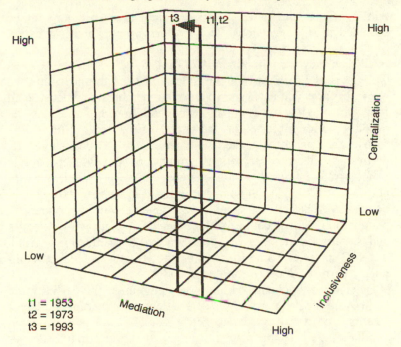

Fig. 8.4. Conservative Party: Organizational change 1953–1993

becoming increasingly difficult to attract any members. Strategists in all three parties thus endorsed increasing inclusiveness as a means to rebuild membership as an electoral resource.

Centralization

At the same time that these parties moved to make their membership rules and procedures more inclusive, they also took steps to decentralize formal control in several important areas of decision-making. In all three parties, the most striking of the recent organizational changes has been the devolution of formal control over candidate selection. Statute changes to this effect have been promoted by party leaders and backed by party conferences. As a result, leaders of local and regional parties and delegates to party conferences are now encouraged or required to surrender their exclusive formal control over selecting candidates for party and public offices; the parties' entire memberships are now to be included in such decisions. These reforms, described in Chapter 6, have made all three contemporary parties much more decentralized than they were in either 1973 or 1953.

Because the main task of this study has been to understand the purposes for which parties have enrolled members, and because all four parties view their constituency and branch parties as the primary building-blocks of the membership organizations, the focus here has not extended to examining the roles played by parties' ancillary organizations (subgroups for women, young people, trade unionists, senior citizens, etc). However, it is worth noting that if the current consideration did include such organizations, the SPD at least would show an even more pronounced picture of recent decentralization. Indeed, the growing strength and statutory privileges of special-interest organizations within the SPD have led some to describe the structure of the contemporary party as 'loosely coupled anarchy'.[2]

Decentralizing changes, like those which made the parties more inclusive, reflected party organizers' attempts to manipulate membership incentives in order to get higher electoral pay-offs from maintaining a party membership. In expanding intra-party democracy, organizers tried simultaneously to boost the attractiveness of party membership and to enhance the legitimacy benefits parties reaped from enrolling their supporters.

Mediation

Finally, all three parties have recently moved in the direction of decreasing levels of mediation between national party élites and enrolled party supporters. The dimension of mediation describes the directness of contacts between individual party members and those who lead the national party. Location upon this dimension depends on the extent to which communication between the top and bottom levels of the party flows through intermediary levels. In recent years, initiatives originating at the top levels of all three parties have had the intended effect of decreasing mediation in intra-party communication. For instance, since 1973 all three parties have created, or at least made expanded use of, central files of members' names and addresses. All three parties have used these address files to send new or reformatted magazines to their entire memberships. The parties' headquarters have used the magazines primarily for top-down communications, but occasionally also to encourage communication in the other direction.[3] In the 1980s and early 1990s, the German parties, like the Labour Party, experimented with another form of direct communication with members: directly contacting individual members to request financial support for national projects, instead of relying on branch-party leaders or on dues collectors to make special fundraising appeals on behalf of the national party.

In decreasing the mediation of relations between central leaders and individual members, parties have taken a significant step away from the hierarchical relations which characterized Duverger's mass/branch model. Duverger's parties were tree-like structures in which the small branches were indirectly joined to the central trunk by intermediary structures (constituency, regional, or state parties); central party leaders relied on these intermediary structures to distribute messages to party supporters. In contrast, today's central party leaders have turned to more efficient, and more reliable, channels for maintaining contacts with enrolled supporters. They have supplemented or bypassed the traditional hierarchical structures in order to communicate directly with members. Messages from the national party are particularly aimed at the many members who have little interest in the activities of local parties or in local political issues, but who instead join a party in order to express national political loyalties.

Decreasing mediation has helped the parties in at least two ways. To begin with, it has provided central party leaders with the means to ensure that non-activist members are regularly contacted by their parties. This was considered to be important because as party organizers became more impressed by the value of the support 'inactive members' could provide, they also became more concerned to ensure that such members had ready access to at least some of the benefits of membership. In addition, decreasing mediation has enabled party leaders to boost the benefits (especially the financial benefits) central parties receive from their membership organizations.

Plotting the direction of party-led efforts at organizational change shows that at least since 1973 three of the four parties have reacted to similar social and technological changes by trying to move party structures and practices in similar directions. In this period, the parties' leaders have introduced or supported initiatives designed to create greater opportunities for direct communication between party headquarters and party members, to create new opportunities for all members to participate in party decision-making, and to lower the barriers which separate members from non-member supporters. Significantly, these similarities emerged in spite of the parties' different ideological and organizational traditions, and in spite of the different institutional environments within which they have competed.

Examining the parties' organizational development at three points in time also makes clear that change is not necessarily either steady or unidirectional. Thus, as CDU leaders in the 1990s exhorted local-party associations to make membership more inclusive, and to nominate more non-party candidates, they were moving the party back towards its incarnation of the 1950s, when it was a more loosely organized party of local notables. Such a reversal in the direction of organizational development is not surprising, because organizational strategies are judged more in terms of their electoral pay-offs than in terms of their novelty or their internal consistency. This mutability is the reason why looking at developments in several periods, instead of just sketching 'before' and 'after' portraits, provides a much better picture of change as an ongoing process.

The Conservative Party

The Conservative Party has stayed conspicuously aloof from many of the trends described above. Indeed, what is striking about the pattern shown in Figure 8.4 is how little this party has moved along any of the organizational dimensions. This idiosyncrasy is more difficult to interpret than the convergence found among the other three parties.

One way partially to account for the Conservative Party's organizational stasis is to argue that this party has had relatively less need to experiment with new methods of winning electoral support. From 1953 to 1993 the Conservative Party was never out of government for more than six consecutive years; indeed, between 1979 and 1992 the party won four consecutive general elections. Even the very successful CDU cannot match this record, because after 1969 the CDU spent thirteen years outside the federal government. If electoral defeat is indeed an important catalyst for organizational reform, it may be premature to draw conclusions about the anomalousness of organizational trends in the Conservative Party. Such judgements should be postponed until some possible future date, if the party ever suffers a sustained series of decisive defeats.

Another way to explain the Conservative Party's immobility on the dimensions of inclusiveness and mediation is to shift the focus away from the direction of organizational movement, and to look instead at its relative location on the organizational dimensions. Even the roughest attempts to place the four parties in relation to one another would undoubtedly suggest the conclusion that one reason that the Conservative Party changed less than the others was because in 1953 it already displayed many of the organizational characteristics that its counterparts only subsequently acquired. For instance, the Conservative Party has always had very inclusive membership policies. It has never had standardized procedures for enrolment, but has instead always permitted local associations to make their own decisions about which supporters should be counted as party members. Local parties have even been able to include on their membership rosters some individuals (casual donors, spouses of those who belong to 'Conservative Clubs') who might not readily describe themselves as party members. Although the other three parties have become more inclusive, the Conservative Party, with its lack of fixed membership dues or of formal enrolment procedures, remains the most inclusive of all the parties.

Given this tradition of inclusiveness, Conservative Party leaders have never been able to rely primarily on mediating party structures to communicate with members. This situation has changed little over the past half century. The party did slightly increase its direct communication with members when it started publishing a membership magazine at the beginning of the 1970s; however, the magazine's circulation is limited to those who pay for a subscription. Indeed, even if it wanted to, the party's Central Office would not be able to send publications to all party members, because it still lacks a complete membership roster. On the other hand, in some ways the party has always been relatively unmediated. Its leaders have never communicated through party channels to the same extent as have the parties of the left in both countries. Local

Conservative associations have generally been more concerned to offer members congenial events than to provide them with political education or with opportunities for sending dissenting messages to party leaders. Instead of sending their messages primarily via association and branch chairs, Conservative leaders have customarily used mass media outlets to communicate with party members and other supporters. Today they can still rely on friendly newspaper editors to publicize their messages. In short, one explanation of why the Conservative Party has not moved in the same ways as the other three parties is that on two of the organizational dimensions the Conservatives started out much closer to the points towards which the other parties were moving.

Does this suggest that the British Conservative Party should be regarded as a kind of organizational model for the other three parties, or for parties in other parliamentary democracies? Put this way, the suggestion is unusual, yet just such a conclusion seems to be implied by several recent discussions of trends in the organizational development of parties. For instance, the contemporary Conservative Party seems to manifest many of the traits which Katz and Mair have identified as being increasingly characteristic of European parties. According to these authors, many party organizations manifest both an increasing dominance of their public-office 'face', and a diminishing independence of their professional apparatus. At the same time, many parties show signs of an ongoing weakening of both the formal and the sentimental ties which once bound national leaders to their locally organized supporters.[4] The Katz and Mair account of trends in party development seems perfectly to describe the organization of the British Conservative Party throughout the past half-century: it is a party which has been led by the parliamentary leadership; it is a party in which Central Office has been the servant of the party's parliamentary leader; it is a party which has always maintained a formal decoupling between party members and the party's parliamentary leadership.

Peter Radunski is a German commentator/practitioner who could also have been thinking of the British Conservative Party when he wrote a recent description of developments in German parties. Radunski, who was earlier encountered in these pages as one of the CDU's organizational experts, lost his long-time job in party headquarters after Kohl removed Heiner Geißler from the party's top organizational spot in 1989. In a 1991 article on party development, he renounced his earlier vision of the 'modern people's party', a vision which he had done much to promote while still employed by the party headquarters. By 1991 Radunski was an elected member of the Berlin Senate, and from this new vantage-point he argued that German parties should embrace their inevitable fate of becoming parties dominated by members of the (federal and state) parliamentary parties. Radunski portrayed this transition as desirable, because legislators are the most legitimate representatives of parties in that they hold a popularly elected mandate, and because they are also generally more competent to speak on policy issues and to make strategic decisions than are those who head the party's non-elected bureaucracy.[5] This vision of the future for German parties is in many respects a good description of the contemporary British Conservative Party, which is likewise dominated by members of its parliamentary delegation.

Yet, although these models imply that the Conservative Party fits a pattern which will be more widely imitated, in one very important way these models seem inappropriate for describing the direction in which at least some parties are heading. The other parties studied here have increasingly diverged from the Conservative Party on the dimension of centralization. In the 1990s the Conservative Party still retained its nineteenth-century structure, which formally separates the party's leader and its professional employees from the membership organization. Given the traditionally high centralization of Conservative Party decision-making, the party's anomalous lack of movement on this dimension can hardly be portrayed as the result of its relative progressiveness. Rather, stasis on this dimension should be explained as the result of two sets of calculations: party organizers have not believed that Conservative members are clamouring for intra-party democracy, nor have they thought it likely that the introduction of such reforms would enhance the party's electoral chances. Under these circumstances, and in the midst of a long period of Conservative election victories, party leaders have had no incentives to surrender real or even symbolic control.

It would, however, be incorrect to suggest that there is either a necessity or a permanence in Conservative Party resistance to shared decision-making. Indeed, one of the broader lessons of these accounts is that party organizers have repeatedly looked to other parties, and to other professions, for ideas about how to define, and how to alter, organizational strategies. There is thus no reason to think that the Conservatives should be permanently immune to the pressures which have prompted leaders of other parties to endorse greater member-democracy. If decentralization were to yield big electoral dividends for the parties which pursue this course, it would not be surprising someday to find the Conservative Party adopting at least symbolic changes in the name of intra-party democracy.

This perspective on organizational change, which emphasizes the frequency and deliberateness of adaptation by imitation, points to two conclusions about the nature of party development. First, it makes clear that, while organizational convergence is facilitated by shared technological opportunities, it is not *caused* by technological change. As they attempt to take advantage of new technologies, party organizers innovate as well as imitate. Indeed, parties may even return to old methods if strategists decide that new technologies are insufficient or ineffective. Second, because this perspective assumes that cross-party and cross-national imitation is common, it suggests that it would be misleading to view organizational similarities within a single country as being merely the legacy of national institutions or organizing traditions. Instead, they should also be seen as the result of deliberate choices to adopt what is, or seems to be, electorally effective. As such, they are likely to be altered whenever new practices come to be seen as more effective.

DEMOCRATIZATION AND THE FUTURE OF MEMBERSHIP PARTIES

This study's investigation of changing ideas about the utility of members has shown the increasing extent to which party leaders and organizers have viewed members as a resource for bolstering party legitimacy, instead of merely as a source of funds or of campaign volunteers. An expanded understanding of the work and worth of members has prompted parties to continue to expend resources on enlisting supporters even if they have ready access to public funding and mass media exposure. Although overall membership totals have declined in recent years in each of the four parties studied here, the parties' reactions to these changes do not conform to a picture of party leaders impatiently trying to hasten the arrival of a future dominated by parties without foot-soldiers.

In short, even if contemporary membership parties are not in the best of health, reports of their death—like reports of their earlier health—have been greatly exaggerated. Of course, to say this is not to say that they will never die: membership parties may disappear in spite of determined efforts to save them. Yet, even if these rescue efforts fail, the form of these attempts may themselves be of interest, because they may ultimately leave a heavy imprint on wider political processes and outputs. Thus, the decentralization of decision-making in the German parties and in the Labour Party, which was noted above and described in more detail in Chapter 6, may not reverse membership losses in any of these parties. It may, however, have a lasting impact outside the parties through its contribution to reshaping citizens' expectations about appropriate roles for leaders and individuals in the processes of political decision-making.

For membership parties, the potential risk of intra-party democratization is that it creates a momentum which is hard to stop and even harder to reverse. If initial efforts in this direction do not stabilize turn-out levels or quell disaffection with established political alternatives, the leaders of losing parties may be tempted to go further in pursuit of their own rhetorical commitment to popular participation. Instituting either open primaries, or closed primaries where the barriers to entry are very low, would be a radical response, but it is a change which could easily be implemented in many countries. Often, the nomination of candidates and the selection of party leaders have remained the special domain of party members not because of legal or constitutional requirements, but rather because of the expectations jointly fostered by all major parties. Currently it is customary for parties in parliamentary democracies to exclude non-members from candidate selection, and such traditions inhibit or block popular demands for broader participation in this initial electoral stage. However, such coalitions of expectations are vulnerable to defection; the dynamics of competitive outbidding may be difficult to control wherever a single party can gain electoral rewards by attacking the existing mechanisms of candidate-selection as procedures which entrench unloved political élites. Indeed, in such situations cartel parties in the Katz and Mair sense may encounter unexpected difficulties, because by definition these are some of the most entrenched actors in a political system.

So far, however, the trend noted in these parties has been towards a kind of intra-party democratization which strengthens the value of members, not towards American-style reforms which blur distinctions between members and other supporters. Organizers in all four parties studied here (even the very inclusive Conservative Party) have recognized that the best way to preserve the attractiveness of membership is to exclude non-members from the most distinctive of the membership privileges—namely, the right to influence personnel decisions. Indeed, in the 1990s the Labour Party tried to increase the value of its privileges for direct members when it excluded affiliated members from voting in local-party candidate selection. Such party-administered closed primaries ensure that the distinction between members and other supporters remains a meaningful one.

As long as British and German party leaders continue to find advantages in paying the costs of enrolling members, the meaning of party membership, and the structures of membership organization, will remain very different from their equivalents in either of the major parties in the United States. It is clear, however, that in responding to voters' apparent interest in symbolic democratization, and to members' apparent interest in meaningful opportunities for participation, the parties are transforming themselves into something quite different from the hierarchical and disciplined mass/branch parties which Duverger described.

This book's discussion of changing relations between parties and their members has thus come full circle from the first chapter, which began with Ostrogorski's dire predictions that newly emerging party organizations would deprive citizens of their political independence. Instead of finding parties in which leaders foster membership organization as a way of gaining better influence over supporters' behaviour, the current investigation has found parties whose leaders are promoting organizational reforms as a way of giving members greater influence over party behaviour. Over the long term, such attempts to rebalance relations between parties and their members could radically alter democratic processes not only within single parties, but also within entire political systems. This is one of the many reasons why the study of membership parties retains its relevance more than a century after Ostrogorski inaugurated the field.

Notes

1. PARTY MEMBERS AND PARTY ORGANIZATION

1. Peter Mair, 'Continuity, Change, and the Vulnerability of Party', *West European Politics*, 12/4 (1989), 180.
2. e.g. scholars writing in the German legal tradition, such as Johann Bluntschli in *Charakter und Geist der politischen Parteien* (Nördlingen: Beckschen Buchhandlung, 1869).
3. Mosei Ostrogorski, *Democracy and the Organization of Political Parties*, trans. Frederick Clarke, ed. Seymour Lipset (Chicago: Quadrangle Books, 1964), 346.
4. Stefano Bartolini, 'The Membership of Mass Parties: The Social Democratic Experience, 1889–1978', in Hans Daalder and Peter Mair (eds.), *Western European Party Systems: Continuity and Change* (Beverly Hills, Calif.: Sage Publications, 1983), 183.
5. Sigmund Neumann, *Die Parteien der Weimarer Republik* (Stuttgart: Kohlhammer Verlag, 1965). Orig. pub. in 1932 as *Die politischen Parteien in Deutschland*. In 1956 Neumann published the better-known English elaboration of this argument in 'Toward a Comparative Study of Political Parties', in Sigmund Neumann (ed.), *Modern Political Parties: A Comparative Approach* (Chicago: University of Chicago Press, 1956).
6. Indeed, Duverger speculated that imitation of socialist-style parties might be over, and that totalitarian parties were the real model of the future. Maurice Duverger, *Political Parties: Their Organization and Activity in the Modern State*, trans. Barbara and Robert North (New York: John Wiley & Sons, 1955).
7. Otto Kirchheimer, 'The Transformation of the Western European Party Systems', in Joseph LaPalombara and Myron Weiner (eds.), *Political Parties and Political Development* (Princeton: Princeton University Press, 1966), ch. 3.
8. Most notably John May, 'Opinion Structure of Political Parties: The Special Law of Curvilinear Disparity', *Political Studies*, 21 (1973), 135–51.
9. This is what Baer refers to as the truncated party model. Denise Baer,

'Who Has the Body? Party Institutionalization and Theories of Party Organization', *American Review of Politics*, 14 (1993), 1–38.

10. Robert McKenzie, *British Political Parties* (Melbourne: William Heinemann, 1955), 591.

11. Leon Epstein, 'Political Parties in Western Democratic Systems', in Roy Macridis (ed.), *Political Parties: Contemporary Trends and Ideas* (New York: Harper & Row, 1967), 148.

12. Ibid.

13. See e.g.: Ian Ward, 'The Changing Organisational Nature of Australia's Political Parties', *Journal of Commonwealth and Comparative Politics*, 29/2 (1991), 153–74; Derek Urwin, 'Norway: Parties between Mass Membership and Consumer-Oriented Professionalism?', in Alan Ware (ed.), *Political Parties: Electoral Change and Structural Response* (Oxford: Basil Blackwell, 1987); Khayyam Zev Paltiel, 'Political Marketing, Party Finance, and the Decline of Canadian Parties', in Alain Gagnon and Brian Tanguay (eds.), *Canadian Parties in Transition: Discourse, Organization, and Representation* (Scarborough: Nelson Canada, 1989); John Meisel, 'The Decline of Party in Canada', in Hugh Thorburn (ed.), *Party Politics in Canada*, 5th edn. (Scarborough: Prentice-Hall Canada, 1985).

14. Hiltrud Naßmacher, 'Die Parteien der Bundesrepublik im Umbau', *Der Bürger im Staat*, 39/4 (1989); Bartolini, 'The Membership of Mass Parties'; Kurt Luther, 'Consociationalism, Parties and the Party System', in id. and Wolfgang Müller (eds.), *Politics in Austria: Still a Case of Consociationalism?* (London: Frank Cass, 1992).

15. Richard Katz, 'Party as Linkage: A Vestigial Function?', *European Journal of Political Research*, 18 (1990), 145–6. Angelo Panebianco, *Political Parties: Organization and Power*, trans. Marc Silver (Cambridge: Cambridge University Press, 1988), 264 ff. See also Richard Katz and Peter Mair, 'The Evolution of Party Organizations in Europe: The Three Faces of Party Organization', *American Review of Politics*, 14 (1993), 593–617.

16. Mark Franklin, Thomas Mackie, and Henry Valen, *Electoral Change* (Cambridge: Cambridge University Press, 1992), pt. 3.

17. Katz, 'Parties as Linkage', 144–5.

18. Leon Epstein, *Political Parties in Western Democracies*, 2nd edn. (New Brunswick: Transaction Books, 1980), 375.

19. Klaus von Beyme, *Parteien in westlichen Demokratien* (Munich: Piper, 1982), 208.

20. Alan Ware, 'Activist–Leader Relations and the Structure of Political Parties: "Exchange" Models and Vote-Seeking Behaviour in Parties', *British Journal of Political Science*, 22 (1992), 71–92.

21. Alistair Cole (ed.), *French Political Parties in Transition* (Aldershot:

Dartmouth, 1990); John Frears, *Parties and Voters in France* (London: St Martin's Press, 1991); Frank Wilson, *French Political Parties under the Fifth Republic* (New York: Praeger Publishers, 1982); Colette Ysmal, *Les Partis politiques sous la Ve République* (Paris: Montchrestien, 1989).

22. These countries included Norway and Canada, which had elsewhere been cited as examples of the decline of membership parties. Jan Sundberg, 'Exploring the Basis of Declining Party Membership in Denmark: A Scandinavian Comparison', *Scandinavian Political Studies*, 10/1 (1987), 17–38; Harold Angell, 'Duverger, Epstein, and the Problem of the Mass Party', *Canadian Journal of Political Science*, 20 (1987), 363–78.

23. Anthony King, 'Political Parties in Western Democracies: Some Sceptical Reflections', *Polity*, 2 (1969), 119.

24. Richard Rose, *Do Parties Make a Difference?* (London: Macmillan, 1980).

25. See e.g. the essays in Frances Castles (ed.), *The Impact of Parties* (London: Sage Publications, 1982); Ian Budge and Hans Keman, *Parties and Democracy* (Oxford: Oxford University Press, 1990); Anthony King, 'What do Elections Decide?', in David Butler, Howard Penniman, and Austin Ranney (eds.), *Democracy at the Polls* (Washington: American Enterprise Institute, 1981).

26. For more on their differences, see 'Roberto Michels and Max Weber: Moral Conviction versus the Politics of Responsibility', in Wolfgang Mommsen, *The Political and Social Thought of Max Weber* (Chicago: University of Chicago Press, 1989).

27. Caps. in original. Robert Michels, *Political Parties*, trans. Eden and Cedar Paul (New York: Dover Publications, 1959), 401.

28. Max Weber, *Staatssoziologie*, ed. Johannes Winckelmann (Berlin: Duncker & Humblot, 1966), 51–84; Ilse Dronberger, *The Political Thought of Max Weber* (New York: Appleton-Century-Crofts, 1971), 84 ff.

29. May, 'Opinion Structure of Political Parties', 135–51. James Bryce made a similar observation fifty years before May: James Bryce, *Modern Democracies*, 2 vols. (New York: Macmillan, 1921), i. 126.

30. For one recent effort to show the electoral effects of party organization in Britain, and for a good bibliog. of earlier studies in Britain and the United States, see Paul Whitely and Patrick Seyd, 'Labour's Vote and Local Activism: The Impact of Constituency Campaigns', *Parliamentary Affairs*, 45 (1992), 582–95. See also Charles Pattie, Paul Whitely, Ron Johnston, and Patrick Seyd, 'Measuring Local Campaign Effects: Labour Party Constituency Campaigning at the 1987 General Election', *Political Studies*, 42 (1994), 469–79; and David

Denver and Gordon Hands, 'Constituency Campaigning', *Parliamentary Affairs*, 45 (1992), 528–44.

31. Ostrogorksi, *Democracy and the Organization of Political Parties*, 304.

32. See e.g. Benjamin Barber, *Strong Democracy* (Berkeley and Los Angeles: University of California Press, 1984), 205 ff.

33. Neumann, 'Toward a Comparative Study of Political Parties'.

34. Mair, 'Continuity, Change and the Vulnerability of Party', 168–87.

35. Sidney Verba, Norman Nie, and Jae-On Kim, *Participation and Political Equality* (Cambridge: Cambridge University Press, 1978), 155.

36. Geraint Parry, George Moyser, and Neil Day, *Political Participation and Democracy in Britain* (Cambridge: Cambridge University Press, 1992), 288–90.

37. A similar distinction is developed by Ruud Koole in *De Opkomst van de Moderne Kaderpartij: Veranderende Partijorganisatie in Nederland 1960–1990* (Utrecht: Het Spectrum, 1992).

38. Lombard League, *Statuto della Lega Lombarda* (n.p.: photocopy, 1992). Thanks are due to Simona Piattoni for her help in providing and translating this document.

39. André Barjonet, *Le Parti communiste français* (Paris: Éditions John Didier, 1969), 87–100; André Laurens and Thierry Pfister, *Les Nouveaux Communistes* (n.p.: Stock, 1973), 129–60.

40. Thomas Poguntke, *Alternative Politics* (Edinburgh: Edinburgh University Press, 1993), 142; id. and Bernard Boll, 'Germany', in Richard Katz and Peter Mair (eds.), *Party Organizations* (London: Sage Publications, 1992).

41. Duverger, *Political Parties*, 63.

42. Indeed, Duverger himself apparently tried to avoid such confusion by substituting 'party of the masses' (*parti des masses*) for the term 'massive party' (*parti massif*), a term he used in an earlier version, and one which puts somewhat greater emphasis on size than on openness to 'the masses'. Maurice Duverger, *Les Partis politiques dans l'État contemporain* (Paris: Les Cours de Droit, 1949), 91 ff.

43. Id., *Political Parties*, 67.

44. Russell Dalton, *Citizen Politics in Western Democracies* (Chatham, NJ: Chatham House, 1984), 188–93. On Germany, see also id. and Robert Rohrschneider, 'Wählerwandel und die Abschwächung der Parteineigungen von 1972 bis 1987', in Max Kaase and Hans-Dieter Klingemann (eds.), *Wahlen und Wähler* (Opladen: Westdeutscher Verlag, 1990). On Britain, see Mark Franklin, *The Decline of Class Voting in Britain* (Oxford: Oxford University Press, 1985).

45. Duverger, *Political Parties*, p. xxiii.

46. Panebianco, *Political Parties: Organization and Power*, ch. 4.
47. Kenneth Janda and Robert Harmel, *Parties and their Environments* (New York: Longman, 1982), ch. 4; von Beyme, *Political Parties in Western Democracies*, trans. Eileen Martin (New York: St Martin's Press, 1985), 189; G. Bingham Powell, 'American Voter Turnout in Comparative Perspective', *American Political Science Review*, 80 (1986), 21.

2. THE COSTS AND BENEFITS OF ENROLLING MEMBERS

1. (London: CCO, 1949), 28.
2. Fred Riggs, 'Comparative Politics and the Study of Parties: A Structural Approach', in William Crotty (ed.), *Approaches to the Study of Party Organization* (Boston: Allyn & Bacon, 1968). His categories were used by Seiler in his reconsideration of Duverger's analysis. Daniel-Louis Seiler, *De la comparaison des partis politiques* (Paris: Economica, 1986), 87 ff.
3. Herbert Kitschelt, *The Logics of Party Formation* (Ithaca, NY: Cornell University Press, 1989).
4. Angelo Panebianco, *Political Parties: Organization and Power*, trans. Marc Silver (Cambridge: Cambridge University Press, 1988).
5. Austin Ranney, 'Candidate Selection', in David Butler, Howard Penniman, and Austin Ranney (eds.), *Democracy at the Polls* (Washington: American Enterprise Institute, 1981), 82–9.
6. This dimension overlaps with, but is broader than, the characteristic which Ranney labels 'direct or indirect participation'.
7. Frank Sorauf, 'Political Parties and Political Analysis', in William Chambers and Walter Dean Burnham (eds.), *The American Party Systems* (New York: Oxford University Press, 1967), 47.
8. James Q. Wilson, *Political Organizations* (New York: Basic Books, 1973), 33–4.
9. Kitschelt, *Logics of Party Formation*, 50 ff.
10. Panebianco, *Political Parties*, p. xii.
11. Ibid. 192.
12. Robert Harmel and Kenneth Janda, 'An Integrated Theory of Party Goals and Party Change', *Journal of Theoretical Politics*, 6 (1994), 261.
13. e.g. in addition to the project led by Harmel and Janda, see the projects described in Andrew Appleton and Daniel Ward, 'Measuring Party Organization in the United States: An Assessment and a New Approach', *Party Politics*, 1 (1995), 113–31; and in Thomas Koelble, 'Economic Theories of Organization and the Politics of Institutional Design in Political Parties', paper presented at APSA annual meeting, New York, Aug. 1994.

14. Gunnar Sjöblom, *Party Strategies in a Multiparty System* (Lund: Berlingska Boktryckeriet, 1968), 49–52.
15. Stefano Bartolini, 'The Membership of Mass Parties: The Social Democratic Experience, 1889–1978', in Hans Daalder and Peter Mair (eds.), *Western European Party Systems: Continuity and Change* (Beverly Hills, Calif.: Sage Publications, 1983), 207.
16. This is in keeping with Kris Deschouwer's argument about the importance of perception as an intervening variable. Kris Deschouwer, 'The Survival of the Fittest: Measuring and Explaining Adaptation and Change of Political Parties', paper presented at European Consortium for Political Research (ECPR) Annual Joint Sessions, Limerick, Mar. 1992, 13 ff.
17. Katz is one notable exception. Richard Katz, 'Party as Linkage: A Vestigial Function', *European Journal of Political Research*, 18 (1990), 145–6.
18. May's 'Special Law of Curvilinear Disparity' is the best-known statement of why members may impose programmatic costs.
19. See e.g. Herbert Kitschelt, 'Austrian and Swedish Social Democrats in Crisis', *Comparative Political Studies*, 27 (1994), 9–10; Paul Whitely, Patrick Seyd, Jeremy Richardson, and Paul Bissell, 'Explaining Party Activism: The Case of the British Conservative Party', *British Journal of Political Science*, 24 (1993), 90.
20. Robert Michels, *Political Parties*, trans. Eden and Cedar Paul (New York: Appleton-Century-Crofts, 1971), 367.
21. Sidney Verba, Norman Nie, and Jae-On Kim, *Participation and Political Equality* (Cambridge: Cambridge University Press, 1978), ch. 8.
22. Paul Lazarsfeld, Bernard Berelson, and Hazel Gaudet, *The People's Choice* (New York: Columbia University Press, 1944).
23. Maurice Duverger, *Political Parties: Their Organization and Activity in the Modern State*, trans. Barbara and Robert North (New York: John Wiley & Sons, 1955).
24. Sjöblom's actor is the party executive: *Party Strategies*, 30.
25. Richard Katz and Peter Mair, 'The Official Story: A Framework for the Comparative Study of Party Organization and Organizational Change', paper presented at the APSA annual meeting, San Francisco, 30 Aug.–1 Sept. 1990.

3. THE DEVELOPMENT OF MEMBERSHIP PARTIES IN GERMANY AND BRITAIN

1. CDU, *Moderne Parteiarbeit in den 90er Jahren* (Bonn: CDU-BGSt, 1989), 469 (author's translation here and throughout).

2. Art. 21 of the Basic Law. Trans. in *The Law on Political Parties* (Bonn: Inter Nationes, 1994), 5.

3. Since 1956, parties have also been eligible to receive *Bundestag* seats in proportion to their share of the popular vote if they win three or more constituency contests.

4. Alf Mintzel, *Die CSU* (Opladen: Westdeutscher Verlag, 1978).

5. Hermann Schmitt, 'Die Sozialdemokratische Partei Deutschlands', in Alf Mintzel and Heinrich Oberreuter (eds.), *Parteien in der Bundesrepublik Deutschland* (Opladen: Leske & Budrich, 1992), 164; Josef Schmid, *Die CDU* (Opladen: Leske & Budrich, 1990).

6. Theo Pirker, *Die SPD nach Hitler* (Munich: Rütten & Loening, 1965), 55.

7. SPD, *Herner Beschlüsse für die Sozialdemokratische Partei Deutschlands* (n.p.: SPD-PV, 1952).

8. SPD, *Propagandatechnik der SPD*, material prepared for the 'Sozialistische Propaganda- und Expertenkonferenz', Dorking, Surrey, 29 Oct.–1 Nov. 1950 (FES: PV Alter Bestand Teil I; HB3 1950).

9. SPD, *Zur Parteidiskussion: Empfehlungen des Parteivorstandes und des Parteiausschüsses* (n.p.: SPD-PV, Parteivorstand, n.d. [1954]); Kurt Klotzbach, *Der Weg zur Staatspartei* (Berlin: Verlag J. H. W. Dietz Nachfolger, 1982), 276–98.

10. Helmut Köser, *Die Grundsatzdebatte in der SPD von 1945/46 bis 1958/59* (Freiburg i.B.: Johannes Kraus, 1971); Peter Lösche and Franz Walter, *Die SPD: Klassenpartei—Volkspartei—Quotenpartei* (Darmstadt: Wissenschaftliche Buchgesellschaft, 1992), 183 ff.

11. Holger Börner, 'Arbeitsbilanz', in SPD, *Jahrbuch 1975–1977*, 221.

12. Herbert Wehner, 'Bericht über die Beratungsergebnisse der Kommission "Reform der Parteiorganisation" ', in SPD, *Außerordentlicher Parteitag 1971: Protokoll*, 19–27.

13. SPD, *Jahrbuch 1973/75*, 252. The magazine has appeared under several names: *Einblick* in early 1974; *Sozialdemokrat Magazin* from 1974 to spring 1989; *Vorwärts* subsequently.

14. SPD, 'Dokumente: zur praktischen Parteiarbeit' (Bonn: SPD-PV, n.d. [1975]); SPD, *Parteitag 1975*, 63–6; SPD, *Jahrbuch 1973/75*, 221–3.

15. This was the controversial Börner/Koschnik study, which was never made public. Eva Kolinsky, *Parties, Opposition and Society in West Germany* (London: Croom Helm, 1984).

16. e.g. in 1984 SPD headquarters produced a new comic strip about recruiting-techniques, published sample letters to send to membership 'targets', and issued prizes for successful recruiters—and net party membership declined by about 10,000. 'Tu was. Mit der SPD', *Sozialdemokrat Magazin*, 10 (1984), 6–7.

17. Russell Dalton and Alexandra Cole, 'The Peaceful Revolution and German Electoral Politics', in Russell Dalton (ed.), *The New Germany Votes* (Providence: Berg Publishers, 1993), 24.

18. Heinrich Tiemann, Josef Schmid, and Frank Löbler, 'Gewerkschaften und Sozialdemokratie in den neuen Bundesländern', *Deutschland Archiv*, 26 (1993), 46.

19. 'Liste Feuerwehr', *Der Spiegel*, 48 (1993), 70–4. For an account of the initial organizational challenges of the eastern SPD, see Stephen Silvia, 'Left Behind: The Social Democratic Party in Eastern Germany', *West European Politics*, 16/2 (1993), 24–48.

20. Karlheinz Blessing (ed.), *SPD 2000: Die Modernisierung der SPD* (Marburg: Schüren Presseverlag, 1993).

21. A. R. L. Gurland, *Die CDU/CSU: Ursprünge und Entwicklung bis 1953* (Frankfurt/M.: Europäische Verlagsanstalt, 1980), 86-92; Geoffrey Pridham, *Christian Democracy in Western Germany* (London: Croom Helm, 1977), 44, 63.

22. Wulf Schönbohm, *Die CDU wird moderne Volkspartei* (Stuttgart: Klett-Cotta, 1985), 40; Bruno Heck, 'Adenauer und die CDU', *Die politische Meinung* (Nov./Dec. 1975), 84–106 .

23. Bruno Heck, 'Der Weg zur Mitgliederpartei', *Deutsches Monatsblatt*, 3/5 (1956), 2, 5.

24. CDU, *Parteitag 1962*, 318.

25. Schönbohm, *Die CDU wird moderne Volkspartei*, 65.

26. Schmid warns against viewing this change as the result of the initiatives of particular individuals, and focuses more on factors in the party's environment and in its federal structure. Schmid, *Die CDU*, 150.

27. Helmut Pütz, Peter Radunski, and Wulf Schönbohm, '34 Thesen zur Reform der CDU', *Sonde*, 2/4 (1969), 5–22. They advocated similar types of reforms after the next election: Helmut Pütz, Peter Radunski, Wulf Schönbohm, and Uwe-Rainer Simon, '18 Thesen zur Reorganisation der CDU', *Sonde*, 6/3–4 (1973), 15–21.

28. Schönbohm, *Die CDU wird moderne Volkspartei*, 187.

29. 'Die CDU auf dem Wege zur Mitgliederpartei', *Deutsches Monatsblatt*, 21/9 (1974), 4.

30. 'Neue Methode bei der Mitgliederwerbung brachten große Erfolge', *Deutsches Monatsblatt*, 20/2 (1973), 16.

31. CDU, 'Modellversuch "Kreisverbandsarbeit" ', reprinted in Norbert Lammert, *Lokale Organisationsstrukturen innerparteilicher Willensbildung: Fallstudie am Beispiel eines CDU-Kreisverbandes im Ruhrgebiet* (Bonn: Eicholz Verlag, 1976), 199–206.

32. CDU, *Moderne Parteiarbeit in den 90er Jahren*.

33. These legacies also created some difficulties for the broader CDU in

figuring out what attitude to take towards collaboration with the previous regime. Clay Clemens, 'Disquiet on the Eastern Front: The Christian Democratic Union in Germany's New Länder', *German Politics*, 2 (1993), 200–23.

34. 'Mehr Power für die Neuen', *Der Spiegel*, 23 (1991), 21–5.
35. Both the Conservative and the Labour Party currently require their parliamentary candidates to obtain the approval of the national party.
36. Known officially as the 'Chairman of the Party'. The Chairman is an officer of Conservative Central Office who is appointed by the leader of the Conservative Party.
37. Richard Kelly, *Conservative Party Conferences* (Manchester: Manchester University Press, 1989).
38. David Butler and Ann Sloman, *British Political Facts 1900–1975* (London: Macmillan, 1975), 183.
39. Henry Pelling, *A Short History of the Labour Party* (London: Macmillan, 1961), 109.
40. 'Committee of Enquiry into Party Organization, Interim Report', reprinted in LabPar, *Report of Conference 1955*, 65.
41. See e.g. the statement of party aims presented to the 1960 Labour Party Conference by party secretary Morgan Phillips: *Labour in the Sixties* (London: LabPar, n.d. [1960]).
42. Patrick Seyd, *The Rise and Fall of the Labour Left* (Basingstoke: Macmillan Education, 1987), 43.
43. Thomas Koelble, *The Left Unraveled* (Durham: Duke University Press, 1991).
44. Constituency Labour Parties were now allowed to affiliate to the national party with only 256 (instead of 1,000) members. This minimum dropped still further in subsequent years.
45. Colin Hughes and Patrick Wintour, *Labour Rebuilt* (London: Fourth Estate, 1990); Patrick Seyd and Paul Whitely, 'Labour's Renewal Strategy', in Martin Smith and Joanna Spear (eds.), *The Changing Labour Party* (London: Routledge, 1992).
46. Larry Whitty, 'Operation Mass Membership', *Labour Party News* (Nov.–Dec. 1988), 6–7.
47. Ralph Atkins, Ivo Dawnay, and Emma Tucker, 'Snags Mar Party's Recruitment Drive', *Financial Times*, 1 Oct. 1991, 14.
48. Butler and Sloman, *British Political Facts 1900–1975*, 183.
49. J. D. Hoffman, *The Conservative Party in Opposition 1945–51* (London: McGibbon & Kee, 1964), 58ff.
50. ConPar, *Minutes of the Committee on Party Reorganisation*, meeting of 7 Oct. (1948) (CCO/500/1/17).
51. Hoffman, *The Conservative Party in Opposition*, 97. For more on the

committee's report, see Robert McKenzie, *British Political Parties* (Melbourne: William Heinemann, 1955), 185–217.

52. ConPar, *Summary Report (1962 Membership Campaign)* (1962) (CCO 500/11/9), 3.

53. ConPar, *Minutes of the Committee on Party Organisation* (Colyton Committee) (1 May 1957) (CCO/500/1/24).

54. Andrew Gamble, 'The Conservative Party', in H. M. Drucker (ed.), *Multi-Party Britain* (London: Macmillan, 1979), 41.

55. Sir Anthony Garner, 'Strengthening the Grass Roots', *Conservative Newsline* (Mar. 1985), 8; Sir Oulton Wade, 'Why We Must Build a Mass Membership', *Conservative Newsline* (Sept. 1984), 6; 'Membership Drive Must Succeed,' *Conservative Newsline* (June 1988), 16.

56. John Lacy, 'Campaigning,' *Conservative Newsline* (Nov. 1989), 8.

57. Paul Whitely, Patrick Seyd, and Jeremy Richardson, *True Blues* (Oxford: Clarendon Press, 1994), 43, 67.

58. Philip Stephens, 'Tory Funders Find Out the Party may be Over', *Financial Times*, 8 July 1993, 8; Gareth Smyth, 'OMOV for Tories?' *New Statesman and Society*, 1 Oct. 1993, 16.

59. Alison Smith, 'Grassroots Rebels Defeat Party Reforms', *Financial Times*, 6/7 Mar. 1993, 6.

4. PARTY MEMBERS AND ELECTIONEERING

1. SPD, *Jahrbuch 1956/57*, 243.

2. V. O. Key, Jr., *Politics, Parties and Pressure Groups*, 4th edn. (New York: Thomas Crowell Co., 1958), 376.

3. Robert Agranoff, *The New Style in Election Campaigns* (Boston: Holbrook Press, 1972), 18.

4. Xandra Kayden and Eddie Mahe, Jr., *The Party Goes On: The Persistence of the Two-Party System in the United States* (New York: Basic Books, 1985), 122. See also Stephen and Barbara Salmore, *Candidates, Parties and Campaigns* (Washington: Congressional Quarterly Press, 1985).

5. A phrase used by Samuel Finer in 'The Decline of Party?', in Vernon Bogdanor (ed.), *Parties and Democracy in Britain and America* (New York: Praeger Publishers, 1984), 4.

6. Peter G. J. Pulzer, *Political Representation and Elections in Britain* (London: George Allen & Unwin, 1967), 87.

7. David Butler and Dennis Kavanagh, *The British General Election of February 1974*, quoted by Howard Penniman, 'Campaign Styles and Methods', in David Butler, Howard Penniman, and Austin Ranney

(eds.), *Democracy at the Polls* (Washington: American Enterprise Institute, 1981), 108–9.

8. Joel Fisher and Sven Groennings, 'German Electoral Politics in 1969', *Government and Opposition*, 5 (1970), 218–34; Henri Menudier, 'La Campagne électorale de la CDU et du FDP', *Revue d'Allemagne*, 9/2 (1987), 108–21.

9. Shaun Bowler and David Farrell, 'Conclusion: The Contemporary Election Campaign', in eid. (eds.), *Electoral Strategies and Political Marketing* (London: Macmillan, 1992), 232–5; David Butler and Austin Ranney, 'Conclusion', in eid. (eds.), *Electioneering: A Comparative Study of Continuity and Change* (Oxford: Clarendon Press, 1992).

10. Samuel Eldersveld, *Political Parties in American Society* (New York: Basic Books, 1982), 415 (emphasis in original). See also James Gibson, Cornelius Cotter, John Bibby, and Robert Huckshorn, 'Whither the Local Parties? A Cross-sectional and Longitudinal Analysis of the Strength of Party Organizations', *American Journal of Political Science*, 29 (1988), 139–60.

11. Alan Ware argued on behalf of this third scenario when he noted that party strategists might retain campaigning by members because they suspect that 'no amount of communication through television can break dominating views or opinions': *Citizens, Parties and the State* (Princeton: Princeton University Press, 1987), 148, 230.

12. Jürgen Falter, 'Kontinuität und Neubeginn: Die Bundestagswahl 1949 zwischen Weimar und Bonn', *Politische Vierteljahresschrift*, 22 (1981), 241; Udo Wengst, 'Die CDU/CSU im Bundestagswahlkampf 1949', *Vierteljahresheft für Zeitgeschichte*, 34 (1986), 1–52; Susanne Hartelt, *Die Wahlkampfführung der SPD 1949–1969* (Master's thesis, Universität Düsseldorf, 1977).

13. SPD, 'Gegen die SPD gerichtete Kräfte und Einflüsse beim Bundestagswahlkampf 1953', Jan. 1994 (FES: PV Alterbestand Teil II #04662), 19; SPD, *Jahrbuch 1956/57*, 301; SPD, 'Werbung und Propaganda der Sozialdemokratischen Partei Deutschlands im Bundestagswahlkampf 1953' (FES: PV Alter Bestand Teil II, #04661), 34; Uwe Kitzinger, *German Electoral Politics: A Study of the 1957 Campaign* (Oxford: Clarendon Press, 1960), 112–16, 141; Eberhard Bitzer, 'Die CDU braucht ein neues Konzept', FAZ, 2 Feb. 1962.

14. SPD, *Jahrbuch 1952/53*, 236.

15. Kitzinger, *German Electoral Politics: A Study of the 1957 Campaign*, 118–22, 135. Wolfgang Hirsch-Weber and Klaus Schütz, *Wähler und Gewählte* (Berlin: Franz Vahlen, 1957).

16. SPD, *Jahrbuch 1968/69*, 42.

17. Kurt Klotzbach, *Der Weg zur Staatspartei* (Berlin: Verlag J. H. W.

Dietz Nachfolger, 1982), 31, 396; Günther Struve, *Kampf um die Mehrheit* (Cologne: Verlag Wissenschaft und Politik, 1971), 53, 141.

18. Monika Bethschneider, *Wahlkampfstrategien: Themen- und Organisationsplanung im Bundestagswahlkampf 1979/80* (Koblenz: Seminar für Politikwissenschaft, 1983), 10. For a general discussion of campaigning in this period, see Werner Wolf, *Wahlkampf und Demokratie* (Cologne: Verlag Wissenschaft und Politik, 1985).

19. Ulrich Duebber and Gerard Braunthal, 'West Germany', *Journal of Politics*, 25 (1963), 780.

20. e.g. organizers of the CDU's 1986 pre-election party conference deliberately imitated techniques they had observed in the United States at Republican Party nominating conventions, techniques intended to maximize the favourable free publicity generated by this expensive event.

21. 'Premiere: Werbe-Spots in den Privaten', *Deutsches Monatsblatt*, 37/5–7 (1989), 5; Fritz Sänger, 'Wahlkampfabkommen und Wahlwerbung', in id. and Klaus Liepelt (eds.), *Wahlhandbuch 1965: Teil 2 Wahlwerber* (n.p.: Institut für Angewandte Sozialwissenschaft, 1965), sect. 2.332, 9; Max Kaase, 'Germany', in Butler and Ranney (eds.), *Electioneering*, 146.

22. CDU, *Bericht der Bundesgeschäftsstelle 1981*, 47; SPD, *Parteitag 1988*, 75.

23. SPD, *Parteitag 1988*, 872; CDU, *Wahlkampfbericht der Bundesgeschäftsstelle zum Bundestagswahlkampf 1986/87* (Bonn: CDU-BGSt, n.d. [1987]), 31.

24. Where not otherwise noted, this description of CDU and SPD national organizers' visions of appropriate local campaign activities is drawn from the following materials (chronologically by party).

SPD: SPD, *Kleines Wahlhelfer A-B-C* (Hanover: SPD-PV, 1947); Arthur Mertins, 'Wahlkampfrichtlinien', reprinted in *Wahlsekretärbesprechung 24. Januar 1947* (FES: PV Alter Bestand Teil II, 05142); SPD, *Der kleine Wahlhelfer* (Bonn, SPD-PV, 1953); SPD, *Der sozialdemokratische Wahlhelfer* (Bonn: SPD-PV, 1953); Arno Scholz, *Das Einmaleins der politischen Werbung* (Berlin: Arani Verlag, 1954); SPD, *Wie führe ich den Wahlkampf?* (Bonn: SPD-PV, 1957; reprinted 1960); 'Werbehelfer', *eilt!*, (1954), 8: 18; 'Werbehelfer', *eilt!*, (1958), 1: 10; 'Werbehelfer', *eilt!*, (1959), 3: 15; Erich Ollenhauer, Willy Brandt, Herbert Wehner, and Alfred Nau, 'An die Mitglieder der Sozialdemokratischen Partei Deutschlands', letter, (SPD-PV, 1962); Klaus Schütz, 'Die Öffentlichkeitsarbeit der Mitgliederpartei', report of Arbeitsgemeinschaft E, *SPD Parteitag 1964*; Herbert Wehner, 'Bundestagswahl 1965', in SPD, *Jahrbuch 1964/65*; Bruno Friedrich, 'Wahlkampf und Parteiorganisation', in Herbert Wehner, Bruno Friedrich, and Alfred Nau, *Parteiorganisation* (Bonn: Verlag Neue Gesellschaft, 1969), 35–41; SPD, *Handbuch Parteiarbeit: Wahlkampfmachen* (Bonn: SPD-PV, n.d. [1976]); SPD, *Jahrbuch 1975/77*; Alex Raulfs, 'Die Wahlkampf- "Instrumente" der SPD', *Neue Gesellschaft*, 23/7 (1976), 560–1; SPD, *Der direkte Draht zum Wähler: Vertrauensarbeit per Telefon* (n.p.: SPD Nordrhein-Westfalen, 1984, and revised 2nd edn., 1990); SPD, *Wahlkampf '90* (Bonn: SPD-PV, 1990). See also the following in *Sozialdemokrat Magazin*: Holger Börner, 'Zeigen, wer wir sind!', 8 (1976), 5; Willy Brandt and Holger Börner, 'Zeig jetzt, daß du Sozialdemokrat bist. Tu was', 9 (1976), insert; 'Wahlkampf: Wie kann ich helfen?', 1 (1978), 10; 'Nicht nur in der Sonne dösen', 7 (1980), 16–17; 'Das 100 000-Mann-Ding', 8 (1980), 28; 'Diskussion im Wohnzimmer', 1 (1983), 14; 'Wahlkampftips des Monats: Direkter Draht zum Wähler', 10 (1986), 10; 'Wahlkampftip des Monats: Video im Winterwahlkampf', 11 (1986), 8; 'Checklist für den Endspurt', 1 (1987), 13; 'Telefonwerbung', 6 (1988), 4–5.

CDU: Günther Triesch, 'Aufmarsch zur Wahlschlacht', *Die politische Meinung*, 92 (1964), 37; CDU, *20 Schritte zum Wahlsieg*, 3rd edn. (Bonn: CDU-BGSt, 1969), 26 (1st edn. 1965); CDU, *Bericht der Organisationskommission: Vorlage für die Sitzung des Bundesvorstandes am 25./26. Mai 1973*; CDU, *Regiebuch 4: Wahlkampfmachen* (Bonn: CDU-BGSt, 1974); CDU, *Neue Wahlkampfformen: Winter Wahlkampf* (Bonn: CDU-BGSt, n.d. [1986]); *Canvassing-Aktionen* (Bonn: CDU-BGSt, 1986); CDU, *CDU aktiv: Sommeraktionen* (Bonn: CDU-BGSt, n.d. [1986]); CDU, *Messen und Ausstellungen* (Bonn: CDU-BGSt, 1986); CDU, *Die CDU ist dabei: Mitmachen bei den Veranstaltungen anderer* (Bonn: CDU-BGSt, 1986); CDU, *Nachbarschaftstreffen* (Bonn: CDU-BGSt, 1986); CDU, *Fit in die Zukunft* (Bonn: CDU-BGSt, 1986); CDU, *Sommeraktionen* (Bonn: CDU-BGSt, 1986); CDU, *Ganz Ohr: Ideenbörse für Aktionswoche im Wahlkampf '90* (CDU-BGSt, 1990); see also the following in *Deutsches Monatsblatt*: Bruno Heck, 'Aufruf zur Wahlspende', 4/6 (1957), 1; and 4/7 (1957), 3; 'Wie Sie Mitbürger überzeugen', 23/10 (1975), 28; 'Ja, ich bin dabei', 23/11 (1975), 20; 'Aus Liebe zu Deutschland: Jeder von uns spendet 10 Mark', 24/7–8 (1976), cover, 1; 'Jetzt den Wahlkampf zur persönlichen Sache machen', 24/9 (1976), 2; 'Mein persönlicher Wahlkampf', 24/9 (1976), 24–5; 'Auto-Aufkleber: Der neue Trend', 26/11 (1978); 'Wir starten den heißen Wahlkampf', 28/8 (1980), 15–18; 'Tip für Ihren persönlichen Wahlkampf', 28/9 (1980), 8; 'Kämpft, Freunde!', 31/1 (1983), 12; 'Was Sie am Tag der Wahl alles tun können', 31, special issue (1983), 3; 'Offensive in den Herbst', 34/10

(1986), 24–5; 'Aktionen im Winter', 34/11 (1986), 4–5; 'Schalten Sie Kleinanzeigen!', 34/12 (1986), 13; 'Sommeraktionen', 34/6 (1986), 17; Peter Radunski, 'Unser Konzept für den Wahlkampf', 34/9 (1986), 7; 'Noch ist jeder vierte Wähler unentschieden', 35/1 (1987), 3–5.

25. SPD, *Wie führe ich den Wahlkampf*, 6.

26. Konrad Kraske, *Die Bundestagswahl 1961: Vorbereitung—Ergebnis—Folgerungen* (Bonn: no publisher, 1962), 18.

27. Id., 'Wähler haben sich verändert', *Die Entscheidung* (Oct. 1966), 13.

28. SPD, *Parteitag 1960*, 483; Schütz, 'Die Öffentlichkeitsarbeit der Mitgliederpartei', 650–2.

29. Bruno Friedrich, 'Bundestagwahlen 1969: Wahlkampf und Parteiorganisation', *Neue Gesellschaft*, 16/2 (1969), 102–7; Hans Jürgen Wischnewski, 'Wahlkampf 1969', ibid. 16/3 (1969), 157–60.

30. CDU, *20 Schritte zum Wahlsieg*, 9.

31. Elisabeth Noelle-Neumann, 'Die Schweigespirale: Über die Entstehung der öffentlichen Meinung', in ead., *Öffentlichkeit als Bedrohung*, 2nd edn. (Freiburg i.B.: Verlag Karl Alber, 1979), 169–203.

32. Wolfgang Falke, 'Partei und Umwelt: Einige Anmerkungen zu Struktur und Aufgabe der Parteiorganisation', in CDU, *Bericht der Organisationskommission* (1973) (KAS: 2/201/5–4).

33. SPD, *Handbuch Parteiarbeit: Wahlkampfmachen*, 6.

34. SPD, *Wahlkampf '90*, 43.

35. This was not an entirely new idea: the CDU had unsuccessfully tried to popularize it in the 1960s. The CDU's *20 Schritte zum Wahlsieg* of 1965 and 1969 included an appendix with scripts for telephone conversations.

36. CDU, *Neue Wahlkampfformen: Telefon-Canvassing* (Bonn: CDU-BGSt, 1986), 2, 5; SPD, *Wahlkampf '90*, 112–14.

37. Edgar Einemann, *Partei-Computer für mehr Demokratie* (Marburg: Schüren Presseverlag, 1991); Jörg Bogumil, *Computer in Parteien und Verbänden* (Opladen: Westdeutscher Verlag, 1991).

38. Raulfs, 'Die Wahlkampf-"Instrumente" der SPD', 560–1.

39. CDU, *Bericht der Bundesgeschäftsstelle 1986*, 34.

40. This is particularly true locally, since laws on campaign finance set very low limits on the budget of the constituency campaign. One result is that parliamentary candidates employ great subterfuges to make clear that they have not actually started to campaign, and that therefore local expenditures should not be booked against the candidate's campaign budget.

41. Martin Harrison, 'Television and Radio', in David Butler and Anthony King, *The British General Election of 1964* (London: Macmillan, 1965), 156–84.

42. Martin Burch, 'The Politics of Persuasion and the Conservative

Leadership's Campaign', in *Political Communications 1983*, 73; David Butler and Dennis Kavanagh, *The British General Election of 1983* (London: Macmillan, 1984), 114; eid., *The British General Election of 1987* (London: Macmillan, 1988), 115.

43. David Butler, 'The Changing Nature of British Elections', in Ivor Crewe and Martin Harrop (eds.), *Political Communications: The General Election Campaign 1983* (Cambridge: Cambridge University Press, 1986), 3.

44. David Butler and Richard Rose, *The British General Election of 1959* (London: Macmillan, 1960), 52, 59.

45. Ibid. 18–24. Kevin Swaddle makes the point that party advertising on billboards and in newspapers had been used prior to 1929, so these techniques were not completely new in 1959. Kevin Swaddle, 'Coping with a Mass Electorate' (doctoral dissertation, Oxford University, 1990), 224.

46. Richard Rose, *Influencing Votes* (New York: St. Martin's Press, 1967).

47. Michael Pinto-Duschinsky, 'Trends in British Political Funding 1983–1987', *Parliamentary Affairs*, 42 (1989), 197–212.

48. David Butler and Dennis Kavanagh, *The British General Election of 1979* (New York: Macmillan, 1980), 139–40; Tim Bell, 'The Conservatives' Advertising Campaign', in Robert Worcester and Martin Harrop (eds.), *Political Communications: The General Election Campaign of 1979* (London: George Allen & Unwin, 1982), 23.

49. Michael Pinto-Duschinsky, 'Financing the British General Election of 1987', in Ivor Crewe and Martin Harrop (eds.), *Political Communications: The General Election Campaign of 1987* (Cambridge: Cambridge University Press, 1989), 24; Michael Harrison, Clare Dobie, and Samir Shah, 'Big Tory Backers Freeze Donations', *Independent*, 16 Mar. 1992, 28; Gary Mead, 'The Man That Will Launch More Than 5,500 Faces', *Financial Times*, 17 Mar. 1992, 10.

50. LabPar, *NEC Report 1988*, 5.

51. Butler and Kavanagh, *The British General Election of 1983*, 34; eid., *The British General Election of 1987*, 27; LabPar, *NEC Report 1988*, 22.

52. Unless otherwise noted, the following account is based on these sources (in chronological order):

Labour Party: Harold Croft, *Conduct of Parliamentary Elections,* 2nd edn. (London: LabPar, 1945); LabPar, *Guide to the Prelude to Victory Campaign* (London: n.d. [1949]); Reg Underhill, 'Get *All* Those Postal Votes', *Labour Organiser*, 50/564 (1970), 70–2; LabPar, *How to Build up the Postal Vote* (London: LabPar; 1970); LabPar, *Conduct of Parliamentary Elections,* 8th edn. (London:

LabPar, 1977); LabPar, *How to Organise for Victory* (London: LabPar, 1984); LabPar, *Campaign to Win* (London: LabPar, 1987); LabPar, *Targeting to Win* (London: LabPar, n.d. [1987]); 'Telephone Canvassing', *Labour Organiser*, 65/638 (1989), 19.

Conservative Party: ConPar, *Organisation of Indoor and Outdoor Meetings* (London: CCO, 1948); ConPar, *The Party Organisation* (London: CCO, 1950); ConPar, *The Voluntary Worker and the Party Organisation* (London: CCO, 1950); ConPar, *Election Manual For Key Workers* (London: CCO, n.d. [1980s]); ConPar, *Polling Day Organisation* (London: CCO, n.d. [1980s]); ConPar, *Local Government Campaigning* (London: CCO, 1987); ConPar, *Your Party* (London: CCO, n.d. [1986]).

53. David Butler and Dennis Kavanagh, *The British General Election of 1992* (London: Macmillan, 1993), 245.
54. R. T. Windle (Labour Party National Agent), 'To the Election Agent', letter, 8 Feb. 1950 (Labour Party Library: Pamphlets 1950).
55. A reported 75% of constituency spending in 1970 was for printing costs. David Butler and Michael Pinto-Duschinsky, *The British General Election of 1970* (New York: Macmillan, 1971), 334.
56. Colin Hart, *Your Party* (London: CCO [1980]), 7. 4.
57. The number of Labour constituency parties using computers in the 1992 general election was about 300, or almost ten times what it had been in 1987. Ian Holdsworth, 'Computers Left, Right and Centre', *Financial Times*, 3 Apr. 1992, 12.
58. David Butler, 'Hi-tech Replaces Rap of the Knocker', *Financial Times*, 31 Mar. 1992, 10; Michael White, 'Parties Plug into Unpredictable Power Points That Could Clinch Victory', *Guardian*, 30 Mar. 1992, 13.
59. ConPar, *Organisation of Indoor and Outdoor Meetings*, 1.
60. Ware, *Citizens, Parties and the State*, 230.

5. PARTY MEMBERS AND INTER-ELECTION ACTIVITIES

1. ConPar, *Your Party* (London: CCO, n.d. [1986]).
2. See e.g. 'Wahlkampfbeginn: Der Tag nach der Wahl', *Union in Deutschland*, 24 May 1962, 1. See also quote at the beginning of this chapter.
3. As Duverger suggests. Maurice Duverger, *Political Parties: Their Organization and Activity in the Modern State*, trans. Barbara and Robert North (New York: John Wiley & Sons, 1955), 63.
4. e.g. Landfried and Patterson allege that this may already have happened in the German parties after the introduction of public

subsidies. Christine Landfried, *Parteifinanzen und politische Macht* (Baden-Baden: Nomos Verlagsgesellschaft, 1990), 70 ff.; William Patterson, 'West Germany: Between Party Apparatus and Basis Democracy', in Alan Ware (ed.), *Political Parties: Electoral Change and Structural Response* (Oxford: Basil Blackwell, 1987), 162; see also Klaus von Beyme, *Political Parties in Western Democracies*, trans. Eileen Martin (New York: St Martin's Press, 1985), 187 ff.

5. On the evolution of such 'contributing memberships' in American parties, see Leon Epstein, *Political Parties in the American Mold* (Madison: University of Wisconsin Press, 1986), 280–1.

6. Anke Fuchs, speaking at the 1991 party conference. SPD, *Parteitag 1991*, 91–2.

7. 'Urwahl und Mitgliederentscheid: Die SPD erprobt die direkte Demokratie', *FAZ*, 20 Nov. 1993, 2.

8. SPD, *Jahrbuch 1979/81*, 343. One possible explanation for this underpayment may be that local parties encourage members to under-pay their dues and then to donate the difference to the local party because contributions, unlike dues, are not shared with the federal party. Ulrich Klose in SPD, *Parteitag 1988*, 63. See also, 'Eine Partei der Armen?', *Vorwärts*, 3 (1991), 14–15.

9. 'Jede Beitragsmark mehr, hilft weiter', *Sozialdemokrat Magazin*, 6 (1985), 12–14; SPD, *Parteitag 1988*, 871.

10. Treasurer Walter Leisler Kiep in CDU, *Bundesparteitag 1987*, 66; CDU, *Moderne Parteiarbeit in den 90er Jahren* (Bonn: CDU-BGSt, 1986), 23–4.

11. Karl Feldmeyer, 'Kiep muß den Parteitag um Geld angehen', *FAZ*, 12 Sept. 1989, 6.

12. *Sozialdemokrat Magazin*, 6 (1977), cover.

13. 'Zehn Mark als Starthilfe', *Union* (Nov.–Dec. 1991), 8.

14. Hans Herbert von Arnim has been one of the most adamant, and best publicized, of these critics. Some of his many publications on this subject are listed in the bibliog. of his 1991 book, *Die Partei, der Abgeordnete und das Geld* (Mainz: Hase & Koehler Verlag, 1991).

15. Helmut Lölhöffel, 'Koalition setzt sich bei Parteifinanzierung durch', *Frankfurter Rundschau*, 13 Nov. 1993, 4; Wolfgang Hoffman, 'Weniger Geld vom Staat', *Die Zeit*, 1 Oct. 1993, 4.

16. Colin Brown, 'Labour Promises to Curb Political Gifts', *Independent*, 14 Apr. 1994, 14. For an overview of pre-1980 discussions, see Michael Pinto-Duschinsky, *British Political Finance 1830–1980* (Washington: American Enterprise Institute, 1981), 273 ff.

17. 'Better for you, and Better for Us', *Labour Organiser*, 12 (Sept.–Oct.

1988), back cover. Also 'Step by Step to National Membership System', *Labour Party News* (Oct. 1990), 28.

18. Teresa Hunter, 'New Card Could Make Carrier a Credit to Labour', *Guardian*, 6 Oct. 1989, 6.

19. 'Now Play your Part in Labour's Victory' (advertisement), *Independent*, 3 Oct. 1990, 1; 'Give £15 to Help Labour Win' (advertisement), ibid. 29 Mar. 1992, 20; 'Urgent Election Appeal' (advertisement), *Guardian*, 25 Mar. 1992, 1.

20. Patrick Wintour, 'Party Facing Cash Crisis Due to Falling Membership', *Guardian*, 30 Sept. 1992, 4.

21. 'Money Matters', *Conservative Newsline* (June 1985), 7–10.

22. Philip Tether, 'Recruiting Conservative Party Members: A Changing Role for Central Office', *Parliamentary Affairs*, 44 (1991), 20–32.

23. J. D. Hoffman, *The Conservative Party in Opposition 1945–51* (London: McGibbon & Kee, 1964), 86.

24. David Butler and Anthony King, *The British General Election of 1966* (London: Macmillan, 1967), 97, 103.

25. David Butler and Dennis Kavanagh, *The British General Election of 1987* (London: Macmillan, 1988), 27. Tether, 'Recruiting Conservative Party Members', 27–32.

26. John Gapper, 'Tories Play the Loyalty Card', *Financial Times*, 6–7 Mar. 1993, 6.

27. SPD, *Wahlkampf '90* (Bonn: SPD-PV, 1990), 70–1; CDU, *Regiebuch 4, Wahlkampfmachen* (Bonn: CDU-BGSt, 1974), 38; Uwe Schleth and Michael Pinto-Duschinsky, 'Why Public Subsidies have Become the Major Source of Party Funds in West Germany, but not in Great Britain', in Arnold Heidenheimer (ed.), *Comparative Political Finance* (Lexington, Mass.: D. C. Heath, 1970).

28. ConPar, *The Party Organisation* (London: CCO, 1950), 23; *Model Rules for Constituency, Branch and European Constituency Councils* (London: CCO, 1986), 2.

29. *House of Lords Debates*, 15 May 1974, vol. 351, col. 1033.

30. ConPar, *Constituency Finance* (London: CCO, 1969) reprinted in John Lees and Richard Kimber (eds.), *Political Parties in Modern Britain: An Organizational and Functional Guide* (London: Routledge & Kegan Paul, 1972).

31. ConPar, *Handbook on Constituency Organisation* (London: The Conservative and Unionist Central Office, 1932); ConPar *Constituency Finance* (London: CCO, 1950); '50 Ideas for Raising Money', *Conservative Agents' Journal*, 516, (1963), 11–21; ConPar, *Your Party*.

32. 'Turning your Votes into Cash', *Conservative Newsline* (Sept. 1984), 8.

33. Sara Barker, 'Beware Competitions!', *Labour Organiser*, 33/382 (1954), 32–3.

34. LabPar, *Your Guide to Fund Raising* (Rochdale: East Midlands Regional Council of the LabPar, 1984); LabPar, *How to Organise for Victory* (London: LabPar, 1984), 67–9; Harold Croft, *Party Organisation*, 7th, 8th, 12th, 14th edns. (London: LabPar, 1946, 1972, 1979); Steve Billcliffe, 'Direct Mail Fundraising', in LabPar, *Your Guide to Fundraising*, 39; LabPar, *Targeting to Win* (London: LabPar, 1987), and *Campaign to Win* (London: LabPar, 1987).

35. 'Du und Wir! Die erste zentrale Werbeaktion der SPD', *SPD Rundschau* (Sept. 1950), 1; SPD, *Mitgliederwerben: Eine leichte Sache* (Bonn: SPD-PV, n.d. [1956]); SPD *Mitglieder werben—leichter gemacht* (Bonn: SPD-PV n.d. [1959]); SPD, *Jahrbuch 1952/53*, 65; SPD, *9 Punkte zur verstärkten Organisationsarbeit* (Bonn: SPD-PV, 1955).

36. SPD, *Jahrbuch 1966/67*, 177; SPD, *Mitgliederwerben—aber wie?* (Bonn: SPD-PV, n.d. [1968]); SPD, *Aktion WIR . . . werben neue Freunde* (Bonn: SPD-PV, n.d. [1971]); SPD, *Hinweise zur Mitgliederwerbeaktion* (Bonn: SPD-PV 1973); SPD, *Jahrbuch 1973/75*, 235–6; SPD, *Handbuch für die Arbeit in sozialdemokratischen Ortsvereinen: Mitglieder werben—Vertrauensarbeit* (Bonn: SPD-PV, n.d. [1978]); SPD, *Tu was. Mit der SPD. Mitgliederwerbung* (Bonn: SPD-PV, n.d. [1984]); 'So wird's gemacht: 15 Schritte zum Erfolg', *Sozialdemokrat Magazin*, 10 (1984), 12; SPD, *Materialien zur innerparteilichen Bildungsarbeit: Neumitgliederschulung* (Bonn: SPD-PV, 1982).

37. 'Jeder ist aufgerufen!', *Union in Deutschland*, 16/21 (1962); Peter Radunski and Alexander Niemetz, *Mitgliederwerbung: Konzept und Praxis* (Frankfurt/M.: CDU Landesverband Hessen, n.d. [1969/1970]); CDU, *Leitfaden für die Mitgliederwerbung* (Bonn: CDU-BGSt, 1972); CDU, *Regiebuch 1: Mitgliederwerbung—Aktion 'CDU-Kontakter'*, (Bonn: CDU-BGSt, n.d. [1973]); CDU, *Mitgliederwerbung leicht gemacht: Erfolgreiche Modelle für CDU-Verbände* (Bonn: CDU-BGSt, 1985); CDU, *Mitgliederwerbung leicht gemacht* (Bonn: CDU-BGSt, 1990).

38. Morgan Phillips, 'Mass Membership Campaign', letter, Jan. 1946 (Labour Party Library: Pamphlets 1946); LabPar, *Victory Membership Campaign* (London: LabPar, 1946); A. L. Williams, 'Now Is the Time for a Big Step Forward!', *Labour Organiser*, 35/408 (1956), 90–1; H. R. Underhill and G. H. Williams, 'A Membership Secretary's Job', *Labour Organiser*, 35/413 (1956), 197–9; LabPar, *Campaign Guide: Labour Party Membership Campaign 1961* (London: LabPar, n.d. [1961]).

39. LabPar, *Make More Members* (London: LabPar, 1979); London Labour Party, 'Membership of the Labour Party', reprinted in *Labour Organiser*, 61/621 (1982).

40. ConPar, *The Voluntary Worker and the Party Organisation*; ConPar, *Campaign '88* (London: CCO, n.d. [1988]); 'Sky's the Limit', *Conservative Newsline* (May 1988), 1; 'How to Boost Membership', *Labour Party News*, 1 (1986), 3–4.

41. 'Um die Aktivierung des Parteilebens', *Neuer Vorwärts*, 6 June 1952; SPD, *9 Punkte zur verstärkten Organisationsarbeit*; 'Abschrift', from SPD-PV 1955 (FES: PV Alter Bestand Teil II, 05137); SPD, *SPD Handbuch für Vertrauensleute* (Stuttgart: SPD Landesverband Baden-Württemberg, n.d. [1964]).

42. Alfred Nau, in SPD, *Parteitag 1952*, 179.

43. Hans Koschnick, 'Bundestagswahlkampf', *Neue Gesellschaft*, 23 (1976), 972; SPD *Jahrbuch 1979/81*, 343.

44. Since then, delegates have been allocated according to paid-up membership only.

45. 'Verbesserung der Beitragsehrlichkeit', *Union in Deutschland*, 7 (1980), unpaginated.

46. 'Do We Deserve Collectors?', *Labour Organiser*, 37/428 (1958), 29.

47. Croft, *Party Organisation*; LabPar, *How to Organise for Victory*.

48. ConPar, *Constituency Finance*, 16; ConPar, *The Voluntary Worker and the Party Organization*, 11; 'Report of the Central Council', in Conservative Party, *Conference 1947*, 21.

49. Sir Anthony Garner, 'Strengthening the Grass Roots', *Conservative Newsline* (Mar. 1985), 8.

50. Arthur Gunlicks, *Local Government in the German Federal System* (Durham: Duke University Press, 1986).

51. 'Marschziele der Union', *Deutsches Monatsblatt*, 7/6 (1960), 8–10.

52. CDU, *Regiebuch 5: Kommunalwahlkampf* (Bonn: CDU-BGSt, 1974), 3.

53. CDU, *Handbuch Ortsverbandsarbeit: Erfolgreich für die CDU* (Bonn: CDU-BGSt, n.d. [1983]), 33. Parties' electioneering obligations do not end with local-government contests. In Germany both parties have always expected their local associations to help in elections for state parliaments, held once every four or five years.

54. Werner Wolf, *Wahlkampf und Demokratie* (Cologne: Verlag Wissenschaft und Politik), 48.

55. Geoffrey Rippon, 'Conservatives and Local Government', *The Councillor*, 1/2 (1948), 13.

56. 'Local Elections Have National Significance', *Labour Organiser*, 35/408 (1956), 83.

57. *Report of the Labour Party Commission of Enquiry 1980* (London: LabPar, n.d. [1980]), 29.

58. John Gyford, *Local Politics in Britain* (London: Croom Helm, 1976), 62; *Conduct of Local Authority Business* (London: HMSO Cmnd 9798, 1986), ii. 42.

59. A. L. Williams, 'Planning for Local Government Elections', *Labour Organiser*, 31/357 (1952), 10, 11, 19; LabPar, *Conduct of Local Elections*, 10th edn. (London: LabPar, 1982); LabPar, *How To Fight Local Elections* (London: LabPar, 1985); ConPar, *Local Government and the Party Organisation* (London: CCO, 1950); ConPar, *Guide to Local Government Elections in England and Wales* (London: CCO, 1987).

60. 'Mach es noch besser!', *SPD Rundschreiben*, 141 (1952); 'Werbehelfer', *eilt!*, 1 (1958); 'Werbehelfer', *eilt!*, 3 (1959); 'Werbehelfer', *eilt!*, 3 (1954), 18.

61. SPD, *9 Punkte zur verstärkten Organisationsarbeit*.

62. See e.g. *Herner Beschlüsse Für die Sozialdemokratische Partei Deutschlands* (Bonn: SPD-PV, 1952); Arno Scholz, *Das Einmaleins der politischen Werbung* (Berlin: Arani Verlag, 1954), 13.

63. Fritz Erler, 'Gedanken zur Politik und inneren Ordnung der Sozialdemokratie', *Neue Gesellschaft*, 5/1 (1956), 3–8.

64. Horst Becker and Bodo Hombach, *Die SPD von Innen* (Bonn: Verlag Neue Gesellschaft, 1983), 3.

65. Josef Hermann Dufhues, speaking at the 1962 CDU party conference: CDU, *Bundesparteitag*, 321; Konrad Kraske, 'Wähler haben sich verändert', *Die Entscheidung* (Oct. 1966), 13–14.

66. Bruno Friedrich, 'Der sozialdemokratische Ortsverein', in Herbert Wehner, Bruno Friedrich, and Alfred Nau, *Parteiorganisation* (Bonn: Verlag Neue Gesellschaft, 1969), 51. Friedrich, who is described by Lösche and Walter as the 'party's true organizational expert' (p. 149), specifically cites the work of Paul Lazarsfeld and Elihu Katz. For the description of members as vote multipliers, see e.g. the SPD Yearbook's description of party campaigning in state elections: SPD *Jahrbuch 1970/72*, 273.

67. Bernd Gugggenberger and Udo Kempf (eds.), *Bürgerinitiativen und repräsentatives System* (Opladen: Westdeutscher Verlag, 1978); Volker Hauff (ed.), *Bürgerinitiativen in der Gesellschaft* (Villingen-Schwenningen: Neckar Verlag, 1980).

68. ConPar, *The Voluntary Worker and the Party Organisation* (London: CCO, 1950), 3; Croft, *Party Organisation*; LabPar, *How to Organise for Victory*, 25; LabPar, *Guide to the Prelude to Victory Campaign* (London: LabPar, n.d. [1949]); Gerald O'Brien, 'The Point of Publicity', *Conservative Agents' Journal* (Oct. 1966), 4.

69. For more on the development of the 'community-politics' approach, see essays in Vernon Bogdanor (ed.), *Liberal Party Politics* (Oxford: Clarendon Press, 1983).

70. Heinrich Geißler, 'Arbeitsschwerpunkte der CDU als Volkspartei der Mitte', CDU press release, 5 Aug. 1987; CDU, *Fit in die Zukunft* (Bonn: CDU-BGSt, 1986); *Regiebuch 7: Vorpolitischer Raum* (Bonn: CDU-BGSt, 1975), 2; CDU, *Regiebuch 3: Mitgliederinitiativen: Das neue Rollenverständnis aktiver CDU-Mitglieder* (Bonn: CDU-BGSt, n.d.[1973]); CDU, *Wahlkampf '76: Maßnahmen und Vorschläge der Bundespartei für die Arbeit in den Wahlkreisen* (Bonn: CDU-BGSt, 1976), unpaginated.

71. Peter Radunski, *Wahlkämpfe: Moderne Wahlkampfführung als politische Kommunikation* (Munich: Günter Olzog Verlag, 1980), 120.

72. Wulf Schönbohm, 'Defizite und konkrete Lösungsmöglichkeiten', *Themen*, 2 (1988), 23.

73. CDU, *Moderne Parteiarbeit in den 90er Jahren*, 12, 14.

74. CDU, *Bürgernahe Formen der Parteiarbeit: Zielgruppenansprache* (Bonn: CDU-BGSt, 1990), 2.

75. e.g. Diane Parness, *The SPD and the Challenge of Mass Politics: The Dilemma of the German Volkspartei* (Boulder, Colo.: Westview Press, 1991).

76. SPD, *Jahrbuch 1975/77*, 459; Holger Börner, 'Bereit sein zum Gespräch mit dem Wähler: Vertrauensarbeit der Partei', *Neue Gesellschaft*, 22/4 (1975), 271.

77. SPD, *Organisationshandbuch: Arbeitshilfen für sozialdemokratische Funktionäre* (Stuttgart: SPD Baden-Württemberg, 1975), 32.

78. 'Wilhelm-Dröscher-Preis: Parteiarbeit zum Anfassen', *Sozialdemokrat Magazin*, 11, 14.

79. SPD, *Politik Lebendig: Handbuch der Parteiarbeit vor Ort* (Bonn: SPD-PV, n.d. [1987 +]), 5.

80. SPD, *Bericht der Kommission zur Prüfung der allgemeinen Organisationsprobleme* (Bonn: SPD-PV, 1958) (FES: PV Alter Bestand Teil II, 04786).

81. SPD, *Organisationshandbuch: Arbeitshilfen für sozialdemokratische Funktionäre*, 32.

82. Basil Feldman, *The Path to Power: From Town Hall to Westminster* (London: Conservative Political Centre, 1975).

83. ConPar, *Survey Canvassing* (London: CCO, 1987), 1.

84. Feldman, *The Path to Power: From Town Hall to Westminster*, 12; Geoffrey Pattie, 'The Tory Antidote to Community Politics', *Crossbow* (Oct. 1973), 17; ConPar, *Your Party*.

85. Joyce Gould, 'Labour's Approach to the Electorate', *Labour Organiser*, 61/621 (1982), 2–3.

86. LabPar, *Campaign Guide for Labour Listens* (London: LabPar, 1987).

87. Ibid.

88. LabPar, *Labour Listens: Campaigning for the 1990s* (London: LabPar, 1987).

89. Patrick Wintour, 'Straw Tries to Nip Lib Dems' Revival in Bud', *Guardian*, 5 Aug. 1993, 2.

90. SPD, *Der rote Faden im Labyrinth: Verbraucherarbeit der Bürgerbüros und Ortsvereine* (Bonn: SPD-PV, 1986); SPD, *Politik lebendig: Handbuch der Parteiarbeit vor Ort*; 'Bürgerbüros—oft die letzte Instanz', *Sozialdemokrat Magazin*, 11–12 (1987), 22.

91. CDU, *Regiebuch 8: Großstadtarbeit* (Bonn: CDU-BGSt, 1976); Peter Radunski, 'Die CDU als moderne Volkspartei: Gedenken zur künftigen Basisorganisation der CDU', *Sonde*, 21/1–2 (1988), 102.

92. ConPar, *Local Government Campaigning* (London: CCO, 1987), 3.

93. LabPar, *Making New Members* (London: LabPar, 1986), unpaginated.

94. e.g. 'Kess & Dott', *Einblick: Sozialdemokratisches Mitgliedermagazin*, 1 (1974), 6; 'Aktion: Stadtteilzeitung', *Sozialdemokrat Magazin*, 3 (1975), 27; CDU, *Regiebuch 10: CDU-Zeitung* (Bonn: CDU-BGSt, n.d. [1977]).

95. CDU, *Handbuch Ortsverbandsarbeit: Erfolgreich für die CDU*, 15.

96. Radunski, 'Die CDU als moderne Volkspartei: Gedanken zur künftigen Basisorganisation der CDU', 106; 'Mit Stadtteilzeitungen macht die SPD Werbung durch die Hintertür', *Die Welt*, 26 Aug. 1985.

97. Otfried Jarren, 'Kommunikation organisieren: Zum Konzept "Bürgerzeitung"', *Neue Gesellschaft*, 25 (1978), 941.

98. SPD, *Parteiarbeit: Zeitung machen*, 2 vols. (Bonn: SPD-PV, n.d. [1981]), i. 7; SPD, *Jahrbuch 1975/77*, 322.

99. SPD, *Jahrbuch 1975/77*, 322.

100. Edgar Einemann, 'Modernes Computer-Netzwerk für die Partei', *Vorwärts*, 8 (1993), 27.

101. 'The Impact Campaign and What It's All About', *Conservative Newsline* (Jan. 1984), 7.

102. Basil Feldman, 'Making an Impact Helps us Win', *Conservative Newsline* (Jan. 1984), 10; ConPar, *Your Party*; ConPar, *Guide to Local Government Elections in England and Wales*, 24; ConPar, *Local Government Campaigning*, 5.

103. LabPar, *Making New Members*; see also LabPar, *Community Newsletters* (London: LabPar, n.d. [1980s]); LabPar, *NEC Report to Conference 1985*, 180.

104. CDU, *Mitgliederwerbung leicht gemacht: Erfolgreiche Modelle für CDU-Verbände*, 44.
105. Bruno Heck, 'Geredet ist genug gewesen', *Die Entscheidung*, 11 (1966), 13.
106. Egon Bahr, in SPD, *Parteitag 1977*, 485.
107. Larry Whitty, 'Operation Mass Membership', *Labour Party News* (Sept.–Oct. 1988), 6.
108. 'Out of the Shadows', *Labour Party News* (Nov.–Dec. 1988), 9.
109. LabPar, *A Year of Labour Party Development: Labour Must Prepare* (London: LabPar, 1944).

6. LINKING PARTY STRATEGIES WITH ORGANIZATIONAL CHANGE

1. SPD, *Ziele und Wege der Parteireform: Die Mitgliederpartei der Zukunft braucht eine moderne Organisation* (Bonn SPD-PV, n.d. (1993), 4.
2. Indeed, at the beginning of the 1990s some party analysts had become convinced that leaders of established parties were becoming ever more insulated from the pressures of member-democracy. Richard Katz and Peter Mair, 'Changing Models of Party Organization and Party Democracy: The Emergence of the Cartel Party', *Party Politics*, 1 (1995), 5–28.
3. Hans Rattinger, 'Abkehr von den Parteien?', *aus Politik und Zeitgeschichte*, 11 (1993), 24–35; Peter Haungs, 'Aktuelle Probleme der Parteiendemokratie', *Jahrbuch für Politik*, 2 (1992), 37–64.
4. Malte Ristau, 'Bewegliche Wähler, dezimierte Volksparteien', *Vorwärts*, 1 (1993), 14.
5. SPD, *Parteitag 1991*, 712–21.
6. CDU, *Moderne Parteiarbeit in den 90er Jahren* (Bonn: CDV-BGSt, 1989), 456.
7. SPD, *Ziele und Wege der Parteireform*, 7.
8. CDU, *Bundesparteitag 1989*; CDU, *Moderne Parteiarbeit in den 90er Jahren*, 459.
9. As the party's general secretary and federal manager later described them. CDU, *Bericht der Bundesgeschäftsstelle 1991*, 2.
10. Karlheinz Blessing (ed.), *SPD 2000; Die Modernisierung der SPD* (Marburg: Schüren Presseverlag, 1993), 194.
11. CDU *Bundesparteitag 1989*, 461.
12. SPD, *Ziele und Wege der Parteireform*, 8.
13. Ibid. 4.
14. CDU, *Bundesparteitag 1989*, 462.
15. CDU, *Bericht der Bundesgeschäftsstelle 1991*, 2. This echoed diag-

noses made almost two decades earlier for the CDU state party in Hessen: 'The modern party must become aware that today it offers only one (of many) opportunities for leisure-time activity. . . . Participation in a party must be interesting and enjoyable.' Peter Radunski and Alexander Niemetz, *Mitgliederwerbung: Konzept und Praxis* (Frankfurt/M.: CDU-Landesverband Hessen, n.d. [1969/70]), 3.

16. Doris Ahnen, 'Organisationspolitische Diskussionen und Maßnahmen der SPD auf Bundesebene seit ihrem Ausscheiden aus der Regierungsverantwortung 1982' (master's thesis, University of Trier, 1990). These are advertised in the membership magazine and are aimed at party members, though non-members may also participate. An article in the SPD membership magazine compared this travel-service with tours the German Automobile Club offers to *its* members; however, party tours were said to be superior because they are vacations which are specifically tailored to the interests of party members. Karlheinz Schonauer, 'Reisen mit Sinn und Verstand', *Vorwärts*, 3 (1991), 19–22.

17. CDU, *Moderne Parteiarbeit in den 90er Jahren*, 459.

18. SPD, *SPD 2000* (Bonn: SPD-PV, 1993), 31.

19. Ibid. 36.

20. Peter Radunski, 'Volksparteien in den 90er Jahren: Die Union vor neuen Herausforderungen', *Sonde*, 22/3 (1989), 25.

21. At its 1994 Conference, the CDU came closer to adopting quotas for female candidates.

22. SPD, *SPD 2000*, 45.

23. CDU, *Moderne Parteiarbeit in den 90er Jahren*, 461.

24. 'In der Partei brauchen auch neue Kräfte ihren Platz', 18. Fourteen years earlier, General Secretary Geißler had also told interviewers that creating new opportunities for participation was the way to combat *Parteienverdroßenheit*. 'Wie kann man der Parteienverdroßenheit begegnen?', *Düsseldorfer Nachrichten*, 19 Apr. 1977.

25. SPD, *SPD 2000*, 44.

26. CDU, *Moderne Parteiarbeit in den 90er Jahren*, 457, 464. Already in 1969, Radunski's and Schönbohm's thirty-four theses on party reform advocated making the party more open to non-members. Peter Radunski, Wulf Schönbohm, and Helmut Pütz, '34 Thesen zur Reform der CDU', *Sonde*, 2/4 (1969), 4–22.

27. SPD, *SPD 2000*, 35.

28. Karsten Plog, 'Ist Schnuppern an der Kieler CDU illegal?', *Frankfurter Rundschau*, 24 Sept. 1993, 4. The party executive of the North Rhine-Westphalian CDU proposed the introduction of free one-year

trial memberships in 1993, but the state party conference rejected the idea. 'Urwahl der Parlamentskandidaten', *FAZ*, 5 July 1993, 4.

29. His resignation was prompted by persistent allegations that he misled a committee which was investigating improprieties in the 1987 election campaign for the Schleswig-Holstein state parliament.

30. The idea of party primaries was mentioned as early as the 1970 party conference, and was mentioned again in 1982 as a possible way of increasing member activity. Peter Lösche and Franz Walter, *Die SPD: Klassenpartei—Volkspartei—Quotenpartei*, (Darmstadt: Wissenschaftliche Buchgesellschaft, 1992), 207; SPD, 'Lebendiger Ortsverein', app. to SPD, *Parteitag 1982*, 4.

31. See e.g. Karlheinz Blessing and Ralf Leinemann, 'Urwahl der Kandidaten', *Vorwärts*, 8 (1992), 11; see also Karlheinz Blessing, 'Mehr Demokratie wagen', ibid. 11 (1991), 38.

32. 'Ohne Kurs und Kapitän', *Der Spiegel*, 19 (1993), 29–35.

33. Over 56% of SPD members participated in the balloting, and the election gave the Rhineland-Palatinate minister president, Rudolf Scharping, slightly more than 40% of the vote in a three-way race. Eckhard Fuhr, 'Sonntag mit Folgen', *FAZ*, 15 June 1993, 1.

34. 'Urwahl und Mitgliederentscheid: Die SPD erprobt die direkte Demokratie', *FAZ*, 20 Nov. 1993, 2.

35. 'Parteireform als Zauberwort', ibid. 29 June 1993, 1; 'Eylman fordert Urwahlen bei der CDU', ibid. 22 June 1993, 1; 'Langen für Befragung unter CDU-Mitglieder', ibid. 25 June 1993, 2; 'Urwahl der Parlamentskandidaten', ibid. 5 July 1993, 'Zur Person: Hans Eichel', *Frankfurter Rundschau*, 24 June 1993, 4.

36. Stuart Weir, 'Operation Scapegoat', *New Statesman and Society*, 4 Sept. 1992, 16.

37. David Denver, 'Britain: Centralized Parties with Decentralized Selection', in Michael Gallagher and Michael Marsh (eds.), *Candidate Selection in Comparative Perspective* (London: Sage Publications, 1988), 47–71.

38. Pippa Norris and Joni Lovenduski, *Political Representation: Gender, Race and Class in the British Parliament* (Cambridge: Cambridge University Press, 1994).

39. Robert Garner and Richard Kelly, *British Political Parties Today* (Manchester: Manchester University Press, 1993), 166–7.

40. LabPar, *Promoting our Values* (London: LabPar, 1988); 'Smith Pulls off High-Risk Gamble', *Guardian*, 30 Sept. 1993, 1.

41. Patrick Wintour, 'Local Party Ballots Show Way to One Member, One Vote', *Guardian*, 8 Oct. 1988, 4.

42. 'Block Voting Reform may be Linked to Membership Drive', *Independent*, 7 Oct. 1989, 7.

43. Patrick Wintour, 'Membership Drive Is On', *Guardian*, 5 July 1988, 6.
44. Richard Heffernan and Mike Marqusee, *Defeat from the Jaws of Victory: Inside Kinnock's Labour Party* (London: Verso, 1992), 330.
45. Heffernan and Marqusee say that the initiative originated with the leftist Tribune Group: ibid. 326.
46. Weir, 'Operation Scapegoat', 16–17. Weir claims that in 1989 only 12,000 trade unionists joined the party under the reduced membership-fee scheme.
47. Patrick Wintour, 'Blair Says Reform Will "Change Party Culture"', *Guardian*, 27 Sept. 1993, 6.

7. MEMBERSHIP SUPPORT FOR POLITICAL PARTIES: HOW MUCH HAS REALLY CHANGED?

1. Reprinted on cover of Harold Croft, *Party Organisation*, 8th edn. (London: LabPar, 1948).
2. Even here, the information is not comparable over time, because the official reporting format has changed several times. Most importantly, since 1984 members' reported contributions have been merged with 'other regular contributions', a category which includes the levies which some parties expect all their elected office-holders to pay.
3. At a conversion rate of £1/DM2.7.
4. At an exchange rate of 2.94 DM/£ *The Times*, 2 July 1987, 26. The difference was even greater than this suggests, because the German campaigns were mostly conducted (though not necessarily fully paid for) in 1986.
5. From *Bundestag* reports, various years. See also Christine Landfried, *Parteienfinanzen und politische Macht* (Baden-Baden: Nomos Verlagsgesellschaft, 1990).
6. Michael Pinto-Duschinsky, *British Political Finance 1830–1980* (Washington: American Enterprise Institute, 1981); id., 'Trends in British Political Funding 1979–1983', *Parliamentary Affairs*, 38 (1985), 328–47; id., 'Trends in British Political Funding 1983–1987', *Parliamentary Affairs*, 42 (1989), 197–212.
7. Michael Harrison, Clare Dobie, and Samir Shah, 'Big Tory Backers Freeze Donations', *Independent*, 16 Mar. 1992, 28.
8. Philip Stephens, 'Tory Funders Find Out the Party may be Over', *Financial Times*, 8 July 1993, 8.
9. Stephanie Münke, *Wahlkampf und Machtverschiebung* (Berlin: Duncker & Humblot, 1952); 'Bis zur letzten Minute: Vorbildlicher Einsatz aller CDU-KV', *Deutsches Monatsblatt*, 8/10 (1961), 4;

Klaus von Beyme, Peter Pawelka, Peter Staisch, and Peter Seibt, *Wahlkampf und Parteiorganisation: Eine Regionalstudie zum Bundestagswahlkampf 1969* (Tübingen: J. C. Mohr, 1974), 53; Norbert Schneider, *Parteien und Kandidaten* (Cologne: Walter Kleikamp, 1972), 237, 245; Kurt Faltlhauser, *Wahlkampf im Wahlkreis* (Augsburg: Dissertationsdruck- und Verlagsanstalt Werner Blasaditch, 1972), 393.

10. Kurt Faltlhauser, 'Aspekte des Wahlkampfes: Image, Öffentlichkeit und Parteiorganisation', in George Golter and Elmar Pieroth (eds.), *Die Union in der Opposition* (Düsseldorf: Econ Verlag, 1970), 45. A similar verdict was reached by an observer of the parliamentary campaigns in Heidelberg in 1969, where, despite their thousands of members, both the local CDU and SPD campaigns were forced to hire professional poster-hangers and leaflet-deliverers. Peter Haungs, 'Abschließende Betrachtungen', in id. (ed.), *Wahlkampf als Ritual?* (Meisenheim am Glan: Verlag Anton Hain, 1975), 311.

11. CDU, *Wahlkampfbericht der Bundesgeschäftsstelle zum Bundestagswahlkampf 1986/87* (Bonn: CDU-BGSt, n.d. [1987]), 11; SPD, *Jahrbuch 1979–1981*, 284.

12. Münke, *Wahlkampf und Machtverschiebung*, 26, 39; Renate Mayntz, *Parteigruppen in der Großstadt* (Cologne: Westdeutscher Verlag, 1959), 39; Nils Diedrich, 'Party Members and Local Party Branches', in Otto Stammer (ed.), *Party Systems, Party Organizations, and the Politics of the New Masses* (Berlin: Freie Universität Berlin, 1968), 108; Claudia Strobel, *Eine lokale Parteigruppe der SPD in einer nordbayerischen Großstadt* (dissertation: Salzburg University, 1976), 95–108; Schneider, *Parteien und Kandidaten*, 104–11, 129; Norbert Lammert, *Lokale Organisationsstrukturen innerparteilicher Willensbildung: Fallstudie am Beispiel eines CDU-Kreisverbandes im Ruhrgebiet* (Bonn: Eicholz Verlag, 1976), 75; Douglas Chalmers, *The Social Democratic Party of Germany* (New Haven: Yale University Press, 1964), 186; Vera Gemmecke, *Parteien im Wahlkampf* (Meisenheim am Glan: Verlag Anton Hain, 1967), 41; Ulrich Lohmar, *Innerparteiliche Demokratie* (Stuttgart: Ferdinand Enke Verlag, 1963), 41; Heino Kaack, 'Die Basis der Parteien: Struktur und Funktion der Ortsvereine', *Zeitschrift für Parlamentsfragen*, 2/1 (1971), 26; Renate Mayntz, 'Lokale Parteigruppe in der kleinen Gemeinde', *Zeitschrift für Politik*, 2/1 (1955), 62; Gerhard Wurzbacher *et al.*, *Das Dorf im Spannungsfeld industrieller Entwicklung* (Stuttgart: Ferdinand Enke Verlag, 1961), 255; Benita Luckman, *Politik in einer deutschen Kleinstadt* (Stuttgart: Ferdinand Enke Verlag, 1970), 195; Bernhard Vogel and Peter Haungs, *Wahlkampf und Wählertradition: Eine Studie zur Bundes-*

tagswahl 1961 (Cologne: Westdeutscher Verlag, 1965), 234; Rüdiger Andel, 'Die CDU in der Bundestagswahl von 1969', in Haungs (ed.), *Wahlkampf als Ritual?*, 28.

13. Wolfgang Falke, *Die Mitglieder der CDU* (Berlin: Duncker & Humblot, 1982); Horst Becker and Bodo Hombach, *Die SPD von Innen* (Bonn: Verlag Neue Gesellschaft, 1983), Oskar Niedermayer, 'Innerparteiliche Partizipation', *aus Politik und Zeitgeschichte*, 11 (1989), 20; SPD, *Jahrbuch 1984/85*, 177.

14. SPD, *Parteitag 1956*, 231; *Parteitag 1960*, 493; *Jahrbuch 1964/65*, 182; *Parteitag 1966*, 240.

15. Becker and Hombach, *SPD von Innen*, 102.

16. INFAS, *Mitglieder und Ortsvereine im SPD-Bezirk Franken* (n.p., n.d. [1981]), 28.

17. SPD, *Jahrbuch*, B28–B29.

18. 'Wintertraining für den Wahlsieg', *Sozialdemokrat Magazin*, 10 (1975), 11; SPD, *Jahrbuch 1984/85*, 209; SPD, *Jahrbuch 1986/87*, 672; 'Mit Stadtteilzeitung macht die SPD Werbung durch die Hintertür', *Die Welt*, 26 Aug. 1985; SPD, *Jahrbuch 1990*, 28–9; Gero Kalt, 'Politik will verkauft sein', *Das Parlament*, 13 Sept. 1986, 18.

19. 'Kess & Dott' , *Einblick: Sozialdemokratisches Mitgliedermagazin*, 1 (1974), 6.

20. Gunlicks, *Local Government in the German Federal System* (Durham, NC: Duke University Press, 1986).

21. Bernhard Beger, 'Das schmale Fundament: Der CDU fehlen die Mitglieder', *Die politische Meinung*, 5/55 (1960), 6; CDU, *Bericht der Bundesgeschäftsstelle 1983*, 78.

22. In the 1970s, this was seen as a particular problem of rural areas. Karl-Heinz Naßmacher and Wolfgang Rudzio, 'Das lokale Parteiensystem auf dem Lande: Dargestellt am Beispiel der Rekrutierung von Gemeinderäten', in Hans-Georg Wehling (ed.), *Dorfpolitik* (Opladen: Leske & Budrich, 1978), 133; Heino Kaack, *Geschichte und Struktur des deutschen Parteiensystems* (Opladen: Westdeutscher Verlag, 1971), 474.

23. SPD, *SPD 2000*, 246. For state-by-state figures on SPD local-government participation, see Heinrich Tiemann, 'Die SPD in den neuen Bundesländern: Organisation und Mitglieder', *Zeitschrift für Parlamentsfragen*, 3 (1993), 415–22.

24. Kaack, *Geschichte und Struktur des deutschen Parteiensystems*, 474.

25. From a survey of 548 CDU and SPD party associations in the state of Rhineland-Palatinate. See Susan Scarrow, 'Does Local Party Organization Make a Difference? Political Parties and Local Government Elections in Germany', *German Politics*, 2/3 (1993), 382–3.

26. Ralph Miliband, 'Socialism and the Myth of the Golden Past', *Socialist Register 1964*, 92–103.

27. These figures come from Swaddle, who discusses differences in the wording of questions and in collection methods: Kevin Swaddle, 'Coping with a Mass Electorate' (doctoral dissertation, Oxford University, 1990), 211.

28. David Butler and Donald Stokes, *Political Change in Britain: Forces Shaping Electoral Choice* (London: Macmillan, 1969), 25; David Butler, *The British General Election of 1951* (London: Macmillan, 1952), 144.

29. Patrick Seyd and Paul Whitely, *Labour's Grass Roots* (Oxford: Clarendon Press, 1992), 95; eid. and Jeremy Richardson, *True Blues* (Oxford: Clarendon Press, 1994), 74.

30. Mark Benney, A. P. Gray, and R. H. Pear, *How People Vote* (London: Routledge & Kegan Paul, 1956), 77–8; H. G. Nichols, *The British General Election of 1950* (London: Macmillan, 1951); *The British General Election of 1951*; id., *The British General Election of 1955* (London: Macmillan, 1955); R. S. Milne and H. C. Mackenzie, *Marginal Seat, 1955* (London: The Hansard Society for Parliamentary Government, 1958).

31. Author's interviews with sixty-nine local, regional, and national party officials and activists from the Labour, Conservative, and (now) Liberal Democratic parties. Interviews, which focused on constituencies in Oxfordshire and Leeds, were conducted with chairs of ward and constituency parties, with local-government representatives, with parliamentary candidates and MPs, and with paid party employees. In addition, the author had access to transcripts of interviews conducted with party agents in Yorkshire constituencies immediately after the 1987 general election. These transcripts were kindly made available by Bob Franklin of Leeds University. For a fuller account of all these interviews, see app. 1 in Susan Scarrow, 'Organizing for Victory: Political Party Members and Party Organizing Strategies in Great Britain and West Germany, 1945–1989' (doctoral dissertation, Yale University, 1991).

32. David Butler and Dennis Kavanagh, *The British General Election of 1987* (London: Macmillan, 1983), 212.

33. Wilfred Fienburgh and Manchester Fabian Society, 'Put Policy on the Agenda', *Fabian Journal* (Feb. 1952), 28.

34. R. L. Borthwick, 'The Labour Party', in H. M. Drucker (ed.), *Multi-Party Britain* (London: Macmillan, 1979), 59.

35. Ibid. 59.

36. Jean Blondel, 'The Conservative Association and the Labour Party in Reading', *Political Studies*, 6/2 (1958), 113–15; Benney, Gray, and

Pear, *How People Vote*, 46–9; D. V. Donnison and D. E. G. Plowman, 'The Functions of Local Labour Parties', *Political Studies*, 2/2 (1954), 162; Julius Gould, ' "Riverside": A Labour Constituency', *Fabian Journal* (Nov. 1954), 14; A. H. Birch, *Small-Town Politics* (London: Oxford University Press, 1959), 48–53, 72–4.

37. Robert McKenzie, *British Political Parties* (Melbourne: William Heinemann, 1955), 548.

38. Ibid. 547; LabPar, *Interim Report of the Committee of Enquiry into Party Organization* (London: LabPar, 1967), 4.

39. 'Survey of South Eastern Area', unpub. document (n.d. [1951]) (CCO/500/11/3); *Final Report of the Committee on Party Organization* (Colyton Committee) (1957) (CCO/500/1/24–5).

40. T. E. M. McKitterick, 'The Membership of the Party', *Political Quarterly*, 31 (1960), 312–19; R. L. Leonard, *Elections in Britain* (London: D. Van Nostrand, 1968), 55; David Berry, *The Sociology of Grass Roots Politics* (London: Macmillan, 1970), 43; ConPar, *Cities Enquiry* (1967) (CCO/500/1/58).

41. Seyd and Whitely, *Labour's Grass Roots*, 88–9.

42. Author's interviews.

43. Birch, *Small-Town Politics*, 48–53, 160–80; Martin Linton, 'The Membership Mystery', *Labour Weekly*, 28 Sept. 1979, 12–13.

44. Geoff Hodgson, *Labour at the Crossroads* (Oxford: Martin Robertson, 1981), 58; Frank Ward, 'Party Membership: Are We Asking the Correct Questions?', *Labour Organiser*, 59/611 (1979), 17.

45. Joyce Gould, 'Towards a Mass Membership', *Labour Organiser*, 65/635 (1985), 2.

46. Whitely, Seyd, and Richardson, *True Blues*, 68.

47. Jude England, 'Attitudes of Councillors', in *Conduct of Local Authority Business* (London: HMSO Cmnd 9798, 1986), ii. 42.

48. Seyd and Whitely, *Labour's Grass Roots*, 93.

49. Whitely, Seyd, and Richardson, *True Blues*, 74.

50. Robert Pinkney, 'An Alternative Political Strategy? Liberals in Power in English Local Government', *Local Government Studies*, 10/3 (1984), 69–84.

51. Author's interviews.

52. It should be noted that the authors reach this conclusion even though they seem to find relatively *high* levels of participation. In one survey, 29% of Conservative Party members and 74% of Labour Party members said they had recently engaged in at least two of the following four activities: attending party meetings, serving on party committees, helping in general elections, helping in local elections. Frank Bealey, Jean Blondel, and W. P. McCann, *Constitu-*

ency Politics: A Study of Newcastle-under-Lyme (London: Faber & Faber, 1965), 405.
53. 'Party Games', *New Society*, 33/668 (1975), 179.

8. THE CHANGING NATURE OF MEMBERSHIP PARTIES

1. Mosei Ostrogorski, *Democracy and the Organization of Political Parties*, trans. Frederick Clarke, ed. Seymour Lipset (Chicago: Quadrangle Books, 1964), p. lxxxii.
2. Peter Lösche and Franz Walter, *Die SPD: Klassenpartei—Volkspartei—Quotenpartei* (Darmstadt: Wissenschaftliche Buchgesellschaft, 1992).
3. e.g. in 1994 the SPD party treasurer promised readers that future issues of the magazine would include reply coupons for members who were unhappy with impending increases in dues, so that members could register this discontent with the party executive. Inge Wettig-Danielmeier, 'Die Mitgliedsbeiträge sind unser finanzielles Rückgrat', *Vorwärts, 2 (1994), 28.*
4. Richard Katz and Peter Mair, 'The Evolution of Party Organizations in Europe: The Three Faces of Party Organization', *American Review of Politics*, 14 (1993), 593–617; eid., 'Changing Models of Party Organization and Party Democracy: The Emergence of the Cartel Party', *Party Politics*, 1 (1995), 5–28.
5. Peter Radunski, 'Fit für die Zukunft?', *Sonde*, 4 (1991), 3–8.

BIBLIOGRAPHY

PARTY AND PARTY-AFFILIATED PUBLICATIONS

Social Democratic Party

(FES numbers refer to documents in the library of the Friedrich-Ebert-Stiftung, Bonn.)

'Aktion: Stadtteilzeitung', *Sozialdemokrat Magazin*, 3 (1975), 27.

BECKER, HORST, and HOMBACH, BODO, *Die SPD von Innen* (Bonn: Verlag Neue Gesellschaft, 1983).

BLESSING, KARLHEINZ, 'Mehr Demokratie wagen', *Vorwärts*, 11 (1991), 38.

——(ed.), *SPD 2000: Die Modernisierung der SPD* (Marburg: Schüren Presseverlag, 1993).

——and LEINEMANN, RALF, 'Urwahl der Kandidaten', *Vorwärts*, 8 (1992), 11.

BÖRNER, HOLGER, 'Bereit sein zum Gespräch mit dem Wähler: Vertrauensarbeit der Partei', *Neue Gesellschaft*, 22/4 (1975), 271–3.

——'Zeigen, wer wir sind!', *Sozialdemokrat Magazin*, 8 (1976), 5.

BRANDT, WILLY, and BÖRNER, HOLGER, 'Zeig jetzt, daß Du Sozialdemokrat bist. Tu was', *Sozialdemokrat Magazin*, 9 (1976), insert.

'Bürgerbüros—oft die letzte Instanz', *Sozialdemokrat Magazin*, 11–12 (1987), 22.

'Checklist für den Endspurt', *Sozialdemokrat Magazin*, 1 (1987), 13.

'Diskussion im Wohnzimmer', *Sozialdemokrat Magazin*, 1 (1983), 14.

'Du und Wir! Die erste zentrale Werbeaktion der SPD', *SPD-Rundschau* Sept. 1950), 1.

'Eine Partei der Armen?', *Vorwärts*, 3 (1991), 14–15.

EINEMANN, EDGAR, 'Modernes Computer-Netzwerk für die Partei', *Vorwärts*, 8 (1993), 27.

ERLER, FRITZ, 'Gedanken zur Politik und inneren Ordnung der Sozialdemokratie', *Neue Gesellschaft*, 5/1 (1958), 3–8.

FRIEDRICH, BRUNO, 'Bundestagwahlen 1969: Wahlkampf und Parteiorganisation', *Neue Gesellschaft*, 16/2 (1969), 102–6.

——'Der sozialdemokratische Ortsverein', in Herbert Wehner, Bruno

Friedrich, and Alfred Nau, *Parteiorganisation* (Bonn: Verlag Neue Gesellschaft, 1969).

——'Wahlkampf und Parteiorganisation', in Herbert Wehner, Bruno Friedrich, and Alfred Nau, *Parteiorganisation* (Bonn: Verlag Neue Gesellschaft, 1969).

JARREN, OTFRIED, 'Kommunikation organiseren: Zum Konzept "Bürgerzeitung"', *Neue Gesellschaft*, 25 (1978), 939–42.

'Jede Beitragsmark mehr, hilft weiter', *Sozialdemokrat Magazin*, 6 (1985), 12–14.

'Kess & Dott', *Einblick: Sozialdemokratisches Mitgliedermagazin*, 1 (1974), 6.

KOSCHNICK, HANS, 'Bundestagswahlkampf', *Neue Gesellschaft*, 23 (1976), 972.

'Mach es noch besser!', *SPD-Rundschreiben*, 141 (1952).

MERTINS, ARTHUR, 'Wahlkampfrichtlinien', reprinted in *Wahlsekretärbesprechung 24. Januar 1947* (FES: PV Alter Bestand Teil II, 05142).

'Nicht nur in der Sonne dösen', *Sozialdemokrat Magazin*, 7 (1980), 16–17.

OLLENHAUER, ERICH, BRANDT, WILLY, WEHNER, HERBERT, and NAU, ALFRED, 'An die Mitglieder der Sozialdemokratischen Partei Deutschlands', letter, (SPD-PV, 1962).

RAULFS, ALEX, 'Die Wahlkampf—"Instrumente" der SPD', *Neue Gesellschaft*, 23/7 (1976), 559–61.

RISTAU, MALTE, 'Bewegliche Wähler, dezimierte Volksparteien', *Vorwärts*, 1 (1993), 14.

SCHONAUER, KARLHEINZ, 'Reisen mit Sinn und Verstand', *Vorwärts*, 3 (1991), 19–22.

SCHÜTZ, KLAUS, 'Die Öffentlichkeitsarbeit der Mitgliederpartei', report of Arbeitsgemeinschaft E, *Parteitag der SPD: Protokoll 1964*.

'So wird's gemacht: 15 Schritte aum Erfolg', *Sozialdemokrat Magazin*, 10 (1984), 12.

Sozialdemokratische Partei Deutschlands, *Jahrbuch der SPD*, various years.

——*Parteitag der SPD: Protokoll*, various years.

——*Kleines Wahlhelfer A-B-C* (Hanover: SPD-PV, 1947).

——*Propagandatechnik der SPD*, material prepared for the 'Socialistische Propaganda- und Expertenkonferenz', Dorking, Surrey, 29 Oct.–Nov. 1950 (FES: PV Alter Bestand Teil I, HB3 1950).

——*Herner Beschlüsse für die Sozialdemokratische Partei Deutschlands* (Bonn: SPD-PV, 1952).

——*Der sozialdemokratische Wahlhelfer* (Bonn: SPD-PV, 1953).

——'Werbung und Propaganda der Sozialdemokratischen Partei

Deutschlands im Bundestagswahlkampf 1953' (n.d. [1953]) (FES: PV Alter Bestand Teil II, 04661).

——'Gegen die SPD gerichtete Kräfte und Einflüsse beim Bundestagswahlkampf 1953', Jan. 1954 (FES: PV Alter Bestand Teil II, 04662).

——*Der kleine Wahlhelfer* (Bonn: SPD-PV, 1953).

——*Zur Parteidiskussion: Empfehlungen des Parteivorstandes und des Parteiausschusses* (Bonn: SPD-PV, n.d. [1954])

——'Abschrift', from SPD-PV, 1955 (FES: PV Alter Bestand Teil II, 05137).

——*9 Punkte zur verstärkten Organisationsarbeit* (Bonn: SPD-PV, 1955).

——*Mitgliederwerben: Eine leichte Sache* (Bonn: SPD-PV, n.d. [1956]).

——*Wie führe ich den Wahlkampf?* (Bonn: SPD-PV, 1957; reprinted 1960).

——*Bericht der Kommission zur Prüfung der allgemeinen Organisationsprobleme* (Bonn: SPD-PV, 1958) (FES: PV Alter Bestand Teil II, 04786).

——*Mitglieder werben—leichter gemacht* (Bonn: SPD-PV, n.d. [1959]).

——*SPD Handbuch für Vertrauensleute* (Stuttgart: SPD-Landesverband, n.d. [1964]).

——*Mitgliederwerben—aber wie?* (Bonn: SPD-PV, n.d. [1968]).

——*Aktion WIR . . . werben neue Freunde* (Bonn: SPD-PV, n.d. [1971]).

——*Hinweise zur Mitgliederwerbeaktion* (Bonn: SPD-PV, 1973).

——'Dokumente: zur praktischen Parteiarbeit' (Bonn: SPD-PV, n.d. [1975]).

——*Organisationshandbuch: Arbeitshilfe für sozialdemokratische Funktionäre* (Stuttgart: SPD Baden-Württemberg, 1975).

——*Handbuch Parteiarbeit: Wahlkampfmachen* (Bonn: SPD-PV, n.d. [1976]).

——*Handbuch für die Arbeit in sozialdemokratischen Ortsvereinen: Mitglieder werben—Vertrauensarbeit* (Bonn: SPD-PV, n.d. [1978]).

——*Parteiarbeit: Zeitung machen* (2 vols) (Bonn: SPD-PV, n.d. [1981]).

——'Lebendiger Ortsverein', app. to SPD, *Parteitag 1982*.

——*Materialien zur innerparteilichen Bildungsarbeit: Neumitgliederschulung* (Bonn: SPD-PV, 1982).

——*Tu was. Mit der SPD. Mitgliederwerbung* (Bonn: SPD-PV, n.d. [1984]).

——*Der rote Faden im Labyrinth: Verbraucherarbeit der Bürgerbüros und Ortsvereine* (Bonn: SPD-PV, 1986).

——*Politik lebendig: Handbuch der Parteiarbeit vor Ort* (Bonn: SPD-PV, n.d. [1987+]).

——*Der direkte Draht zum Wähler: Vertrauensarbeit per Telefon* (n.p.: SPD Nordrhein-Westfalen, 1984, and revised 2nd edn. 1990).

——*Wahlkampf '90* (Bonn: SPD-PV, 1990).

——*SPD 2000* (Bonn: SPD-PV, 1993).

——*Ziele und Wege der Parteireform: Die Mitgliederpartei der Zukunft braucht eine moderne Organization* (Bonn: SPD-PV, n.d. [1993]).

'Telefonwerbung', *Sozialdemokrat Magazin*, 6 (1988), 4–5.

'Das 100 000-Mann-Ding', *Sozialdemokrat Magazin*, 8 (1980), 28.

'Tu was. Mit der SPD', *Sozialdemokrat Magazin*, 10 (1984), 6–7.

'Um die Aktivierung des Parteilebens', *Neuer Vorwärts*, 6 June 1952.

'Wahlkampf: Wie Kann ich helfen?', *Sozialdemokrat Magazin*, 1 (1978), 10.

'Wahlkampftip des Monats: Direkter Draht zum Wähler', *Sozialdemokrat Magazin*, 10 (1986), 10.

'Wahlkampftip des Monats: Video im Winterwahlkampf', *Sozialdemokrat Magazin*, 11 (1986), 8.

WEHNER, HERBERT, 'Bundestagswahl 1965', in SPD, *Jarbuch 1964/65*.

——'Bericht über die Beratungsergebnisse der Kommission "Reform der Parteiorganisation"', in SPD, *Außerordentlicher Parteitag 1971: Protokoll*, 19–27.

'Wilhelm-Dröscher-Preis: Parteiarbeit zum Anfassen', *Sozialdemokrat Magazin*, 11 (1981), 14.

'Wintertraining für den Wahlsieg', *Sozialdemokrat Magazin*, 10 (1975), 6–13.

WISCHNEWSKI, HANS JÜRGEN, 'Wahlkampf 1969', *Neue Gesellschaft*, 16/3 (1969), 157–60.

Christian Democratic Union

(KAS numbers refer to documents in the archives of the Konrad-Adenauer-Stiftung, St. Augustin.)

'Aktionen im Winter', *Deutsches Monatsblatt*, 34/11 (1986), 4–5.

'Aus Liebe zu Deutschland: Jeder von uns spendet 10 Mark', *Deutsches Monatsblatt*, 24/7–8 (1976), cover.

'Auto-Aufkleber: Der neue Trend', *Deutsches Monatsblatt*, 26/11 (1978), 25.

BEGER, BERNHARD, 'Das schmale Fundament: Der CDU fehlen die Mitglieder', *Die politische Meinung*, 5/55 (1960), 3–8.

'Bis zur letzten Minute: Vorbildlicher Einsatz aller CDU-KV', *Deutsches Monatsblatt*, 8/10 (1961), 4.

'Die CDU auf dem Wege zur Mitgliederpartei', *Deutsches Monatsblatt*, 21/9 (1974), 4.

Christlich-Demokratische Partei Deutschlands, *Bericht der Bundesgeschäftsstelle*, various years.

——*Bundesparteitag der CDU*, various years.

——*Mitgliederwerben: Eine leichte Sache* (Bonn: CDU-BGSt [1956]).

——*20 Schritte zum Wahlsieg*, 3rd edn. (Bonn: CDU-BGSt, 1969). (1st edn. 1965.)

——*Leitfaden für die Mitgliederwerbung* (Bonn: CDU-BGSt, 1972).

——*Bericht der Organisationskommission Vorlage für die Sitzung des Bundesvorstandes am 25./26. Mai 1973.*

——*Regiebuch 1: Mitgliederwerbung—Aktion 'CDU-Kontakter'*, (Bonn: CDU-BGSt, n.d. [1973]).

——*Regiebuch 3: Mitgliederinitiativen: Das neue Rollenverständnis aktiver CDU-Mitglieder* (Bonn: CDU-BGSt, n.d. [1973]).

——*Regiebuch 4: Wahlkampfmachen* (Bonn: CDU-BGSt, 1974).

——*Regiebuch 5: Kommunalwahlkampf* (Bonn: CDU-BGSt, 1974).

——*Regiebuch 7: Vorpolitischer Raum* (Bonn: CDU-BGSt, 1975).

——'Modellversuch "Kreisverbandsarbeit"', reprinted in Norbert Lammert, *Lokale Organisationsstrukturen innerparteilicher Willensbildung: Fallstudie am Beispiel eines CDU-Kreisverbandes im Ruhrgebiet* (Bonn: Eicholz Verlag, 1976)

——*Regiebuch 8: Großstadtarbeit* (Bonn: CDU-BGSt, 1976).

——*Wahlkampf '76: Maßnahmen und Vorschläge der Bundespartei für die Arbeit in den Wahlkreisen* (Bonn: CDU-BGSt, 1976).

——*Regiebuch 10: CDU-Zeitung* (Bonn: CDU-BGSt, n.d. [1977]).

——*Handbuch Ortsverbandsarbeit: Erfolgreich für die CDU* (Bonn: CDU-BGSt, n.d. [1983]).

——*Mitgliederwerbung leicht gemacht: Erfolgreiche Modelle für CDU-Verbände* (Bonn: CDU-BGSt, 1985).

——*Canvassing-Aktionen* (Bonn: CDU-BGSt, 1986).

——*CDU aktiv: Sommeraktionen* (Bonn: CDU-BGSt, n.d. [1986]).

——*Die CDU ist dabei: Mitmachen bei den Veranstaltungen anderer* (Bonn: CDU-BGSt, 1986).

——*Fit in die Zukunft* (Bonn: CDU-BGSt, 1986).

——*Messen und Ausstellungen* (Bonn: CDU-BGSt, 1986)

——*Nachbarschaftstreffen* (Bonn: CDU-BGSt, 1986).

——*Neue Wahlkampfformen: Telefon-Canvassing* (Bonn: CDU-BGSt, 1986).

——*Neue Wahlkampfformen: Winter Wahlkampf* (Bonn: CDU-BGSt, 1986).

——*Sommeraktionen* (Bonn: CDU-BGSt, 1986).

——*Wahlkampfbericht der Bundesgeschäftsstelle zum Bundestags- wahlkampf 1986/87* (Bonn: CDU-BGSt, n.d. [1987]).

——*Moderne Parteiarbeit in den 90er Jahren* (Bonn: CDU-BGSt, 1989).

——*Bürgernahe Formen der Parteiarbeit: Zielgruppenansprache* (Bonn: CDU-BGSt, 1990).

——*Ganz Ohr: Ideenbörse für Aktionswoche im Wahlkampf '90* (Bonn: CDU-BGSt, 1990).

——*Mitgliederwerbung leicht gemacht* (Bonn: CDU-BGSt, 1990).

FALKE, WOLFGANG, 'Partei und Umwelt: Einige Anmerkungen zu Struktur und Aufgabe der Parteiorganisation', in CDU, *Bericht der Organisationskommission* (1973) (KAS: 2/201/5–4).

GEIßLER, HEINRICH, 'Arbeitsschwerpunkte der CDU als Volkspartei der Mitte', CDU press release, 5 Aug. 1987.

HECK, BRUNO, 'Der Weg zur Mitgliederpartei', *Deutsches Monatsblatt*, 3/5 (1956), 2, 5.

——'Aufruf zur Wahlspende', *Deutsches Monatsblatt*, 4/6 (1957), 1; and 4/7 (1957), 3.

——'Geredet ist genug gewesen', *Die Entscheidung*, 11 (1966), 13.

——'Adenauer und die CDU', *Die politische Meinung*, (Nov./Dec. 1975), 84–106.

'Ja, ich bin dabei', *Deutsches Monatsblatt*, 23/11 (1975), 20.

'Jeder ist aufgerufen', *Union in Deutschland*, 16/21 (1962), 1–2.

'Jetzt den Wahlkampf zur persönlichen Sache machen', *Deutsches Monatsblatt*, 24/9 (1976), 2.

'Kämpft, Freunde!', *Deutsches Monatsblatt*, 31/1 (1983), 12.

KRASKE, KONRAD, 'Wähler haben sich verändert', *Die Entscheidung* (Oct. 1966), 13–14.

'Marschziele der Union', *Deutsches Monatsblatt*, 7/6 (1960), 8–10.

'Mein persönlicher Wahlkampf', *Deutsches Monatsblatt*, 24/9 (1976), 24–5.

'Neue Methode bei der Mitgliederwerbung brachten große Erfolge', *Deutsches Monatsblatt*, 20/2 (1973), 16.

'Noch ist jeder vierte Wähler unentschieden', *Deutsches Monatsblatt*, 35/1 (1987), 3–5.

'Offensive in den Herbst', *Deutsches Monatsblatt*, 34/10 (1986), 24–5.

'Premiere: Werbe-Spots in den Privaten', *Deutsches Monatsblatt*, 37/5–7 (1989), 5.

PÜTZ, HELMUT, RADUNSKI, PETER, and SCHÖNBOHM, WULF, '34 Thesen zur Reform der CDU', *Sonde*, 4/4 (1969), 5–22.

————————and SIMON, UWE-RAINER, '18 Thesen zur Reform der CDU', *Sonde*, 6/3–4 (1973), 15–21.

RADUNSKI, PETER, 'Die Parteien- und Mobilisierungskampagne', *Sonde*, 2/3 (1980), 90–102.

———'Unser Konzept für den Wahlkampf', *Deutsches Monatsblatt*, 34/9 (1986), 7.

———'Die CDU als moderne Volkspartei: Gedanken zur künftigen Basisorganisation der CDU', *Sonde*, 21/1–2 (1988), 99–106.

———'Volksparteien in den 90er Jahren: Die Union vor neuen Herausforderungen', *Sonde*, 22/3 (1989), 21–9.

———and NIEMETZ, ALEXANDER, *Mitgliederwerbung: Konzept und Praxis* (Frankfurt/M.: CDU Landesverband Hessen, n.d. [1969/70]).

'Schalten Sie Kleinanzeigen!', *Deutsches Monatsblatt*, 34/12 (1986), 13.

'Sommeraktionen', *Deutsches Monatsblatt*, 34/6 (1986), 17.

'Tip für Ihren persönlichen Wahlkampf', *Deutsches Monatsblatt*, 28/9 (1980), 8.

TRIESCH, GÜNTHER, 'Aufmarsch zur Wahlschlacht', *Die politische Meinung*, 92 (1964), 37.

'Verbesserung der Beitragsehrlichkeit', *Union in Deutschland*, 7 (1980), not paginated.

'Wahlkampfbeginn: Der Tag nach der Wahl', *Union in Deutschland*, 24 May 1962, 1.

'Was Sie am Tag der Wahl alles tun können', *Deutsches Monatsblatt*, 31, special issue (1983), 3.

'Werbehelfer', *eilt!*, 8 (1954), 18.

'Werbehelfer', *eilt!*, 1 (1958), 10.

'Werbehelfer', *eilt!*, 3 (1959), 15.

'Wie Kann man der Parteienverdroßenheit begegnen?', *Düsseldorfer Nachrichten*, 19 Apr. 1977.

'Wie Sie Mitbürger überzeugen', *Deutsches Monatsblatt*, 23/10 (1975), 28.

'Wir starten den heißen Wahlkampf', *Deutsches Monatsblatt*, 28/8 (1980), 15–18.

'Zehn Mark als Starthilfe', *Union* (Nov./Dec. 1991), 8.

Labour Party

BARKER, SARA, 'Beware Competitions!', *Labour Organiser*, 33/382 (1954), 32–3.

'Better for You, and Better for Us', *Labour Organiser*, 12 (Sept.–Oct. 1988), back cover.

CROFT, HAROLD, *Conduct of Parliamentary Elections*, 2nd edn. (London: LabPar, 1945).

———*Party Organisation*, 7th, 8th, 12th, 14th, edns. (London: LabPar, 1946, 1948, 1972, 1979).

'Do We Deserve Collectors?', *Labour Organiser*, 37/428 (1958), 29.

GOULD, JOYCE, 'Labour's Approach to the Electorate', *Labour Organiser*, 61/621 (1982), 2–4, 10–12.

———— 'Towards a Mass Membership', *Labour Organiser*, 65/635 (1988), 2–4, 10–12.

'How to Boost Membership', *Labour Party News*, 1 (Oct. 1986), 3–4.

Labour Party, *NEC Report to Conference*, various years.

———— *Report of Conference* (London: LabPar, various years).

———— *A Year of Labour Party Development: Labour Must Prepare* (London: LabPar, 1944).

———— *Victory Membership Campaign* (London: LabPar, 1946).

———— *Guide to the Prelude to Victory Campaign* (London: LabPar, n.d. [1949]).

———— 'Committee of Enquiry into Party Organization, Interim Report', reprinted in *Report of Conference 1955* (London: LabPar, 1955).

———— *Campaign Guide: Labour Party Membership Campaign 1961* (London: LabPar, n.d. [1961]).

———— *Interim Report of the Committee of Enquiry into Party Organisation* (London: LabPar, 1967).

———— *How to Build up the Postal Vote* (London: LabPar, 1970).

———— *Conduct of Parliamentary Elections*, 8th edn. (London: LabPar, 1977).

———— *Make More Members* (London: LabPar, 1979).

———— *Community Newsletters* (London: LabPar, n.d. [1980s]).

———— *Report of the Labour Party Commission of Enquiry 1980* (London: LabPar, n.d. [1980]).

———— *Conduct of Local Elections*, 10th edn. (London: LabPar, 1982).

———— *How to Organise for Victory* (London: LabPar, 1984).

———— *Your Guide to Fund Raising* (Rochdale: East Midlands Regional Council of the Labour Party, 1984).

———— *How to Fight Local Elections* (London: LabPar, 1985).

———— *Making New Members* (London: LabPar, 1986).

———— *Campaign Guide for Labour Listens* (London: LabPar, 1987).

———— *Campaign to Win* (London: LabPar, 1987).

———— *Labour Listens: Campaigning for the 1990s* (London: LabPar, 1987).

———— *Labour Party Rule Book 1987/88* (London: LabPar, 1987).

———— *Targeting to Win* (London: LabPar, 1987).

———— *Promoting Our Values* (London: LabPar, 1988).

———— 'Now Play your Part in Labour's Victory' (advertisement), *Independent*, 3 Oct. 1990, 1.

———— 'Give £15 to Help Labour Win' (advertisement), *Independent*, 29 Mar. 1992, 20.

————'Urgent Election Appeal' (advertisement), *Guardian*, 25 Mar. 1992, 1.

LINTON, MARTIN, 'The Membership Mystery', *Labour Weekly*, 28 Sept. 1979, 12–13.

'Local Elections Have National Significance', *Labour Organiser*, 35/408 (1956).

London Labour Party, 'Membership of the Labour Party', reprinted in *Labour Organiser*, 61/621 (1982).

'Out of the Shadows', *Labour Party News* (Nov./Dec. 1988), 9.

PHILLIPS, MORGAN, 'Mass Membership Campaign', letter, Jan. 1946 (Labour Party Library—Pamphlets 1946).

————*Labour in the Sixties* (London: LabPar, n.d. [1960]).

'Step by Step to National Membership System', *Labour Party News* (Oct. 1990), 28.

'Telephone Canvassing', *Labour Organiser*, 65/638 (1989), 19.

UNDERHILL, REG, 'Get *All* Those Postal Votes', *Labour Organiser*, 50/564 (1970), 70–2.

UNDERHILL, H. R., and WILLIAMS, G. H., 'A Membership Secretary's Job', *Labour Organiser*, 35/413 (1956), 197–9.

'Urgent Election Appeal', advertisement, *Guardian*, 25 Mar. 1992, 1.

WARD, FRANK, 'Party Membership: Are We Asking the Correct Questions?', *Labour Organiser*, 59/611 (1979), 13–19.

WHITTY, LARRY, 'Operation Mass Membership', *Labour Party News*, (Sept.–Oct. 1988), 6–7.

WILLIAMS, A. L., 'Planning for Local Government Elections', *Labour Organiser*, 31/357 (1952), 10–11, 19.

————'Now is the Time for a Big Step Forward!', *Labour Organiser*, 35/408 (1956), 90–1.

WINDLE, R. T., 'To the Election Agent', letter, 8 Feb. 1950 (Labour Party Library: Pamphlets 1950).

Conservative Party

(CCO numbers refer to documents in Conservative Party Archives, Oxford.)

Conservative Party, *Annual Conference Report*, various years.

————*Handbook on Constituency Organisation* (London: The Conservative and Unionist Central Office, 1932).

————*Evidence of Col. Stanley Bell Hon. Treasurer for North-Western Area*, 19 Feb. 1948 (CCO/500/1/20).

————*Minutes of the Committee on Party Reorganisation*, meeting of 7 Oct. 1948 (1948) (CCO/500/1/17).

————*Organisation of Indoor and Outdoor Meetings* (London: CCO, 1948).

————*Final Report of the Committee on Party Organisation* (London: CCO, 1949).

————*Constituency Finance* (London: CCO, 1950).

————*Local Government and the Party Organisation* (London: CCO, 1950).

————*The Party Organisation* (London: CCO, 1950).

————*The Voluntary Worker and the Party Organisation* (London: CCO, 1950).

———— 'Survey of South Eastern Area' (n.d. [1951]) (CCO/500/11/3).

————*Final Report of the Committee on Party Organisation* (Colyton Committee) (1957) (CCO/500/1/24–25).

————*Minutes of the Committee on Party Organisation* (Colyton Committee) (1 May 1957) (CCO/500/1/24).

————*Summary Report (1962 Membership Campaign)* (1962) (CCO 500/11/9).

————*Cities Enquiry* (1967) (CCO/500/1/58).

————*Constituency Finance* (London: CCO, 1969) reprinted in John Lees and Richard Kimber (eds.), *Political Parties in Modern Britain: An Organizational and Functional Guide* (London: Routledge & Kegan Paul, 1972).

————*Election Manual for Key Workers* (London: CCO, n.d. [1980s]).

————*Polling Day Organisation* (London: CCO, n.d. [1980s])

————*Model Rules for Constituency, Branch and European Constituency Councils* (London: CCO, 1986).

————*Your Party* (London: CCO, n.d. [1986]).

————*Guide to Local Government Elections in England and Wales* (London: CCO, 1987).

————*Local Government Campaigning* (London: CCO, 1987).

————*Survey Canvassing* (London: CCO, 1987).

————*Campaign 88* (London: CCO, n.d. [1988]).

FELDMAN, BASIL, *The Path to Power: From Town Hall to Westminster* (London: Conservative Political Centre, 1975).

———— 'Making an Impact Helps us Win', *Conservative Newsline* (Jan. 1984), 10.

'50 Ideas for Raising Money', *Conservative Agents' Journal*, 516 (1963), 11–21.

GARNER, SIR ANTHONY, 'Strengthening the Grass Roots', *Conservative Newsline* (Mar. 1985), 8.

HART, COLIN, *Your Party* (London: CCO [1980]).

'The Impact Campaign and What It's All about', *Conservative Newsline* (Jan. 1984), 7.

LACY, JOHN, 'Campaigning', *Conservative Newsline* (Nov. 1989), 8.

'Membership Drive Must Succeed', *Conservative Newsline* (June 1988), 16.

'Money Matters', *Conservative Newsline* (June 1985), 7–10.

O'BRIEN, GERALD, 'The Point of Publicity', *Conservative Agents' Journal* (Oct. 1966), 4.

PATTIE, GEOFFREY, 'The Tory Antidote to Community Politics', *Crossbow* (Oct. 1973), 17.

RIPPON, GEOFFREY, 'Conservatives and Local Government', *The Councillor*, 1/2 (1948), 13.

'Sky's the Limit', *Conservative Newsline* (May 1988), 1.

'Turning your Votes into Cash', *Conservative Newsline* (Sept. 1984), 8.

WADE, SIR OULTON, 'Why We Must Build a Mass Membership', *Conservative Newsline* (Sept. 1984), 6.

SECONDARY SOURCES

AGRANOFF, ROBERT, *The New Style in Election Campaigns* (Boston: Holbrook Press, 1972).

AHNEN, DORIS, 'Organisationspolitische Diskussionen und Maßnahmen der SPD auf Bundesebene seit ihrem Ausscheiden aus der Regierungsverantwortung 1982' (master's thesis, University of Trier, 1990).

ANDEL, RÜDIGER, 'Die CDU in der Bundestagswahl von 1969', in Peter Haungs (ed.), *Wahlkampf als Ritual?* (Meisenheim am Glan: Hain, 1987).

ANGELL, HAROLD, 'Duverger, Epstein, and the Problem of the Mass Party', *Canadian Journal of Political Science*, 20 (1987), 363–78.

APPLETON, ANDREW and WARD, DANIEL, 'Measuring Party Organization in the United States: An Assessment and a New Approach', *Party Politics*, 1 (1995), 113–31.

ARNIM, HANS HERBERT von, *Die Partei, der Abgeordnete und das Geld* (Mainz: Hase & Koehler, 1991).

ATKINS, RALPH, DAWNAY, IVO, and TUCKER, EMMA, 'Snags Mar Party's Recruitment Drive', *Financial Times*, 1 Oct. 1991, 14.

BAER, DENISE, 'Who Has the Body? Party Institutionalization and Theories of Party Organization', *American Review of Politics*, 14 (1993), 1–38.

BALL, ALAN, *British Political Parties* (London: Macmillan, 1980).

BARBER, BENJAMIN, *Strong Democracy* (Berkeley and Los Angeles: University of California Press, 1984).

BARJONET, ANDRÉ, *Le Parti communiste français* (Paris: Éditions John Didier, 1969).

BARTOLINI, STEFANO, 'The Membership of Mass Parties: The Social

Democratic Experience, 1889–1978', in Hans Daalder and Peter Mair (eds.), *Western European Party Systems: Continuity and Change* (Beverly Hills, Calif.: Sage, 1983).

——and MAIR, PETER, *Identity, Competition and Electoral Availability* (Cambridge: Cambridge University Press, 1990).

BEALEY, FRANK, BLONDEL, JEAN, and MCCANN, W. P., *Constituency Politics: A Study of Newcastle-under-Lyme* (London: Faber & Faber, 1965).

BELL, TIM, 'The Conservatives' Advertising Campaign', in Robert Worcester and Martin Harrop (eds.), *Political Communications: The General Election Campaign of 1979* (London: George Allen & Unwin, 1982).

BENNEY, MARK, GRAY, A. P., and PEAR, R. H., *How People Vote* (London: Routledge & Kegan Paul, 1956).

BERRY, DAVID, *The Sociology of Grass Roots Politics* (London: Macmillan, 1970).

BETHSCHNEIDER, MONIKA, *Wahlkampfstrategien: Themen- und Organisationsplanung im Bundestagswahlkampf 1979/80* (Koblenz: Seminar für Politikwissenschaft, 1983).

BEYME, KLAUS VON, *Parteien in westlichen Demokratien* (Munich: Piper, 1982).

——*Political Parties in Western Democracies*, trans. Eileen Martin (New York: St Martin's Press, 1985).

——PAWELKA, PETER, STAISCH, PETER, and SEIBT, PETER, *Wahlkampf und Parteiorganisation: Eine Regionalstudie zum Bundestagswahlkampf 1969* (Tübingen: J. C. Mohr, 1974).

BIRCH, A. H., *Small-Town Politics* (London: Oxford University Press, 1959).

BITZER, EBERHARD, 'Die CDU braucht ein neues Konzept', *FAZ*, 2 Feb. 1962.

'Block Voting Reform may be Linked to Membership Drive', *Independent*, 7 Oct. 1989, 7.

BLONDEL, JEAN, 'The Conservative Association and the Labour Party in Reading', *Political Studies*, 6/2 (1958), 101–19.

BLUNTSCHLI, JOHANN, *Charakter und Geist der politischen Parteien* (Nördlingen: Beckschen Buchhandlung, 1869).

BOGDANOR, VERNON (ed.), *Liberal Party Politics* (Oxford: Clarendon Press, 1983).

BOGUMIL, JÖRG, *Computer in Parteien und Verbänden* (Opladen: Westdeutscher Verlag, 1991).

BORTHWICK, R. L., 'The Labour Party', in H. M. Drucker (ed.), *Multi-Party Britain* (London: Macmillan, 1979).

BOWLER, SHAUN, and FARRELL DAVID, 'Conclusion: The Contemporary

Election Campaign', in eid. (eds.) *Electoral Strategies and Political Marketing* (London: Macmillan, 1992).

BROWN, COLIN, 'Labour Promises to Curb Political Gifts', *Independent*, 14 Apr. 1994, 14.

BRYCE, JAMES, *Modern Democracies*, 2 vols. (New York: Macmillan, 1921).

BUCHAN, DAVID, 'French Socialists Seek a Gallant Loser', *Financial Times*, 3 Feb. 1995, 2.

BUDGE, IAN, and KEMAN, HANS, *Parties and Democracy* (Oxford: Oxford University Press, 1990).

BURCH, MARTIN, 'The Politics of Persuasion and the Conservative Leadership's Campaign', *Political Communications 1983*, 65–76.

BUTLER, DAVID, *The British General Election of 1951* (London: Macmillan, 1952).

——*The British General Election of 1955* (London: Macmillan, 1955).

——'The Changing Nature of British Elections', in Ivor Crewe and Martin Harrop (eds.), *Political Communications: The General Election Campaign 1983* (Cambridge: Cambridge University Press, 1986).

——'Hi-tech Replaces Rap of the Knocker', *Financial Times*, 31 Mar. 1992, 10.

——and KAVANAGH, DENNIS *The British General Election of October 1974* (New York: Macmillan, 1975).

————*The British General Election of 1979* (New York: Macmillan, 1980).

————*The British General Election of 1983* (London: Macmillan, 1984).

————*The British General Election of 1987* (London: Macmillan, 1988).

————*The British General Election of 1992* (London: Macmillan, 1993).

——and KING, ANTHONY, *The British General Election of 1964* (London: Macmillan, 1965).

————*The British General Election of 1966* (London: Macmillan, 1967).

——and PINTO-DUSCHINSKY, MICHAEL, *The British General Election of 1970* (New York: Macmillan, 1971).

——and RANNEY, AUSTIN, 'Conclusion', in eid. (eds.), *Electioneering: A Comparative Study of Continuity and Change* (Oxford: Clarendon Press, 1992).

——and ROSE, RICHARD, *The British General Election of 1959* (London: Macmillan, 1960).

——and SLOMAN, ANN, *British Political Facts 1900-1975* (London: Macmillan, 1975).

——and STOKES, DONALD, *Political Change in Britain: Forces Shaping Electoral Choice* (London: Macmillan, 1969).

CASTLES, FRANCES (ed.), *The Impact of Parties* (London: Sage Publications, 1982).

'CDU/CSU und FDP können mit knapper Mandatsmehrheit weiterregieren', *Deutschland Nachrichten*, 21 Oct. 1994, 1.

CHALMERS, DOUGLAS, *The Social Democratic Party of Germany* (New Haven: Yale University Press, 1964).

CLEMENS, CLAY, 'Disquiet on the Eastern Front: The Christian Democratic Union in Germany's New Länder', *German Politics*, 2 (1993), 200–23.

COLE, ALISTAIR (ed.), *French Political Parties in Transition* (Aldershot: Dartmouth, 1990).

Conduct of Local Authority Business, 2 vols. (London: HMSO Cmnd 9798, 1986).

DALTON, RUSSELL, *Citizen Politics in Western Democracies* (Chatham, NJ: New Chatham House, 1984).

——and COLE, ALEXANDRA, 'The Peaceful Revolution and German Electoral Politics', in Russell Dalton (ed.), *The New Germany Votes* (Providence: Berg Publishers, 1993).

——and ROHRSCHNEIDER, ROBERT, 'Wählerwandel und die Abschwächung der Parteineigungen von 1972 bis 1987', in Max Kaase and Hans-Dieter Klingemann (eds.), *Wahlen und Wähler* (Opladen: Westdeutscher Verlag, 1990).

DENVER, DAVID, 'Britain: Centralized Parties with Decentralized Selection', in Michael Gallagher and Michael Marsh (eds.), *Candidate Selection in Comparative Perspective* (London: Sage Publications, 1988), 47–71.

——and HANDS, GORDON, 'Constituency Campaigning', *Parliamentary Affairs*, 45 (1992), 528–44.

DESCHOUWER, KRIS, 'The Survival of the Fittest: Measuring and Explaining Adaptation and Change of Political Parties', paper presented at ECPR annual joint session, Limerick, Mar. 1992.

DEUTSCHER BUNDESTAG, *Rechenschaftsberichte der Parteien* (1967–83 in *Bundesanzeiger*; 1984–92 in *Bundestag Drucksachen*), various years.

DIEDRICH, NILS, 'Party Members and Local Party Branches', in Otto Stammer (ed.), *Party Systems, Party Organizations, and the Politics of the New Masses* (Berlin: Freie Universität Berlin, 1968).

DONNISON, D. V., and PLOWMAN, D. E. G., 'The Functions of Local Labour Parties', *Political Studies*, 2/2 (1954), 154–67.

DRONBERGER, ILSE, *The Political Thought of Max Weber* (New York: Appleton-Century-Crofts, 1971).

DUEBBER, ULRICH and BRAUNTHAL, GERARD, 'West Germany', *Journal of Politics*, 25 (1963), 774–89.

DUVERGER, MAURICE, *Les Partis politiques dans L'État contemporain* (Paris: Les Cours de Droit, 1949).

——*Political Parties: Their Organization and Activity in the Modern State*, trans. Barbara and Robert North (New York: John Wiley & Sons, 1955).

EINEMANN, EDGAR, *Partei-Computer für mehr Demokratie* (Marburg: Schüren Presseverlag, 1991).

ELDERSVELD, SAMUEL, *Political Parties in American Society* (New York: Basic Books, 1982).

ENGLAND, JUDE, 'Attitudes of Councillors', in *Conduct of Local Authority Business*, 2 vols. (London: HMSO Cmnd 9798, 1986), ii.

EPSTEIN, LEON, *Political Parties in Western Democracies* (New York: Praeger Publishers, 1967).

——'Political Parties in Western Democratic Systems', in Roy Macridis (ed.), *Political Parties: Contemporary Trends and Ideas* (New York: Harper & Row, 1967).

——*Political Parties in Western Democracies*, 2nd edn. (New Brunswick: Transaction Books, 1980).

——*Political Parties in the American Mold* (Madison: University of Wisconsin Press, 1986).

'Eylman fordert Urwahlen bei der CDU', *FAZ*, 22 June 1993, 1.

FALKE, WOLFGANG, *Die Mitglieder der CDU* (Berlin: Duncker & Humblot, 1982).

FALTER, JÜRGEN, 'Kontinuität und Neubeginn: Die Bundestagswahl 1949 zwischen Weimar und Bonn', *Politische Vierteljahresschrift*, 22 (1981), 236–42.

FALTLHAUSER, KURT, 'Aspekte des Wahlkampfes: Image, Öffentlichkeit und Parteiorganisation', in George Golter and Elmar Pieroth (eds.), *Die Union in der Opposition* (Düsseldorf: Econ Verlag, 1970).

——*Wahlkampf im Wahlkreis* (Augsburg: Dissertationsdruck- und Verlagsanstalt Werner Blasaditch, 1972).

FELDMEYER, KARL, 'Kiep muß den Parteitag um Geld angehen', *FAZ*, 12 Sept. 1989, 6.

FIENBURGH, WILFRED, and Manchester Fabian Society, 'Put Policy on the Agenda', *Fabian Journal*, (Feb. 1952), 25–33.

FINER, SAMUEL, 'The Decline of Party?', in Vernon Bogdanor (ed.) *Parties and Democracy in Britain and America* (New York: Praeger Publishers, 1984).

FISHER, JOEL, and GROENNINGS, SVEN, 'German Electoral Politics in 1969', *Government and Opposition*, 5 (1970), 218–34.

FRANKLIN, MARK, *The Decline of Class Voting in Britain* (Oxford: Oxford University Press, 1985).

——MACKIE, THOMAS, and VALEN, HENRY, *Electoral Change* (Cambridge University Press, 1992).

FREARS, JOHN, *Parties and Voters in France* (London: St Martin's Press, 1991).

FUHR, ECKHARD, 'Sonntag mit Folgen', *FAZ*, 15 June 1993, 1.

GALLUP, GEORGE (ed.), *The Gallup International Public Opinion Polls: Great Britain 1937–1975* (New York: Random House, 1976).

GAMBLE, ANDREW, 'The Conservative Party', in H. M. Drucker (ed.), *Multi-Party Britain* (London: Macmillan, 1979).

GAPPER, JOHN, 'Tories Play the Loyalty Card', *Financial Times*, 6–7 Mar. 1993, 6.

GARNER, ROBERT, and KELLY, RICHARD, *British Political Parties Today* (Manchester: Manchester University Press, 1993).

GEMMECKE, Vera, *Parteien im Wahlkampf* (Meisenheim am Glan: Verlag Anton Hain, 1967).

GIBSON, JAMES, COTTER, CORNELIUS, BIBBY, JOHN, and HUCKSHORN, ROBERT, 'Whither the Local Parties? A Cross-sectional and Longitudinal Analysis of the Strength of Party Organizations', *American Journal of Political Science*, 29 (1988), 139–60.

GOULD, JULIUS, '"Riverside": A Labour Constituency', *Fabian Journal* (Nov. 1954), 12–18.

GUGGENBERGER, BERND, and KEMPF, UDO (eds.), *Bürgerinitiativen und repräsentatives System* (Opladen: Westdeutscher Verlag, 1978).

GUNLICKS, ARTHUR, *Local Government in the German Federal System* (Durham, NC: Duke University Press, 1986).

GURLAND, A. R. L., *Die CDU/CSU: Ursprünge und Entwicklung bis 1953*, (Frankfurt/M.: Europäische Verlagsanstalt, 1980).

GYFORD, JOHN, *Local Politics in Britain* (London: Croom Helm, 1976).

HARMEL, ROBERT and JANDA, KENNETH, 'An Integrated Theory of Party Goals and Party Change', *Journal of Theoretical Politics*, 6 (1994), 259–88.

HARRISON, MARTIN, 'Television and Radio', in David Butler and Anthony King, *The British General Election of 1964* (London: Macmillan, 1965).

HARRISON, MICHAEL, DOBIE, CLARE, and SHAH, SAMIR, 'Big Tory Backers Freeze Donations', *Independent*, 16 Mar. 1992, 28.

HARTELT, SUSANNE, 'Der Wahlkampfführung der SPD 1949–1969' (master's thesis, Universität Düsseldorf, 1977).

HASTINGS, ELIZABETH HANN, and HASTINGS, PHILIP K., (eds.), *Index to International Public Opinion 1983–84* (Westport, Conn.: Greenwood Press, 1985).

——*Index International to Public Opinion 1987–88* (Westport, Conn.: Greenwood Press, 1989).

HAUFF, VOLKER (ed.), *Bürgerinitiativen in der Gesellschaft* (Villingen-Schwenningen: Neckar Verlag, 1980).

HAUNGS, PETER (ed.), *Wahlkampf als Ritual?* (Meisenheim am Glan: Verlag Anton Hain, 1974).

——'Aktuelle Probleme der Parteiendemokratie', *Jahrbuch für Politik*, 2 (1992), 37–64.

HEFFERNAN, RICHARD, and MARQUSEE, MIKE, *Defeat from the Jaws of Victory: Inside Kinnock's Labour Party* (London: Verso, 1992).

HIRSCH-WEBER, WOLFGANG, and SCHÜTZ, KLAUS, *Wähler und Gewählte* (Berlin: Franz Vahlen, 1957).

HODGSON, GEOFF, *Labour at the Crossroads* (Oxford: Martin Robertson, 1981).

HOFFMAN, J. D., *The Conservative Party in Opposition 1945–51* (London: McGibbon & Kee, 1964).

HOFFMANN, WOLFGANG, 'Weniger Geld vom Staat', *Die Zeit*, 1 Oct. 1993.

HOLDSWORTH, IAN, 'Computers Left, Right and Centre', *Financial Times*, 3 Apr. 1992, 12.

House of Lords Debates, 15 May 1974, vol. 351, col. 1033.

HUGHES, COLIN, and WINTOUR, PATRICK, *Labour Rebuilt* (London: Fourth Estate, 1990).

HUNTER, TERESA, 'New Card Could Make Carrier a Credit to Labour', *Guardian*, 6 Oct. 1989, 6.

INFAS (Institute für angewandte Sozialforschung), *Mitglieder und Orts-vereine im SPD-Bezirk Franken* (n.p., n.d. [1981]).

INGLEHART, RONALD, *Culture Shift in Advanced Industrial Societies* (Princeton: Princeton University Press, 1990).

JANDA, KENNETH, and HARMEL, ROBERT, *Parties and their Environments* (New York: Longman, 1982).

KAACK, HEINO, 'Die Basis der Parteien: Struktur und Funktion der Ortsvereine', *Zeitschrift für Parlamentsfragen*, 2/1 (1971), 23–38.

——*Geschichte und Struktur des deutschen Parteiensystems* (Opladen: Westdeutscher Verlag, 1971).

KAASE, MAX, 'Germany', in David Butler and Austin Ranney (eds.), *Electioneering* (Oxford: Clarendon Press, 1992), 146.

KALT, GERO, 'Politik will verkauft sein', *Das Parlament*, 13 Sept. 1986, 18.

KATZ, RICHARD, 'Party as Linkage: A Vestigial Function?', *European Journal of Political Research*, 18 (1990), 143–61.

——and MAIR, PETER, 'The Official Story: A Framework for the Comparative Study of Party Organization and Organizational Change', paper presented at APSA annual meeting, San Francisco, 30 Aug.–1 Sept. 1990.

——'The Evolution of Party Organizations in Europe: The Three Faces of Party Organization', *The American Review of Politics*, 14 (1993), 593–617.

——'Changing Models of Party Organization and Party Democracy: The Emergence of the Cartel Party', *Party Politics*, 1 (1995), 5–28.

KAYDEN, XANDRA, and MAHE, EDDIE JR., *The Party Goes On: The Persistence of the Two-Party System in the United States* (New York: Basic Books, 1985).

KELLY, RICHARD, *Conservative Party Conferences* (Manchester: Manchester University Press, 1989).

KEY, V. O. JR., *Politics, Parties and Pressure Groups*, 4th edn. (New York: Thomas Crowell Co., 1958).

KING, ANTHONY, 'Political Parties in Western Democracies: Some Sceptical Reflections', *Polity*, 2 (1969), 111–41.

——'What do Elections Decide?', in David Butler, Howard Penniman, and Austin Ranney (eds.), *Democracy at the Polls* (Washington: American Enterprise Institute, 1981).

KIRCHHEIMER, OTTO, 'The Transformation of the Western European Party Systems', in Joseph LaPalombara and Myron Weiner (eds.), *Political Parties and Political Development* (Princeton: Princeton University Press, 1966).

KITSCHELT, HERBERT, *The Logics of Party Formation* (Ithaca, NY: Cornell University Press, 1989).

——'Austrian and Swedish Social Democrats in Crisis', *Comparative Political Studies*, 27 (1994), 3–39.

KITZINGER, UWE, *German Electoral Politics: A Study of the 1957 Campaign* (Oxford: Clarendon Press, 1960).

KLOTZBACH, KURT, *Der Weg zur Staatspartei* (Berlin: J. H. W. Dietz Nachfolger, 1982).

KOELBLE, THOMAS, *The Left Unraveled* (Durham, NC: Duke University Press, 1991).

——'Economic Theories of Organization and the Politics of Institutional Design in Political Parties', paper presented at APSA annual meeting, New York, Aug. 1994.

KOLINSKY, EVA, *Parties, Opposition and Society in West Germany* (London: Croom Helm, 1984).

KOOLE, RUUD, *De Opkomst van de Moderne Kaderpartij: Veranderende Partijorganisatie in Nederland 1960–1990* (Utrecht: Spectrum, 1992).

KÖSER, HELMUT, *Die Grundsatzdebatte in der SPD von 1945/46 bis 1958/59* (Freiburg i.B.: Johannes Kraus, 1971).

KRASKE, KONRAD, *Die Bundestagswahl 1961: Vorbereitung—Ergebnis—Folgerungen* (Bonn: no publisher, 1962).

——'Wähler haben sich verändert', *Die Entscheidung*, (Oct. 1966), 13–14.

LAMMERT, NORBERT, *Lokale Organisationsstrukturen innerparteilicher Willensbildung: Fallstudie am Beispiel eines CDU-Kreisverbandes im Ruhrgebiet* (Bonn: Eichholz Verlag, 1976).

LANDFRIED, CHRISTINE, *Parteifinanzen und politische Macht* (Baden-Baden: Nomos Verlagsgesellschaft, 1990).

'Langen für Befragung unter CDU-Mitglieder', *FAZ*, 25 June 1993, 2.

LAURENS, ANDRÉ and PFISTER, THIERRY, *Les Nouveaux Communistes* (n.p.: Stock, 1973).

The Law on Political Parties (Bonn: Inter Nationes, 1994).

LAZARSFELD, PAUL, BERELSON, BERNARD, and GAUDET, HAZEL, *The People's Choice* (New York: Columbia University Press, 1944).

LEONARD, R. L., *Elections in Britain* (London: D. Van Nostrand, 1968).

LINTON, MARTIN, and TIRBUTT, SUSAN, 'Winning Foray against Size of Block Vote', *Guardian*, 6 Oct. 1988, 6.

'Liste Feuerwehr', *Der Spiegel*, 48 (1993), 70–4.

LOHMAR, ULRICH, *Innerparteiliche Demokratie* (Stuttgart: Ferdinand Enke Verlag, 1963).

LÖLHÖFFEL, HELMUT, 'Koalition setzt sich bei Parteifinanzierung durch', *Frankfurter Rundschau*, 13 Nov. 1993, 4.

LOMBARD LEAGUE, *Statuto della Lega Lombarda* (n.p.: photocopy, 1992).

LÖSCHE, PETER and WALTER, FRANZ, *Die SPD: Klassenpartei—Volkspartei—Quotenpartei* (Darmstadt: Wissenschaftliche Buchgesellschaft, 1992).

LUCKMAN, BENITA, *Politik in einer deutschen Kleinstadt* (Stuttgart: Ferdinand Enke Verlag, 1970).

LUTHER, KURT, 'Consociationalism, Parties and the Party System', in Kurt Luther and Wolfgang Müller (eds.), *Politics in Austria: Still a Case of Consociationalism?* (London: Frank Cass, 1992).

MAIR, PETER, 'Continuity, Change and the Vulnerability of Party', *West European Politics*, 12/4 (1989), 168–87.

MAY, JOHN, 'Opinion Structure of Political Parties: The Special Law of Curvilinear Disparity', *Political Studies*, 21 (1973), 135–51.

MAYNTZ, RENATE, 'Lokale Parteigruppe in der kleinen Gemeinde', *Zeitschrift für Politik*, 2/1 (1955), 59–74.

——*Parteigruppen in der Großstadt* (Cologne: Westdeutscher Verlag, 1959).

MCKENZIE, ROBERT, *British Political Parties* (Melbourne: William Heinemann, 1955).

McKitterick, T. E., 'The Membership of the Party', *Political Quarterly*, 31 (1960), 312–23.

Mead, Gary, 'The Man that will Launch More than 5,500 Faces', *Financial Times*, 17 Mar. 1992, 10.

'Mehr Power für die Neuen', *Der Spiegel*, 23 (1991), 21–5.

Meisel, John, 'The Decline of Party in Canada', in Hugh Thorburn (ed.) *Party Politics in Canada*, 5th edn. (Scarborough: Prentice-Hall Canada, 1985).

'Membership Drive Disappointment', *Independent*, 1 Oct. 1990.

Menudier, Henri, 'La Campagne électorale de la CDU et du FDP', *Revue d'Allemagne*, 9/2 (1987), 108–21.

Michels, Robert, *Political Parties*, trans. Eden and Cedar Paul (New York: Dover Publications, 1959).

Miliband, Ralph, 'Socialism and the Myth of the Golden Past', *Socialist Register 1964*, 92–103.

Milne, R. S., and Mackenzie, H. C., *Marginal Seat, 1955* (London: The Hansard Society for Parliamentary Government, 1958).

Mintzel, Alf, *Die CSU* (Opladen: Westdeutscher Verlag, 1978).

——and Oberreuter, Heinrich (eds.), *Parteien in der Bundesrepublik Deutschland* (Opladen: Leske & Budrich, 1992).

'Mit Stadtteilzeitung macht die SPD Werbung durch die Hintertür', *Die Welt*, 26 Aug. 1985.

Mommsen, Wolfgang, *The Political and Social Thought of Max Weber* (Chicago: University of Chicago Press, 1989).

Münke, Stephanie, *Wahlkampf und Machtverschiebung* (Berlin: Duncker & Humblot, 1952).

Naßmacher, Hiltrud, 'Die Parteien der Bundesrepublik im Umbau', *Der Bürger im Staat*, 39/4 (1989), 231–6.

Naßmacher, Karl-Heinz, and Rudzio, Wolfgang, 'Das lokale Parteiensystem auf dem Lande: Dargestellt am Beispiel der Rekrutierung von Gemeinderäten', in Hans-Georg Wehling (ed.), *Dorfpolitik* (Opladen: Leske & Budrich, 1978).

Neumann, Sigmund, 'Toward a Comparative Study of Political Parties', in id. (ed.), *Modern Political Parties: A Comparative Approach* (Chicago: University of Chicago Press, 1956).

——*Die Parteien der Weimarer Republik* (Stuttgart: Kohlhammer Verlag, 1965).

Nichols, H. G., *The British General Election of 1950* (London: Macmillan, 1951).

Niedermayer, Oskar, 'Innerparteiliche Partizipation', *aus Politik und Zeitgeschichte*, 11 (1989), 15–25.

Noelle-Neumann, Elisabeth, 'Die Schweigespirale. Über die Entstehung der Öffentlichen Meinung', in ead., *Öffentlichkeit als Bedrohung*, 2nd edn. (Freiburg i.B.: Verlag Karl Alber, 1979).

NORRIS, PIPPA, and LOVENDUSKI, JONI, *Political Representation: Gender, Race and Class in the British Parliament* (Cambridge: Cambridge University Press, 1994).

'Ohne Kurs und Kapitän', *Der Spiegel*, 19 (1993), 29–35.

OSTROGORSKI, MOSEI, *Democracy and the Organization of Political Parties*, trans. Frederick Clarke, ed. Seymour Lipset (Chicago: Quadrangle Books, 1964).

PALTIEL, KHAYYAM ZEV, 'Political Marketing, Party Finance, and the Decline of Canadian Parties', in Alain Gagnon and Brian Tanguay (eds.), *Canadian Parties in Transition: Discourse, Organization, and Representation* (Scarborough: Nelson Canada, 1989).

PANEBIANCO, ANGELO, *Political Parties: Organization and Power*, trans. Marc Silver (Cambridge: Cambridge University Press, 1988).

PARNESS, DIANE, *The SPD and the Challenge of Mass Politics: The Dilemma of the German Volkspartei* (Boulder, Colo.: Westview Press, 1991).

PARRY, GERAINT, MOYSER, GEORGE, and DAY, NEIL, *Political Participation and Democracy in Britain* (Cambridge: Cambridge University Press, 1992).

'Parteireform als Zauberwort', *FAZ*, 29 June 1993, 1.

'Party Games', *New Society*, 33/668 (1975), 179.

PATTERSON, WILLIAM, 'West Germany: Between Party Apparatus and Basis Democracy', in Alan Ware (ed.), *Political Parties: Electoral Change and Structural Response* (Oxford: Basil Blackwell, 1987).

PATTIE, CHARLES, WHITELY, PAUL, JOHNSTON, RON, and SEYD, PATRICK, 'Measuring Local Campaign Effects: Labour Party Constituency Campaigning at the 1987 General Election', *Political Studies*, 42 (1994), 469–79.

PELLING, HENRY, *A Short History of the Labour Party* (London: Macmillan, 1961).

PENNIMAN, HOWARD, 'Campaign Styles and Methods', in David Butler, Howard Penniman, and Austin Ranney (eds.) *Democracy at the Polls* (Washington: American Enterprise Institute, 1981).

PINKNEY, ROBERT, 'An Alternative Political Strategy? Liberals in Power in English Local Government', *Local Government Studies*, 10/3 (1984), 69–84.

PINTO-DUSCHINSKY, MICHAEL, *British Political Finance 1830–1980* (Washington: American Enterprise Institute, 1981).

——— 'Trends in British Political Funding 1979–1983', *Parliamentary Affairs*, 38 (1985), 328–47.

——— 'Financing the British General Election of 1987', in Ivor Crewe and Martin Harrop (eds.), *Political Communications: The General Election Campaign of 1987* (Cambridge: Cambridge University Press, 1989).

——'Trends in British Political Funding 1983–1987', *Parliamentary Affairs*, 42 (1989), 197–212.

PIRKER, THEO, *Die SPD nach Hitler* (Munich: Rütten & Loening, 1965).

PLOG, KARSTEN, 'Ist Schnuppern an der Kieler CDU illegal?', *Frankfurter Rundschau*, 24 Sept. 1993, 4.

POGUNTKE, THOMAS, *Alternative Politics* (Edinburgh: Edinburgh University Press, 1993).

——'Explorations into a Minefield: Anti-Party Sentiment. Conceptual Thoughts and Empirical Evidence', paper presented at ECPR annual joint session, Madrid, Apr. 1994.

—— and BOLL, BERNARD, 'Germany', in Richard Katz and Peter Mair (eds.), *Party Organizations* (London: Sage Publications, 1992).

POWELL, G. BINGHAM, 'American Voter Turnout in Comparative Perspective', *American Political Science Review*, 80 (1986), 17–43.

PRIDHAM, GEOFFREY, *Christian Democracy in Western Germany* (London: Croom Helm, 1977).

PULZER, PETER G. J., *Political Representation and Elections in Britain* (London: George Allen & Unwin, 1967).

RADUNSKI, PETER, *Wahlkämpfe: Moderne Wahlkampfführung als politische Kommunikation* (Munich: Günter Olzog Verlag, 1980).

RANNEY, AUSTIN, *Curing the Mischiefs of Faction* (Berkeley: University of California Press, 1975).

——'Candidate Selection', in David Butler, Howard Penniman, and Austin Ranney (eds.), *Democracy at the Polls* (Washington: American Enterprise Institute, 1981).

RATTINGER, HANS, 'Abkehr von den Parteien?', *aus Politik und Zeitgeschichte*, 11 (1993), 24–35.

RIGGS, FRED, 'Comparative Politics and the Study of Parties: A Structural Approach', in William Crotty (ed.), *Approaches to the Study of Party Organization* (Boston: Allyn & Bacon, 1968).

ROSE, RICHARD, *Influencing Votes* (New York: St Martin's Press, 1967).

——*Do Parties Make a Difference?* (London: Macmillan, 1980).

SÄNGER, FRITZ, 'Wahlkampfabkommen und Wahlwerbung', in id. and Klaus Liepelt (eds.), *Wahlhandbuch 1965: Teil 2 Wahlwerber* (n.p.: Institut für angewandte Sozialwissenschaft, 1965).

SALMORE, STEPHEN and SALMORE, BARBARA, *Candidates, Parties and Campaigns* (Washington: Congressional Quarterly Press, 1985).

SCARROW, SUSAN, 'Organizing for Victory: Political Party Members and Party Organizing Strategies in Great Britain and West Germany, 1945–1989' (doctoral dissertation, Yale University, 1991).

————'Does Local Party Organization Make a Difference? Political Parties and Local Government Elections in Germany', *German Politics*, 2/3 (1993), 377–92.

SCHLETH, UWE, and PINTO-DUSCHINSKY, MICHAEL, 'Why Public Subsidies have Become the Major Source of Party Funds in West Germany, but not in Great Britain', in Arnold Heidenheimer (ed.), *Comparative Political Finance* (Lexington, Mass.: D. C. Heath, 1970).

SCHMID, JOSEF, *Die CDU* (Opladen: Leske & Budrich, 1990).

SCHMIDT, UTE, 'Christlich Demokratische Union Deutschlands', in Richard Stöss (ed.), *Parteien-Handbuch* (Opladen: Westdeutscher Verlag, 1983).

SCHMITT, HERMANN, 'Die Sozialdemokratische Partei Deutschlands', in Alf Mintzel and Heinrich Oberreuter (eds.), *Parteien in der Bundesrepublik Deutschland* (Opladen: Leske & Budrich, 1992).

SCHNEIDER, NORBERT, *Parteien und Kandidaten* (Cologne: Walter Kleikamp, 1972).

SCHOLZ, ARNO, *Das Einmaleins der politischen Werbung* (Berlin: Arani Verlag, 1954).

SCHÖNBOHM, WULF, *Die CDU wird moderne Volkspartei* (Stuttgart: Klett-Cotta, 1985).

————'Defizite und konkrete Lösungsmöglichkeiten', *Themen*, 2 (1988), 23.

SEILER, DANIEL-LOUIS, *De la comparaison des partis politiques* (Paris: Economica, 1986).

SEYD, PATRICK, *The Rise and Fall of the Labour Left* (Basingstoke: Macmillan Education, 1987).

————and WHITELY, PAUL, *Labour's Grass Roots* (Oxford: Clarendon Press, 1992).

————————'Labour's Renewal Strategy', in Martin Smith and Joanna Spear (eds.), *The Changing Labour Party* (London: Routledge, 1992).

SILVIA, STEPHEN, 'Left Behind: The Social Democratic Party in Eastern Germany', *West European Politics*, 16/2 (1993), 24–48.

SJÖBLOM, GUNNAR, *Party Strategies in a Multiparty System* (Lund: Berlingska Boktryckeriet, 1968).

SMITH, ALISON, 'Grassroots Rebels Defeat Party Reforms', *Financial Times*, 6/7 Mar. 1993, 6.

'Smith Pulls off High-Risk Gamble', *Guardian*, 30 Sept. 1993, 1.

SMYTH, GARETH, 'OMOV for Tories?' *New Statesman and Society*, 1 Oct. 1993, 16.

SORAUF, FRANK, 'Political Parties and Political Analysis', in William Chambers and Walter Dean Burnham (eds.), *The American Party Systems* (New York: Oxford University Press, 1967).

STEPHENS, PHILIP, 'Tory Funders Find Out the Party may be Over', *Financial Times*, 8 July 1993, 8.

STROBEL, CLAUDIA, 'Eine lokale Parteigruppe der SPD in einer nord-bayerischen Großstadt' (dissertation, Salzburg University, 1976).

STROM, KAARE, 'A Behavioral Theory of Competitive Political Parties', *American Journal of Political Science*, 34 (1990), 565–98.

STRUVE, GÜNTHER, *Kampf um die Mehrheit* (Cologne: Verlag Wissenschaft und Politik, 1971).

SUNDBERG, JAN, 'Exploring the Basis of Declining Party Membership in Denmark: A Scandinavian Comparison', *Scandinavian Political Studies*, 10/1, (1987), 17–38.

SWADDLE, KEVIN, 'Coping with a Mass Electorate' (doctoral dissertation, Oxford University, 1990).

TETHER, PHILIP, 'Recruiting Conservative Party Members: A Changing Role for Central Office', *Parliamentary Affairs*, 44 (1991), 20–32.

TIEMANN, HEINRICH, 'Die SPD in den neuen Bundesländern: Organisation und Mitglieder', *Zeitschrift für Parlamentsfragen*, 3 (1993), 415–22.

——SCHMID, JOSEF, and LÖBLER, FRANK, 'Gewerkschaften und Sozialdemokratie in den neuen Bundesländern', *Deutschland Archiv*, 26 (1993), 46.

'Urwahl der Parlamentskandidaten', *FAZ*, 5 July 1993, 4.

'Urwahl und Mitgliederentscheid: Die SPD erprobt die direkte Demokratie', *FAZ*, 20 Nov. 1993, 2.

URWIN, DEREK, 'Norway: Parties between Mass Membership and Consumer-Oriented Professionalism?', in Alan Ware (ed.), *Political Parties: Electoral Change and Structural Response* (Oxford: Basil Blackwell, 1987).

VERBA, SIDNEY, NIE, NORMAN, and KIM, JAE-ON, *Participation and Political Equality* (Cambridge: Cambridge University Press, 1978).

VOGEL, BERNHARD, and HAUNGS, PETER, *Wahlkampf und Wählertradition: Eine Studie zur Bundestagswahl 1961* (Cologne: Westdeutscher Verlag, 1965).

WARD, IAN, 'The Changing Organisational Nature of Australia's Political Parties', *Journal of Commonwealth and Comparative Politics*, 29/2 (1991), 153–74.

WARE, ALAN, *Citizens, Parties and the State* (Princeton: Princeton University Press, 1987).

——'Activist-Leader Relations and the Structure of Political Parties: "Exchange" Models and Vote-Seeking Behaviour in Parties', *British Journal of Political Science*, 22 (1992), 71–92.

WEBER, MAX, *Staatssoziologie*, ed. Johannes Winckelmann (Berlin: Duncker & Humblot, 1966).

WEIR, STUART, 'Operation Scapegoat', *New Statesman and Society*, 4 Sept. 1992, 16–17.

WENGST, UDO, 'Die CDU/CSU im Bundestagswahlkampf 1949', *Vierteljahresheft für Zeitgeschichte*, 34 (1986), 1–52.

WHITE, MICHAEL, 'Parties Plug into Unpredictable Power Points That Could Clinch Victory', *Guardian*, 30 Mar. 1992, 13.

WHITELY, PAUL, and SEYD, PATRICK, 'Labour's Vote and Local Activism: The Impact of Constituency Campaigns', *Parliamentary Affairs*, 45 (1992), 582–95.

——and RICHARDSON, JEREMY, *True Blues* (Oxford: Clarendon Press, 1994).

——and BISSELL, PAUL, 'Explaining Party Activism: The Case of the British Conservative Party', *British Journal of Political Science*, 24 (1993), 79–94.

'Wie kann man der Parteienverdroßenheit begegnen?', *Düsseldorfer Nachrichten*, 19 Apr. 1977.

WILSON, FRANK, *French Political Parties under the Fifth Republic* (New York: Praeger Publishers, 1982).

WILSON, JAMES Q., *Political Organizations* (New York: Basic Books, 1973).

WINTOUR, PATRICK, 'Membership Drive Is On', *Guardian*, 5 July 1988, 6.

——'Local Party Ballots Show Way to One Member, One Vote', *Guardian*, 8 Oct. 1988, 4.

——'Party Facing Cash Crisis Due to Falling Membership', *Guardian*, 30 Sept. 1992, 4.

——'Straw Tries to Nip Lib Dems' Revival in Bud', *Guardian*, 5 Aug. 1993, 2.

——'Blair Says Reforms Will "Change Party Culture"', *Guardian*, 27 Sept. 1994, 6.

WOLF, WERNER, *Wahlkampf und Demokratie* (Cologne: Verlag Wissenschaft und Politik, 1985).

WOOD, NICHOLAS, 'Tories Hope for 10% Rise in Membership', *Times*, 11 Oct. 1988.

WURZBACHER, GERHARD, et al., *Das Dorf im Spannungsfeld industrieller Entwicklung* (Stuttgart: Ferdinand Enke Verlag, 1961).

YSMAL, COLETTE, *Les Partis politiques sous la Ve République* (Paris: Montchrestien, 1989).

'Zur Person: Hans Eichel', *Frankfurter Rundschau*, 24 June 1993, 4.

Index